P9-CPX-058

JULIUS STREICHER

Julius Streicher (far left) and Adolf Hitler at the 1927 Nuremberg Rally.

JULIUS STREICHER

**Nazi Editor of the Notorious Anti-Semitic
Newspaper *Der Stürmer***

by **Randall L. Bytwerk**

with a new afterword

Cooper Square Press

First Cooper Square Press Edition 2001

This Cooper Square Press paperback edition of *Julius Streicher* is an unabridged republication of the edition published in New York in 1983, with fifty textual emendations and the addition of a new afterword by the author. It is reprinted by arrangement with the author.

Published by Cooper Square Press
An Imprint of the Rowman & Littlefield Publishing Group
150 Fifth Avenue, Suite 817
New York, New York 10011

Distributed by National Book Network

Library of Congress Cataloging-in-Publication Data

Bytwerk, Randall L.
    Julius Streicher : Nazi Editor of the notorious anti-Semitic newspaper Der Stürmer / Randall L. Bytwerk.—1st Cooper Square Press ed.
        p. cm.
    Originally published: New York : Stein and Day, 1983.
    Includes bibliographical references and index.
    ISBN 0-8154-1156-1 (alk. paper)
        1. Antisemitism—Germany. 2. Streicher, Julius, 1885–1946. 3. Stérmer. 4. Germany—Ethnic relations. I. Title.

DS146.G4 B98 2001
305.892'4043—dc21   2001028990

⊖™ The paper used in this publication meets the minimum requirements of
American National Standard for Information Sciences—Permanence of
Paper for Printed Library Materials, ANSI/NISO Z39.48–1992.
Manufactured in the United States of America.

TO
Sharon Van Haitsma Bytwerk,
"Heaven's last best gift,
my ever new delight"

Contents

Illustrations between pages 77 and 100

Preface

Why did the Germans kill six million Jews? There are dozens of books on what one might call the technology of the Holocaust, the operation of the death camps, but far fewer on the forces that led a civilized nation to commit, condone, or ignore genocide. Most Germans, of course, had no part in the death camps, indeed did not know that Jews were being annihilated by the millions. Yet almost all Germans had seen the intensifying persecution of the Jews that began in 1933. Few Germans had protested. Few Germans had been interested in knowing where all the Jews had gone.

This book looks at part of what persuaded Germans to stand by while their Jewish fellow citizens were persecuted—the anti-Semitic propaganda of Julius Streicher, "World Jew-baiter No. 1," the most vicious and prolific of the Nazi anti-Semites. Streicher and his like did not persuade all or even most Germans to hate Jews. But they did establish an attitude of indifference toward Jews without which the Holocaust could not have occurred.

I owe thanks to many people who have helped me to write this book. Professor Robert D. Brooks first interested me in the subject and has given much help over the years. Professor David Zarefsky had valuable advice. Northwestern University and Southern Illinois

University at Carbondale gave travel support. My colleagues of the Department of Speech Communication at SIU made my work easier by their example and good cheer. The book was finished during a sabbatical semester provided by Southern Illinois University.

Librarians and archivists have made their usual quiet but essential contributions. I owe particular thanks to the splendid staff at the Wiener Library, and to the late Dr. Arnd Müller of Nuremberg, whose guide to the Stürmerarchiv saved me much work. The Hoover Institution at Stanford University provided many of the illustrations. Jim Jennings helped out with photography.

The editors of the *Wiener Library Bulletin* and *Journalism History* gave permission to incorporate material into this book that originally appeared in their journals, and the editor of the *Christian Vanguard* allowed me to use material from his newspaper.

JULIUS STREICHER

I

The Making of an Anti-Semite

Julius Streicher was the seventh of ten Nazi war criminals to hang on the morning of October 16, 1946. All had been among the most powerful and dangerous of Hitler's agents in Germany's war against the world. Streicher remained loyal to the end. Only he shouted the old cry "Heil Hitler!" as he neared the gallows. On the platform, glaring at the Allied press correspondents gathered to watch the hangings, he yelled "Purim Festival 1946!"—referring to the biblical Book of Esther, which describes how Haman was executed on the gallows he had intended for the Jews. "The Bolshevists will hang you one day," he added as final preparations were made. His body was cremated with those of the other Nazi leaders and the ashes, ironically under the cover name Abraham Goldberg, were scattered into a small stream near Munich.

He had been among the most despicable men of the Nazi movement, scorned and hated by the broader world and even by many of his fellow Nazis. For twenty-five years he had hated the Jews. Called "World Jew-baiter No. 1," "the biggest bigot in the world," and "the high priest of stupidity," Streicher's weekly newspaper *Der Stürmer* had been devoted entirely to rousing racial hatred. It had been one of the most widely circulated papers in Germany, the one paper Hitler

1

himself claimed to read from cover to cover. The Allies brought him to trial not because of his central role in the Nazi government or because of any direct part in implementing the Holocaust, but because in the words of the indictment his propaganda had left "a legacy of almost a whole people poisoned with hate, sadism, and murder." Others had carried out the Holocaust; Streicher had prepared the ground.

Julius Streicher's early life hardly suggested that he would die universally despised. Born on February 12, 1885, in Fleinhausen, a small village fifteen miles west of the Bavarian town of Augsburg, he was the ninth child of the village schoolmaster. An ill-paid man with so large a family could scarcely support it easily, but Streicher's memories of his childhood were happy. His mother, whom he later called "the fortress of my childhood," cheerfully accepted the view that women should be concerned with children, kitchen, and church, a model of what the Nazis were later to urge on all German womanhood.[1] Herr Streicher, a firm father, had the respect and admiration of his children, it seems, since five of his seven surviving children followed him into the teaching profession.

The rural village in which Streicher grew up was strongly Catholic. Its citizens were poorly educated men and women with no false confidence in human nature. Jews were not often seen, but the villagers thought they knew a great deal about them. Generations of rumor and myth had made Jews into mysterious and dangerous creatures, capable of the worst behavior. Early in his life Streicher absorbed the prevailing anti-Semitism. When he was five his mother ordered fabric from a Jewish shop in a neighboring town; on delivery, the fabric was adjudged of inferior quality. That, Streicher's mother told her son in tears, was just like a Jew. The village priest in his regular periods of religious instruction in the school explained how the Jews had fought Christ bitterly, finally crucifying him. "That was my first inkling that the nature of the Jews was peculiar," he later wrote.[2] These incidents, and surely there were others, did not make Streicher the blustering anti-Semite he would become, but they helped to establish the foundation for his Jew-baiting career.

At thirteen he completed his basic education and entered a teacher training institute, where his performance was unremarkable but acceptable. The five-year course was followed by a year of supervised student teaching, after which Streicher began service at the bottom of the teaching heirarchy as a substitute teacher in January 1904. Filling in as needed, he taught in six Bavarian villages within seven months. As a teacher Streicher was expected to attend to the spiritual as well as to the intellectual development of his pupils. Particularly in the small towns in which he taught, the local priest often had supervisory authority over the schoolmaster. Now, Streicher was never to be a man who easily accepted interference in his affairs, and his childhood had not left him a loyal Catholic. In July 1904 he decided to change the time at which the Sunday school (for which the schoolmaster was also responsible) met, against the wishes of the parish priest. Having other complaints against the troublesome nineteen-year-old as well, the priest made a formal complaint to Streicher's superiors. The altercation did Streicher's career no harm, for he soon after received more permanent teaching assignments.

By 1907 he was sufficiently established to take a year's leave from teaching to serve as an army volunteer. Peacetime military service failed to discipline him, for his file noted that he had demonstrated his unsuitability to become an officer. Part of the problem had been a three-day jail term, apparently the result of a brawl that Streicher later said resulted from his refusal to tolerate an insult. But such conduct was not that of a German officer.

His army service completed, he resumed teaching in 1908. Trying to keep him out of difficulty, his superiors gave him a post in a larger town, where clerical supervision would be less direct, but in August 1909 Streicher seems to have thrown a visiting priest out of his classroom. Such behavior could not be tolerated, but in the end it worked to Streicher's advantage. The nearby Nuremberg school system was headed by an administrator himself not sympathetic to religious involvement in public instruction. Hearing of Streicher's difficulties, he offered Streicher a job that he quickly accepted. Twenty-five years later, Streicher would become Nuremberg's uncrowned ruler.

Nuremberg in 1909 was a splendid and prosperous city; its medieval walls and buildings showed the German past to good advantage, and made it a prime tourist attraction. Its citizens were for good reason proud of their city. Nuremberg's history spanned a thousand years. Albrecht Dürer, Germany's finest artist, had been born there and

refused lucrative offers to leave. As a free city, Nuremberg for generations stood independent of outside domination through good times
and bad. Its citizens had accepted the Reformation with alacrity,
making Nuremberg an island of Protestantism in a predominantly
Catholic region.

During the nineteenth century Nuremberg recovered from a long
decline to become a major industrial center. The first German railroad
line connected Nuremberg with its neighbor Fürth; soon Nuremberg
was the hub of a railroad network. The goods of the growing town left
by rail for every part of civilization. By 1871, the year Wilhelm I
became emperor of the consolidated Second Reich, Nuremberg was a
healthy city with a population of eighty-three thousand, growing to
three hundred thousand by Streicher's arrival. With the growth in
population came a change in the city's religious makeup. In 1800
nearly all its citizens had been Protestant. By 1910 a third were
Catholic, and almost eight thousand were Jews. Expansion brought
with it the problems of social change and industrialization that contributed to the appeal Nazism shortly would have.

Streicher took to Nuremberg. By now he was an experienced and
capable teacher who rapidly earned the confidence of his superiors.
Now he decided to become active politically. He may well have had
socialist leanings, for the poor working-class children he taught won
his sympathy, but the political limits placed on state employees
prevented any thought of joining the Social Democratic Party, whose
Marxist rhetoric was anathema to most Germans. Certainly the more
moderate Democratic Party was acceptable, and as it had as one goal
the elimination of clerical supervision of public education, it attracted
some teachers. For even in Nuremberg the schools were not free of
religion. Responding to the increasing Catholic population, the
Nurembergers had adopted combined schools that all students
attended regardless of religious confession, but at which separate
classes were held to provide religious instruction. By 1912 Streicher
had joined that party.

Recognizing his promise as a speaker, the Democratic Party put
him to work addressing meetings outside Nuremberg. His first
speech, guided by an "inner voice" to which Streicher often referred,
went well. The new orator blushed when he was applauded with
enthusiasm. But as he later remembered, not everyone in the audience

applauded. Some, most of them Jews, had kept silent. Returning to Nuremberg that evening with an employee of a Nuremberg bank, he was warned to avoid offending Jews in the future:

> Streicher, let me give you some advice. I work in a Jewish firm. I have learned to be silent at times when my German heart gladly would have spoken, and often I speak when I would rather be silent. The Jews are few in number, but great in the economic and political power they have achieved, and their power is dangerous. You, my dear Streicher, are still young and cocky, and don't mince words. But never forget what I am telling you: the Jews have *great* power, and that power is dangerous, very dangerous.[3]

That fellow surely was not the only anti-Semite Streicher met. Though impressed by the words, Streicher was not yet persuaded to join any of the anti-Jewish groups Nuremberg sheltered.

By 1913 he seemed ready to settle down to a comfortable life. That year he married Kunigunde Roth, daughter of a respected Nuremberg baker, in a marriage slightly higher than was to be expected for him. She proved a proper and most long-suffering wife, a model German *Hausfrau,* who never interfered in her husband's affairs, whether business or romantic. Their first son, Lothar, later to write for his father's *Der Stürmer,* was born in 1915. A second son, Elmar, followed in 1918.

Before either son was born, however, Streicher's life took an abrupt turn. When World War I began, he promptly reenlisted in the army. Like such fellow Nazis as Adolf Hitler and Hermann Göring, he relished combat and saw a startling amount of it. His unit, among the first to be sent to the front, met heavy fighting as the German army marched through France. Streicher sought out dangerous missions, one of which made him the first man in his company to win the Iron Cross. Carrying a crucial message through heavy enemy fire, he prevented an encirclement. By 1915 he had been selected as part of an elite machine-gun company, and soon, despite his previous record, he was accepted as an officer candidate.

In 1916 Romania joined the Allied cause, and Streicher's unit was transferred to the Carpathian front for a short, happy campaign that ended victoriously against the new enemy. Now he returned to Germany for training as a machine-gun platoon leader, part of his rise to officer status. His promotion demonstrated real merit. His past had hampered his rise, but almost as serious an impediment was the fact that he was an elementary-school teacher. Officers generally came from more elevated stock. Yet Streicher's superb performance under fire, his excellent recommendations from the Nuremberg school system, and the support of the officers whose company he wished to join resulted in his surprising advancement.

By July 1917 he was a lieutenant in the reserves. After additional training in the use of machine guns, he fought on the Italian front in the winter of 1917. By early 1918 he was back in France, where he added the Iron Cross, First Class, to his growing list of decorations. This medal, the highest German military award commonly given, was not rare—several million first- and second-class Iron Crosses were awarded—but it nonetheless conveyed genuine distinction. Both Streicher and another Iron Cross recipient, Adolf Hitler, were to wear their medals regularly after the war. With the collapse of German resistance in November 1918, Streicher was demobilized and returned immediately to Nuremberg.

His military career had been consistent with his character. Like many of his generation, he found in the community of the trenches satisfactions unavailable in peacetime. An excellent combat leader, he was dependable as long as the requirements were courage and constancy under fire. His willingness to follow other people's orders off the battlefield was less impressive. Even after he became an officer he found it difficult to stay out of trouble. While returning to Germany in 1917, for example, an altercation with a health officer in Salzburg led to a formal letter of complaint in his file.[4]

The Nuremberg to which Streicher returned in November 1918 was a city far different from what he had left in 1914. World War I had left its citizens—indeed, the whole nation—confused and disoriented. In a mistake the Allies were not to repeat in 1945, Germany had not been defeated clearly on the battlefield. To the German military leadership the fact that the war was lost was plain; but to German civilians, who could see their armies standing on French soil and could recall the total defeat of Russia in 1917, it was incredible that Germany now was subject to the Allied will. Hindenburg and Ludendorff, the very military leaders who had informed the civilian government that defeat was certain, were later to explain the German collapse by proposing the "stab in the back" legend, by which the nation had been ruined by traitors at home more than by enemy armies. It would be a satisfying theory.

In winter 1918 Nurembergers watched their once orderly society show decay unknown under the comfortable reign of the Kaiser, who now lived in exile in Holland. Allied soldiers occupied Germany, riding free wherever they wished on the state railroad. Prices more than doubled, and even then, essential goods often were unavailable. A new form of government, democracy, began to rule the nation, its officials conducting the business of a nation prepared neither intellectually nor culturally for self-government. A new constitution was proposed by an elected assembly meeting in Weimar. And the opposing forces of the right and left, gaining new strength in an unstable nation, brought to German cities a series of battles and assassinations that formerly were characteristic phenomena of the front line, not the streets of a civilized nation.

The confusion was complicated by the nature of the November Armistice, which had ended the fighting but left the terms of peace to later deliberation. Utterly powerless, the German representatives to the Versailles peace conference had little choice but to accept the terms of their nation's unforgiving enemies. When in May 1919 the text of the treaty was released, Germans independent of party reacted with amazed disbelief. No one had expected an easy treaty, but Woodrow Wilson's Fourteen Points had led many Germans to hope for a tolerable peace. The Treaty of Versailles held Germany wholly to blame for the devastation visited on Europe. The German army was limited to 100,000 men; the high-seas fleet, veteran of a single major battle, was scuttled. Large areas of previously German soil became foreign territory. And the Allies demanded war reparations so substantial that they were as yet unable to agree on the final sum. The wisdom of Churchill's maxim "in victory: magnanimity" is plain in the consequences of Versailles. However justified the Allied peace terms were, the sums they received from Germany after World War I were hardly sufficient to meet the smallest fraction of the costs of the next generation's battle with a resurgent Germany.

Julius Streicher's first year back in Nuremberg, then, was a hard one. Unlike many of his compatriots, he at least had his job as a schoolteacher waiting for him. And he had not lost interest in politics. At about the time another German veteran named Adolf Hitler was beginning his political career in Munich, Streicher resumed his, but in a new direction. Exactly what happened to him in 1919 is not clear, but by the end of the year he had become a radical anti-Semite.[5] His own later accounts are somewhat contradictory, and he was not yet sufficiently important to leave tracks in the files of the assiduous Nuremberg police, who regularly attended political meetings and wrote detailed reports of the goings-on. It is clear that by January 1919 he was attending meetings of the Schutz und Trutz Bund (Protective and Defensive Society), a rapidly growing anti-Semitic alliance that had as a primary goal persuading Germans to oppose Jews. After hearing the group's speakers, Streicher began reading a profusion of anti-Semitic pamphlets and books. Chief among them was Theodor Fritsch's *Handbuch der Judenfrage (Handbook of the Jewish Question),* an arsenal of anti-Jewish material that had an enormous influence on him. Streicher found in it and similar works a cogent explanation for the turmoil Germany was suffering: The Jews, he concluded, were guilty.

Soon he had resumed his career as a public speaker, at first addressing left-wing meetings during the discussion periods that most German parties allowed following the main speech. Questions could be put to the speaker, but often extended responses from audience members were permitted. Streicher later claimed to have spoken during many discussion periods, becoming so popular that he was refused the floor. He then called his own public meeting in the summer of 1919 to proclaim his anti-Semitism. During the Nuremberg trials he recalled that thousands packed the hall, and thousands more were turned away. The whole account is questionable, since the Nuremberg police failed to report Streicher's activity. They might have missed his discussion speaking but would not have ignored the major public meeting Streicher claimed to have held. Whatever the events of the year, he had by its end absorbed in full the idea that Jews were a separate race engaged in a sinister plot to rule the world, the conviction that governed the remaining years of his life.

With the enthusiasm of a new convert, Streicher looked for an organization of like-minded people. The Schutz und Trutz Bund he found inadequate, since it depended more on the printed word than on the mass meetings that Streicher thought vital if anti-Semitism were to spread. In January 1920, he turned to the newly established Nuremberg branch of a tiny political party, the Deutschsozialistische Partei (German Socialist Party). Though the DSP lacked a clear anti-Jewish platform, it was despite its name a right-wing group holding many of the traditional values that Streicher supported, and its very smallness gave him opportunity to influence its development. By April 1920 he was the Nuremberg delegate to the first national DSP convention. He joined those urging the party to run candidates for the June national parliamentary elections, and himself headed the Nuremberg party list of candidates.

In Nuremberg he found enough time outside his teaching duties to campaign energetically for the party, which soon had over three hundred members in his district and founded local groups in neighboring towns. But the election results were discouraging. Nationally the DSP vote was insignificant. In Nuremberg it was slightly more than 1 percent.

Meanwhile Streicher had added another task to his already busy days. A sign of a reputable German political party was the publication of a newspaper. At the April DSP convention a Nuremberg schoolteacher had been authorized to begin such a paper, but nothing had come of his work. Streicher took on the assignment, publishing the first issue of the *Deutsche Sozialist* on June 4, 1920. He immediately began to develop the style of popular journalism that later made the *Stürmer* infamous. His goal was to provide short articles in simple language that explained to a popular audience the intricacies of politics and economics. As he reported to the August 1920 DSP national meeting: "Gentlemen, let us not forget that we want to speak primarily to the workers. Brevity is the seasoning. . . . The contents must have a popular style."[6]

His lead article in the newspaper's first issue is a good example of his early writing. Addressed to Communists and Socialists, it began by saluting them as brothers:

> Yes! You are brothers. German mothers bore you on German soil. The same German blood flows in our veins.
> We and you have nothing to lose, but everything to gain. We have the same desire: to escape our present misery as fast as possible. We want

the same solutions. We too want our part of German soil. A small lot
with a little garden, just like so many others of our race. It is the right of
being born a German. And we want to be free of the usurious yoke of big
money!

Later in the article Streicher turned to the Jews:

Do you really think the Rothschilds, Mendelsohns, Bleichroders,
Warburgs and Cohns worry about your poverty? As long as the blood
brothers of the Mendelsohns, the Bleichroders and the Cohns are your
leaders, and as long as your party officials are Jewish lackeys, you will
be no threat to the big money men. As long as you yourself do not lead
the way, and as long as the black shadow of foreign blood is behind you,
you will be betrayed and deceived. The black shadow cares for itself, not
for you.[7]

The prose was not of particularly high quality, but it was simple.
Readers had no difficulty determining whom Streicher thought was
to blame for their ills.

With a newspaper under his control, the rebellious spirit that made
enemies of priests now began to make enemies of party colleagues.
The DSP, relatively moderate as right-wing parties went, found
quickly that Streicher followed his own line. And to their surprise, the
party leaders learned that they had no direct control over what
Streicher published, since he had seen to it that he personally owned
the newspaper. The complaints were many at the August DSP meeting. One delegate reported that some Catholics had left his group after
Streicher's first issue attacked the Jesuits. Others complained about
Streicher's increasing Jew-baiting. Streicher himself reported that
"some of the readers have written me, urging that the word 'Jew' be
avoided. I chose that term after careful thought. I knew it would
probably bring opposition." But he replied by observing that the
newspaper was his, and that he would do what he thought necessary.
"Were it otherwise, all that needed to be said might not be said."[8] A
week later Alfred Brunner, the DSP national leader, wrote Streicher
that he would not be permitted to rise to the party central leadership,
though his services as a propagandist were still welcome.

Streicher clearly had failed to turn his party in what he thought to be the correct direction. The problem he faced was that, from his perspective, no one was on the right track. He wanted a party willing to resort to mass propaganda to spread anti-Semitism, but his views were too radical for most other anti-Jewish groups to accept. Reluctantly he remained with the DSP, reporting at the third national DSP meeting in March 1921 that his local group now had over eight hundred members.

Throughout the party squabbling, the continuing economic and political uncertainties, and despite his full-time job, Streicher continued to put out the paper. It sold no more than two or three thousand copies a week, not enough to make it profitable. Shortages of paper and cash regularly hampered publication. Streicher solved the latter problem by finding a new printer whenever the old one pressed too insistently for payment. Nuremberg fortunately had many of that worthy trade.

His hectic life mirrored what was going in on the larger society. The shaky German democracy confronted a series of crises during the early 1920s only marginally less severe than those of 1919. The heavy economic demands of the Treaty of Versailles reduced production and encouraged inflation. There was a disconcerting chain of violence from the political left and right, the best-known case of which was the 1920 Kapp *Putsch,* a right-wing revolt in Berlin that had considerable support. That attempt failed, but a simultaneous rebellion in Bavaria established the supremacy of the right there. The continuing chaos contributed to the growing popularity of radical movements, as many Germans concluded that democracy was incapable of governing the nation.

One of those growing radical movements was Adolf Hitler's National Socialist German Workers Party (NSDAP), whose membership was limited to the Munich area. Since the DSP and the Nazis had much in common, members of the parties began to work for union. In May 1921 a Munich Nazi wrote to Streicher claiming that Hitler would welcome a merger, which in fact he may have then supported.[9] At a gathering of right-wing movements the previous August, Hitler had strongly supported cooperation. But by summer 1921 Hitler's views had changed markedly. He was not yet the absolute party leader he would soon become, and some of those working for merger saw it as a way of keeping Hitler from seizing complete control. The proposed headquarters of the united party, for example, was to be Berlin, far from Hitler's Munich power base.

Hitler's opposition became clear when, to the astonishment of the other Nazi leaders, he resigned from the party in July 1921 after the Augsburg groups of both parties had worked out a cooperative arrangement that threatened Hitler's control. Hitler made it known he would return only if given what amounted to absolute authority. Realizing his indispensability, the party surrendered. Merger negotiations ended immediately, for Hitler would tolerate no rivals. By September 1921, Otto Dickel, an Augsburg DSP leader involved in the earlier dealings, wrote Streicher enclosing a letter from Hitler which, Dickel thought, would destroy his political career. Dickel was willing to allow Hitler to continue to make propaganda, the role Brunner had been willing to give Julius Streicher in the DSP.[10]

The same Dickel began yet another right-wing group in the fall of 1921, the Deutsche Werkgemeinschaft (German Working Community). Not a party, its announced intention was to unite all racial right-wing movements, a frequent and always unsuccessful goal. One of its symbols, used by several German and Austrian groups, was the swastika. Streicher by now realized that he would not significantly influence the direction the DSP was taking and decided to join Dickel's new organization. Knowing he was more radical than most Deutsche Werkgemeinschaft members, he hoped to take a commanding position in a new movement. Changing the name of his paper to the *Deutscher Volkswille* with its October 1, 1921 issue and bringing most of his Nuremberg followers with him, Streicher soon was at work in a new cause.

The first energies went into a campaign for members in the towns surrounding Nuremberg. New groups were founded and hundreds of members won over. Streicher's rhetoric was becoming more vehement. Formerly he had made the usual broad accusations against Jews. Now he began supplementing them with claims of specific Jewish crimes in the Nuremberg region, the kind of tactic that would make him famous. During the spring of 1921, for example, he had accused Jews of ritual murder, the ceremonial killing of Christians to secure their blood for religious purposes. The charge was ancient, but Streicher added that several children disappeared annually in Nuremberg, the victims of the frightful Jewish crime. Such an outrageous accusation was too much even for the predominantly right-wing Bavarian judiciary. Brought to trial for the first of numerous times, Streicher was convicted of malicious slander and ordered to pay a small fine.

Speaking to meetings in outlying areas was not Streicher's favorite way of spreading anti-Semitism. Since his days with the DSP he had been convinced that mass meetings were the most powerful method of propaganda. The Deutsche Werkgemeinschaft leadership preferred less flashy methods of persuasion, but Streicher finally convinced them to authorize a mass meeting in Nuremberg on April 4, 1922. Several thousand people turned out to hear Streicher outline the new organization's platform. Streicher explained that he had fought in World War I thinking he was doing battle for Germany. Only later, he said, did he discover that the Jews controlled everything. "The racial question is the key to world history," he explained, using a favorite quotation from one of Benjamin Disraeli's novels. Already Streicher was using the sexual rhetoric that would become his trademark. "Stand in front of a hotel and see who takes the arms of the German girls," he suggested. "Not the German worker. We know they give themselves to the Orientals. . . ." His unusual racial theories were developing: "When a Negro or a black soldier on the Rhine misuses a German girl, she is lost to the race." The audience responded with enthusiasm, and Streicher promised to speak the week following on the goals of the Deutsche Werkgemeinschaft.[11]

The next meeting went poorly. The Socialists and Communists sent hundreds of men to the meeting with the intention of breaking it up. The two thousand attendees witnessed a debacle. After the meeting had been disrupted repeatedly by catcalls and jeers, Streicher declared it over. The result was a general melee. Even after massive police intervention, four people were wounded. The embarrassed Deutsche Werkgemeinschaft blamed Streicher for the affair, and he, never tolerating opposition well, left a meeting of Deutsche Werkgemeinschaft leaders angrily.

The unpleasantness made it plain to Streicher that he needed a more congenial organization. While continuing to speak for the Deutsche Werkgemeinschaft in the towns outside Nuremberg (no more mass meetings were authorized), he could see his influence declining. He had lost full control of the *Deutscher Volkswille,* probably for financial reasons, though the new editor, Walther Keller-bauer, for the time being Streicher's friend, continued to print his articles. In August 1922 the Augsburg group canceled its standing order for two hundred copies of the newspaper, a significant part of the total circulation, claiming the paper was not in accord with the views of most members, that constructive economic and political articles were lacking, and that the scope was too narrow, an admirable analysis.[12] The Deutsche Werkgemeinschaft did not want to lose Streicher's propagandistic talents—several letters from Augsburg urged him to remain loyal—but neither was it willing to give him the leadership role he wanted.

Now Streicher considered Hitler's Nazis. The Augsburgers, hoping to scuttle the attempt, sent Hitler a letter vehemently attacking Streicher, which Hitler cleverly passed on to Streicher (almost guaranteeing he would break with them). Hitler wrote the Augsburgers that he had a much better opinion of Streicher than he had of them, whom he still had not forgiven for the previous year's challenge to his leadership.[13] In May 1922, perhaps already thinking of Hitler, Streicher had written a lead article entitled "The Longing for a Strong Hand," a call for Germans to subordinate themselves to a leader who could give direction.[14] Streicher apparently had realized that he would not be that leader. Already he had failed to dominate two quite insignificant political groups, while Hitler clearly controlled the Nazis, and his movement was growing.

It is not clear when the two first met. Certainly they knew of each other by 1920. Shortly after Hitler put an end to the NSDAP-DSP merger negotiations in 1921, he had sent Streicher a friendly letter on the matter. Apparently the two did not meet until sometime in 1922, however, when Streicher heard Hitler speak in Munich. The result was dramatic. Streicher's most detailed account, written near the end of his life and showing clear lapses of memory, still shows the kind of appeal Hitler exerted on many Germans. Streicher described the enormous tension that filled the packed meeting hall:

> Suddenly a voice cried "Hitler is coming!" As if filled with some mysterious power, the many thousands of men and women lifted their right arms as in a blessing. Again and again, with primitive power the

chant "Heil Hitler!" swelled up to greet his arrival. . . . I felt this Adolf Hitler must be something special. . . .

Now he spoke. First slowly, hardly audible, then faster and more powerfully, and finally with overpowering strength. . . . He revealed an enormous treasure trove of thought in a speech of more than three hours, clothed with the beauty of inspired language.

Each person felt it: this man spoke from a godly calling, he spoke as a messenger from heaven at a time when hell threatened to swallow up everything.

And everyone understood him, whether with the brain or the heart, whether man or woman. He had spoken for everyone, for the entire German people. Just before midnight his speech concluded with the inspiring call: "Workers, blue collar or white! To you is extended the hand of a German people's community of heart and action."

"We Pray to the God of Justice." Never before had I heard that song sung so imploringly, so filled with faith and hope. And never before had the singing of "Deutschland über Alles" moved me as deeply as it did in that mass meeting where I first saw Adolf Hitler and heard him speak. I felt it: In this moment destiny calls to me a second time! I hurried through the jubilant masses to the podium, stood before him, and said: "I am Julius Streicher. At this moment I know I can be only a follower. But you are a *leader*! I give to you the popular movement which I have built in Franconia."[15]

The truth is a little less spectacular. Before handing over his movement Streicher conducted a series of negotiations, including at least one personal meeting with Hitler to work out the details. Streicher secured financial assistance to help cover the debts he had accumulated in two years of political combat. But there is no doubt that Hitler made of Streicher one of his many converts. Streicher's friendship with Hitler remained solid for the rest of his life, forming the basis of his personal power. Hitler was hardly an admirable human being, but he could be loyal to those who had helped him, particularly his earliest followers. In *Mein Kampf,* Streicher is one of the few people Hitler praises by name, calling his willingness to hand over his movement "a decision that was personally as hard as it was thoroughly decent."

On October 20, 1922, two thousand of Streicher's supporters

gathered to establish the Nuremberg group of the Nazi party. After Streicher had traced the development of the right-wing movement in Franconia and attacked the Jews, Hitler himself spoke, expressing appreciation for Streicher's work. The base which Streicher gave Nazism in Nuremberg was of critical importance to its early growth. Previously Hitler had limited the party to the Munich area. With his power established he was now ready for major expansion. Nuremberg was the "bridge to the north," the first major stronghold outside Munich.

Becoming a Nazi did not improve Streicher's unpleasant personality. Even though he finally had found a party radical enough to accept his extreme views, he was still unable to get along with anyone not willing to follow his wishes. It even took time before Hitler was able to bring him to submission. Within a month of the establishment of Nazism in Nuremberg Streicher was battling his new allies. The major opponent was Walther Kellerbauer, a former friend and a man by any standards pleasanter than Streicher. Resisting Streicher's attempt to dictate to the Nuremberg Nazis, Kellerbauer found supporters, among them the leaders of the Nuremberg Storm Troopers, Nazism's paramilitary organization. The struggle became bitter and by May 1923 was ruining the effectiveness of the entire party in Nuremberg. Hitler, who had previously and unsuccessfully tried to settle the matter, now took direct action. He sent the reliable and tough-minded Helmuth Klotz to Nuremberg. Klotz took control of the Storm Troopers and soon found that the bulk of the Nuremberg Nazis, having irregular contact with Streicher, supported him. Klotz thus arranged to have Kellerbauer removed as editor of the party news-paper and reduced in power. But he also made sure the Storm Troopers remained outside of Streicher's control. Ultimately Hitler established a separate Storm Trooper command, leaving local party leaders like Streicher outside the hierarchy. By fall 1923 Streicher was in firm control of Nuremberg Nazism.[16]

The attractiveness of the party to nonmembers naturally had been lessened by the well-publicized infighting, yet Streicher through it all continued a heavy schedule of mass meetings in Munich, frequent speaking engagements in neighboring towns, and of course his teaching. Perhaps the most significant outcome of the battle, however, was the beginning of Streicher's newspaper *Der Stürmer,* which we will examine in more detail in Chapter III.

The Nazi bickerings were very much overshadowed by the culmination of the great German inflation in the summer and fall of 1923. The currency had been inflating since the end of the war, but a combination of factors led to a dramatic increase in prices after May 1923. In six months, the price Streicher charged for an issue of *Der Stürmer* increased from 250 marks to 1.5 billion (see Table 1). A photograph of the period shows a child standing next to the enormous pile of banknotes it took to equal an American dollar. Destroying savings and public confidence in democracy's ability to govern Germany, the inflation led many to look to more radical solutions. To this day, any German government that adopts an inflationary policy will invite political defeat.

Table 1

Der Stürmer Price Increases: 1923

Issue and Month	Price in Marks
No. 1 (May)	250
No. 7 (July)	800
No. 8 (July)	1,500
No. 9 (August)	2,000
No. 10 (August)	10,000
No. 11 (August)	100,000
No. 12 (September)	200,000
No. 13 (September)	500,000
No. 14 (October)	3,000,000
No. 15 (October)	15,000,000
No. 16 (October)	20,000,000
No. 17 (October)	200,000,000
No. 18 (November)	1,500,000,000

Such catastrophic inflation together with what Hitler perceived to be favorable political conditions led to the inglorious Beer Hall

Putsch of November 8–9, 1923, Hitler's attempt to seize power through revolution. Streicher was centrally involved. He had been traveling regularly to Munich throughout the fall to give speeches at mass meetings. When on November 8 he received a message ordering him to Munich, he later testified that he thought he was wanted for another speech. Other evidence suggested he had a better idea of Hitler's plans. In any event, upon reaching the beer hall where Hitler's revolution was in progress, Streicher immediately joined in. Confident of Streicher's abilities, Hitler appointed him acting head of the Nazi party and director of propaganda.[17] Streicher went to work, first speaking to the assembled Storm Troopers.

The next day he drove about Munich in the company of a brigade of Nazis, speaking in public squares to large crowds of understandably curious citizens (see figure 2). A Munich newspaper summarized the tone of his remarks:

> German men and women! The national government has been established. Soon you will see action. Revolution races through the country. Profiteers, whether Christian or Jewish, will be hanged. The stock exchange will be closed and the banks will be supervised by the government. The new government will give you food, but you must have patience with its leaders. Adolf Hitler has thrown those who betrayed you into prison. Minister Schweyer sits in the same cell where Adolf Hitler was once imprisoned. The time of shame is over. The time of freedom has arrived. After this there will be but two parties, one of the poor, free and loyal German people, the other that of the usurious Jew. To which party do you want to belong? . . . He who does not obey the national government will be hanged, but he who does will be happy.[18]

The short, absurd history of the revolt is well known. Upon completing his speaking tour Streicher joined the main body of Hitler's followers in their march through Munich. When the procession reached the Feldherrnhalle, a prominent public monument on a large open square, the police opened fire. Sixteen of Hitler's followers died, the revolt collapsed, and Hitler went to jail.

Streicher returned to Nuremberg on an evening train. He urged his excited Nuremberg followers to remain calm and avoid causing difficulties for the police. The police meanwhile decided to arrest Streicher, and the government decided that he had overstepped the political boundaries established for state employees. Suspended from his teaching position on November 12, Streicher instituted legal appeals that continued until he was permanently suspended in 1928, but at two-thirds salary. The court decided he had been a good teacher before the *Putsch* and had earned a pension.

Leading armed rebellion against the state is generally thought to be a serious offense, but neither Hitler nor his followers were punished severely. The Bavarian judiciary was concerned more with rebellion from the left. Hitler served only fourteen months in prison, and Streicher was released on February 27, 1924, after serving a month with Hitler at the Landsberg prison. The jail term had done nothing to diminish Streicher's political fervor, and freed now from his teaching duties he could devote full energy to holding Nuremberg Nazism together. The party was officially outlawed, so Hitler's followers organized new groups having the same goals but with different names. Streicher initially joined the Deutscher Arbeiter Partei (DAP), on whose ticket he was elected to the Bavarian parliament in the April 6, 1924 elections. The seat carried with it a modest salary, a railroad pass good throughout Bavaria, and parliamentary immunity, a valuable fringe benefit for so regular a patron of the courts as Streicher would soon become.

Following the usual pattern, Streicher was quickly fighting with other DAP leaders. The squabbling had Hitler's tacit approval. Operating on the principle of dividing the potential opposition, the imprisoned Hitler refrained from giving his followers clear guidance on how to conduct the movement in his absence. As a result, the various groups each claimed to be following the silent Führer's wishes. Without Hitler's direct backing Streicher found himself in much the old position—unable to dominate and unwilling to subordinate himself. On July 21, 1924, he was expelled from the DAP, though he was as eager to leave as it was to be rid of him. Joining with Hermann Esser, another unsavory early Nazi, Streicher now formed the Nuremberg chapter of a second Nazi successor group, the Grossdeutsche Volksgemeinschaft (GVG).

His oratorical abilities rapidly gave his new party the leading role in radical right-wing Nuremberg politics. An average DAP meeting in August 1924 drew four hundred people, half of whom were Streicher supporters out to cause mischief. Streicher, meanwhile, consistently drew audiences of two thousand. Part of the problem was that, at least in comparison to Streicher, the DAP leadership had scruples. Walther Kellerbauer, Streicher's former friend and now the DAP leader, charged that Streicher regularly attacked in the crudest ways anyone who disagreed with him.[19] Kellerbauer could speak from experience. Calumny may not be polite, but it draws audiences. Streicher also began feuding with his comrades in the state legislature, being expelled in October 1924 from the Völkisch Block, a Nazi coalition. Streicher and his supporters in turn accused the coalition of a series of errors, including the dastardly crime of "parliamentarian intellectualism."[20]

In Nuremberg Streicher decided to run for the city council, securing easy election in the fall 1924 elections. There he proved as unhelpful a politician as he had been in the Bavarian legislature. Gregor Strasser, a prominent early Nazi with no liking for Streicher, was to criticize his conduct harshly in 1930. According to a police observer, Strasser "raised the general reproach against Streicher of Nuremberg that, even though he had been a member of the city council for five years, he had not done anything. Streicher should insult people less and do more practical work in the city council."[21] But Streicher really was not interested in doing productive work. For one thing, it would mean putting up with opposing ideas, but more importantly Streicher saw it as a waste of time. The purpose of securing political office was to gain a propaganda platform, not to give over long hours to patching up the Weimar Republic. As Joseph Goebbels put it, to invest hard work in Weimar politics only attacked a small part of a large problem. The better solution was to destroy what existed and start afresh.

Streicher's general conduct was evident from his first day as a city councilman. The initial meeting of the new council was on January 1, 1925. Streicher and his fellow Nazi councilmen made so much noise that Mayor Hermann Luppe, an active proponent of democracy, was forced to end the meeting. Luppe met with the leaders of the other parties before the next council meeting to plan ways of dealing with the obstreperous Nazis; all agreed to a change in the rules that permitted the mayor to eject members after calling them to order three times. Luppe also secured a new and louder bell, the German equivalent of the chairman's gavel. The old one could not be heard above Streicher's shouting. Having made his preparations, Luppe called a second meeting. Early in the meeting Streicher took the floor. Observing that Luppe had called him and his supporters psychopaths and that mentally deficient people were by law ineligible to serve on city councils, Streicher accused the mayor of being remiss in his duties, as he had done nothing to prevent Streicher from being seated. He then attacked Luppe in a typical display of calumny and concluded that he would be willing to work constructively as long as someone other than Luppe was mayor. The meeting degenerated into a shouting match, and Luppe called the waiting police, who escorted Streicher out.[22]

One hundred people were waiting for him outside City Hall. They accompanied him to a previously announced public meeting on the theme "Battle in City Hall," where twenty-five hundred Nurembergers were waiting. The fact that so many people would attend a meeting even before anything had happened testifies both to Streicher's drawing power and to the confidence Nuremberg's citizens had in his ability to provoke a fight.

The affair received considerable press coverage and supplied Streicher with material for several speeches during the following weeks. His subsequent conduct was no better. On February 4 he was again ejected. Thereafter, council meetings were more peaceful, largely because Streicher skipped most of them. There were no propaganda benefits to be won from continued disruption, and Streicher certainly did not want to take the duties of a councilman seriously.

Hitler secured early release from his quite pleasant prison and at the end of February 1925 moved to unify his disorganized followers. Streicher was one of the first, Hitler later recalled, to renew his oath of allegiance: "I have tried to do my best during your absence," Streicher said. "I do not know whether I have succeeded. If I made mistakes, and that is possible, I did not do so intentionally. Now that you are here, I place my work in your hands."[23] The GVG was officially dissolved at a February 27 meeting. Five days later the Nuremberg Nazis turned out in force to hear Hitler's first public speech there in over a year. Three parallel meetings were arranged, to which forty-seven hundred people came. Hitler appeared at each. Streicher was now appointed Nazi *Gauleiter* (regional leader) for Franconia, the region surrounding Nuremberg.

Streicher's willingness to subordinate himself to Hitler in 1922, together with his loyalty to the imprisoned Hitler in 1924, gave Streicher the political security he had lacked earlier in his career. His personality had not changed; indeed, a regular series of complaints and rebellions against his leadership continued throughout the remaining Weimar years. At least six anti-Streicher newspapers were published after 1923, most seeing several issues at best. Streicher once remarked that, had he been given all the money people had spent putting out newspapers that attacked him, he could have built a country villa.[24] Hitler now and again became angry with Streicher's blunders but never seriously considered withdrawing his support. As a result, all the various challenges to Streicher's leadership collapsed.

He was also becoming a regular visitor to the Nuremberg courtrooms. Most cases concerned charges of libel or slander, and several received remarkable publicity—notably the Luppe-Streicher trials of 1924 and 1925. Hermann Luppe had been appointed lord mayor of Nuremberg in 1920. Having established an excellent record of municipal leadership in Frankfurt, and being a well-educated man with strong democratic convictions who did not fear political battle, he was well suited to be the leading proponent of democracy in northern Bavaria. Streicher had been fighting with the mayor since 1922, when Streicher had demanded that Luppe correct a false statement that had been made about Streicher during a city council meeting. Luppe made the sensible response that to correct every misstatement made there would be an unreasonably demanding task, certainly not an answer likely to quiet the hot-tempered Streicher. When Streicher accused Luppe of having Jewish ancestry, he replied that Streicher should be happy were his ancestry as solidly Aryan as Luppe's. Streicher responded with an increasingly severe series of attacks, culminating in libelous charges in early issues of *Der Stürmer*. The mayor first sensibly decided that no good would come of bringing suit; eventually Streicher's persistence and the urgings of Luppe's friends got the better of his patience, and he instituted suit in the fall of 1924.

The trial was distinctly unpleasant from Luppe's perspective. The courtroom regularly was filled with Streicher's vocal and insulting supporters. The judge, a well-meaning man entirely unsuited to the task of dealing with a political showman like Streicher, was unable to maintain order. As Luppe later put it, "he was the founder of a private choir. In music circles he was thought to be a good jurist, and in legal circles to be a good musician."[25] Having no regular occupation, Streicher could put more effort into the case than Luppe, who could not ignore his duties as mayor for the month the trial took. Streicher defended himself by raising a variety of charges against Luppe, mostly groundless, though some were embarrassing. The most memorable issue was the coat Luppe had purchased from the city used-clothing office, frequented mostly by the poor. Though Luppe violated no law in the purchase, it was an ill-advised acquisition which Streicher was to make noise about for years (see figure 4). The trial ended with Streicher's conviction.

The lengthy appeal, which also ended with a conviction, was held late in 1925. Adolf Hitler even appeared to testify that in attacking Luppe, Streicher was following the party's orders. Once again Nazis packed the courtroom, and again Luppe suffered their rude conduct. He heard Streicher's usual lengthy speeches. The worst came when the mayor was temporarily suspended from office on suspicion of perjury. Though he was quickly absolved, the contrast between the treatment he endured and the brief prison term Streicher received was discouraging. Streicher meanwhile went to trial for an unrelated offense. Convicted again, the two sentences were combined into a 3½-month term, which he served between August and December 1926.

Both trials were extraordinarily valuable propaganda from the Nazi point of view. The leading Nuremberg newspapers gave regular and extensive publicity, making Streicher seem far more significant than he in fact was. As Goebbels noted of his similar experiences in Berlin, the important thing was to be noticed. Only then could one win supporters. Since Streicher's followers were convinced of his innocence, frequent court appearances only proved that Streicher was being persecuted by the Jews. As he put it: "When one visits a courtroom these days, it is just like walking into a synagogue."[26] Ironically, the oftener Streicher went to court, the more his followers thought of him.

The Luppe-Streicher trials were only the most prominent of Streicher's courtroom visits. He was brought to court himself at least a dozen times during the Weimar era for his own speaking and writing, and he instituted a number of suits against others. His newspaper was seized or banned more than thirty times between 1923 and 1933. During a single eleven-day period in 1928, five lawsuits against *Stürmer* staff members commenced. It would perhaps be going too far to say that Streicher welcomed the opportunity to visit the courts so often, as his legal expenses were high. Still, he could always appeal to his supporters for assistance and count on getting it. His files contain long lists of those who gave to his legal defense fund. Prison terms were not welcome either, but he could trust the Bavarian courts to award lenient sentences. Despite his consistent calumnies, Streicher served a total of about eight months in prison. His legal standing was particularly improved by his election to the Bavarian legislature, which carried parliamentary immunity. That immunity could be revoked, as it in fact was several times, but the process was difficult and the authorities often decided that prosecution was not worth the effort.

Streicher's growing effectiveness became plain toward the end of the Weimar period, when victims found it increasingly difficult to persuade the authorities to prosecute him. Walter Berlin, chairman of the Nuremberg chapter of the Central Union of German Citizens of the Jewish Faith, repeatedly attempted to persuade the public prosecutor to go after Streicher. As Berlin later wrote: "Generally, the Public Prosecutor, though often not contesting my opinion, was rather reluctant to act, particularly, as was intimated to me, because juries became more and more influenced by the very articles on which the prosecution had to be based."[27] Anti-Semitism was becoming more acceptable.

The regular revolts against his leadership within the party and his frequent court cases were generally no more than minor annoyances. Most of Streicher's energies after 1925 went into two related goals: building support for Nazism and spreading anti-Semitism. In his political speaking and newspaper writing, he perfected the propaganda skills that were to make him the world's leading Jew-baiter after 1933.

Public speaking was one of the most valuable of his skills. Since so much of his time went into making speeches, it is worth looking at his performance. The Nazis in general put astonishing energy into oratory. Hitler's lucid discussion of mass propaganda in *Mein Kampf* claimed that all great changes in world history were the result of the spoken word, and he made sure Nazism relied on speeches more than on any other means of propaganda. Hundreds of thousands of Nazi meetings were held prior to 1933, fifty thousand in the two weeks before the April 1932 presidential elections alone.[28]

The practice in Nuremberg was consistent with the overall policy. Nuremberg Nazis held over one hundred meetings during their first year, not counting those held outside the city proper. During 1931 Streicher's region held more than three thousand meetings. He of course did not speak at all or even most of them, but throughout his career he maintained an average of more than one major speech a week. In 1930 he was named an NSDAP national speaker, the top tier of the party's extensive and well-developed speaker system, and he was one of the most requested Nazi orators. Although he was an abysmal correspondent and his surviving personal files have large gaps, dozens of requests for his services as a speaker remain.

What was it about Streicher that made such an unpleasant man such a popular speaker? His regular appearance in the newspapers did make him a Nazi celebrity; some invitations came from people who simply wanted to see what he looked like. More than that, he was an accomplished popular speaker who put on lively and entertaining meetings. Radio was only developing and television was scarcely imagined in the 1920s. Political speeches were for many Germans a form of entertainment, a way of passing the evening at modest cost. Streicher's ability to be entertaining is indicated by the regularity with which Nurembergers came to hear him say essentially the same things every week for ten years.

Nazi mass meetings were spectacular affairs. They combined bands, marching men, colorful decorations, vendors hawking the Nazi press, and two thousand or more people. All that joined with lively oratory made for an evening worth the price of admission. That admission charge was critical, by the way. Multiplied by the thousands who regularly attended his meetings and added to the revenues from the *Stürmer* and Streicher's rich mistresses (for whom he had a peculiar attraction), it made him one of Hitler's most dependable sources of money after 1925. "If all Gauleiters were as efficient in raising money as my old fighting comrade Julius Streicher," Hitler once said, "half my worries would disappear immediately."[29]

On his own, Streicher had reached the discouragingly accurate analysis of mass propaganda outlined by Hitler in *Mein Kampf.* Both realized that propaganda had to be simple, repetitious, and emotional. The result in Streicher's case was summarized by a policeman who attended one of his meetings: "The intellectual level of the evening... was extraordinarily coarse and vulgar."[30] But it worked. A more flattering description comes from a 1935 article by a Nazi journalist describing Streicher's Berlin speech that year: "Julius Streicher spoke simply and directly in the language of the people. Everyone understood him, for he used the simplest, crystal clear language."[31] Streicher himself amused audiences by explaining that he spoke so simply so as to be understood even by a university professor.

His delivery was lively and varied. *The New York Times,* describing one of his frequent speeches to children, observed that "his smile never fails to throw young children into convulsions,"[32] and police reporters regularly commented on his forceful style. One of Streicher's superiors in the Nuremberg school system made a comment about his teaching which applies as well to his oratory:

> I have to say that teacher Streicher possesses all the qualities that are necessary to be a good teacher. Above all, he has the rare ability to captivate his students. This ability stems from his strong emotions and will, as well as from a rare gift of emotionally vivid and lively illustration. He has an extraordinary ability to speak extemporaneously, and can adapt so as to hold the interest of his students.[33]

Those abilities were as valuable in a public meeting as they were in a schoolroom.

A hallmark of effective propaganda is to say the same thing in different ways. The effective propagandist looks not for new arguments but for new evidence, new examples. Thus Streicher presented the citizens with a steady supply of material demonstrating the depravity of the Jews and the ineffectualness of the Weimar Republic. In 1927, for example, he told his audience of a poor forester he had met while in jail. Forced to poach to feed his family, he was now serving a three-year term. Though the Nuremberg police doubted the truthfulness of the story (the newspaper clipping in their files that reports the story has a question mark in the margin), his audience was not likely to doubt the truth of so touching a tale.[34] On the same theme three years later, he told of a tailor jailed because he could not pay a ten-mark debt. These kinds of stories were well suited to his audience, primarily farmers, workers, and the middle class, the levels of society most threatened by economic hardship. Streicher made it clear that they too faced financial ruin: "Today the German middle class, the poor German man, sits in prison beside criminals, ground under by this government. If the prisons are not yet overflowing, it is only because there are thousands who have not yet chanced to fall into the morass of laws. One can determine the state of this nation from the state of its prisons."[35]

If his material was emotionally appealing, it was from a critical perspective less admirable. His rhetoric was simple to the point of numbness. His arguments were few: Jews were responsible for the world's ills, Adolf Hitler and Nazism were Germany's salvation. As early as 1922 a police reporter wrote that Streicher "delivered his familiar exposition against the Jews, without adding anything particularly new," and ten years later a colleague commented: "Streicher raised his old complaints against the Jews."[36] Streicher was far more interested in getting old ideas across than beginning on new ones. Nor was he interested in providing solutions, always dangerous things to propose. Instead Streicher gave visionary descriptions of a marvelous future under Nazism, without making it clear what that future involved. As he told the 1927 party rally in Nuremberg:

> Into this night of horror came the rescuing rays of National Socialism. It was the Gospel of recovery for our German fatherland, again bringing clarity into the chaos of opinions, to the maelstrom of political discord. It preached the coming day of freedom, and gave expression to the hope that the time is no longer distant when the swastika flag will be draped over the coffin of Marxism. When that day comes, it will once again be fitting to call upon the Almighty in the words of the hymn: "Now Thank We All Our God."[37]

The police reporter noted that spontaneous and long-lasting applause greeted his speech, not surprising given the audience. In 1931, he was telling audiences of a secret agreement between Hitler and officials in Britain and Italy which would end war reparations payments when Hitler became chancellor, a claim a government report noted was gladly believed though entirely false.[38] The plainest evidence for Streicher's simpleminded view of the universe is, of course, his anti-Semitism. As will become clear in later chapters, his fundamental argument was that most of the world's ills would vanish with the Jews.

Streicher naturally relied heavily on such standard themes as sex, religion, and violence. His sexual rhetoric we will consider at length in Chapter VII. From the religious appeals he used, one might almost think him a devout Christian. The Nazi program spoke of the party's support for a "positive Christianity" without in any way commiting Nazism to the ancient body of Christian doctrine. Similarly, though Streicher had long since left the Catholicism of his childhood by the 1920s, he knew that many in his audience were still faithful and could be reached with religious language. "The Christian religion no longer carries a true view of Christianity," he argued, apparently a devout reformer. "Christ was a fighter, not a weakling."[39] Sometimes speaking with a Bible in hand, he claimed to be attacking not Christianity, rather the perverted Jewish version of it that the Jews had foisted on Germany. He even announced a new Christ in the person of Adolf Hitler, rather a common Nazi theme. "I bow down to him; he is sent by God." Both Hitler and Christ had much in common, he thought. Both had walked the road to Golgatha and both had been betrayed.[40]

Consciously or not, Streicher was following what became official Third Reich policy. As a later Nazi writer put it, Christianity had taken over Germany by adopting the old pagan religious symbols but giving them new meaning, slowly transforming pagans to Christians through familiar rituals.[41] Nazism developed an impressive set of ceremonies which, having clear Christian analogies, were intended ultimately to replace the Gospel of Christ with the Gospel of Hitler. When Streicher turned to Christian images or suggested that the Church had long sanctioned attacks on Jews, the uncritical hearer could easily assume he was a loyal son of the Church. As early as 1922 one woman praised him as an "example of a genuine Christian man," and a later writer announced that he was praying that God "would lead your spirit in the right ways, allowing you to speak without fear or terror, using your gifts for the benefit of humanity."[42]

Violence was another standby. From the earliest days of the movement, Nazism realized the appeal of force. More than four hundred Nazis died in political violence before 1933, many during political meetings, and thousands more were wounded. Post-1933

Nazi literature glorified the days when regular fights were the consequence of party membership. As Otto Strasser, a leading early Nazi put it, such warfare advanced the Nazi cause. Describing one meeting hall brawl, he wrote:

> The battle . . . rather than destroying the purpose of our meeting actually strengthened it enormously. All those who still remained with us in the hall after the fight had taken our side in a sort of spontaneous partnership. The bitter struggle brought about the spirit of camaraderie which is engendered whenever men go through physical combat together. A short time before they had been doubtful of us, suspicious. . . . Now that attitude was changed. We had become allies, if only by force of circumstances.[43]

Streicher was in full agreement. In 1924 he told an audience that Nazis would fight Jews and Marxists "with German fists, weapons and daggers, and we shall not rest until the last of these strangers is defeated."[44] In 1926 he chaired a meeting in Munich. The audience, which included many Socialists and Communists, had been well behaved until one person heckled. The speaker ignored the interruption, but Streicher stood up, stopped him, and said: "One moment, please. The disturber should stand up. Who laughed? The dog has to leave." The culprit, reluctant to draw the attentions of a brigade of Storm Troopers, held silent. Streicher then ordered the Storm Troopers to "clear the hall of Marxists." Before returning the floor to the speaker, he remarked that "terror from the left can be combated only by still firmer terror from the right."[45] Such provocative behavior, and more examples could be given, had a dual function, both enhancing the image of the NSDAP as an aggressive movement and giving the audience the satisfying experience of being on the winning side.

A final element that made Streicher a popular speaker was his ability to use invective and find scandal. The eagerness with which people hear gossip is hard to overestimate, as the Nazis knew well. Goebbels claimed that "Berlin needs scandal like a fish needs water," a statement equally true of Nuremberg. Disgruntled city employees and loyal Nazis provided a reliable supply of lively material. Konrad Heiden, one of the earliest and best historians of Nazism, noted that Streicher "provided at short intervals a grand scandal for the people of Nuremberg who, like the inhabitants of all great cities, enjoyed a scandal. If he attacked an opponent—and it was generally a Jew—for any kind of misbehavior, he was always right up to a point, despite exaggerations and generalizations."[46] Heiden is too generous to Streicher's love of truth, but it is true that his scandalmongering had an element of truth often enough to build his credibility and to draw audiences confident of his ability to reveal fresh gossip.

All told, Streicher was dramatic, exciting to listen to, armed with tantalizing charges and amazing stories. He put complicated happenings into simple form, giving his audiences the illusion that he (and they) had a clear understanding of local events and world politics. All that was a lot to get for the price of admission, often only about the price of a glass of the excellent Nuremberg beer.

Despite Streicher's activity as a speaker, journalist, and politician, he was not a particularly influential Nazi after 1925. Increasingly Hitler turned to cleverer men like Joseph Goebbels and Hermann Göring instead of reliable but less capable men like Streicher. Hitler realized well enough that Streicher simply was not very bright. Nonetheless, Streicher's limited abilities were used. Hitler made Nuremberg the site of the party rallies in 1927 and 1929, partly because Nuremberg was a city rich in tradition, partly because it was a Nazi stronghold with Julius Streicher there to arrange details. In 1932 Streicher was elected to the Reichstag, the national legislature. And his newspaper gained increasing national circulation as Nazism grew.

As Hitler was conducting his final drive for power, the last and most serious of the pre-1933 revolts against Streicher's leadership broke out. Wilhelm Stegmann, who as a Storm Trooper leader stood outside Streicher's direct control, began a campaign in August 1932 to drive Streicher out. Stegmann not only published the by now obligatory anti-Streicher newspaper, making the customary charges of sexual misconduct, financial mismanagement, and political ineffectiveness, he also used the Storm Troopers to wage what sometimes became open warfare. Several men on both sides were killed. The outraged Hitler, who found the negative publicity harmful to his January 1933 negotiations for the chancellorship, ordered Stegmann deposed. Streicher was fully victorious, as he so regularly had been in the past. Once again Hitler had saved him. And now, with Hitler as chancellor, whole new courses of action were available.

II

The Bloody Czar
of Franconia

For most Nazis, 1933 was final victory. After years of fierce struggle they now could enjoy the rewards of power. Soon Hitler refused to hold the Nuremberg party rally meeting of the party's political leaders during the day—too many had new paunches. Albert Speer accordingly designed his stunning "cathedral of light"—hundreds of spotlights pointing straight up—to illuminate an evening meeting and conceal the fat. For Julius Streicher, however, 1933 was only a beginning. With Hitler in power, policies for which he long had argued had excellent chances of becoming national law.

Unlike many party bigwigs, Streicher did not immediately take on a state position to complement his party office. He despised bureaucrats, and to become one would require moving to the smaller town of Ansbach, seat of the Franconian government. That did not mean Streicher lacked influence on what happened. In the peculiar parallel structure of party and state in the Third Reich, the government official who ignored the wishes of his *Gauleiter* generally found party more powerful than state. It did mean that Streicher could remain in Nuremberg, running his district with a strong if disorganized hand.

Streicher never had been a good administrator. He had, it is true, done a competent job of arranging the pre-1933 Nuremberg rallies, but he was really better suited for war than for peace. Just as he had been a poor soldier off the battlefield and a good one on it, he was better at fighting for political power than he was at using it. Indeed, the almost absolute power of a *Gauleiter* of the Third Reich exacerbated the flaws in his personality. He could not tolerate the orders of others, nor would he tolerate disobedience on the part of his subordinates. As Edward N. Peterson observes:

> Probably more so than any of his peers, Streicher combined the elements of a dictator who would brook no opposition with those of the anarchist, the lover of chaos, who would accept no orders from superiors. This inability to fit into an organization, even his own, was his greatest weakness as Gauleiter. His lack of control made him enemies above, such as Goering and Himmler, and drove honorable men out of his organization below, leaving miserable toadies who had to crawl at his feet. There was constant turmoil in Franken because there was constant turmoil in Streicher.[1]

The pleasures of power Streicher enjoyed. Those bureaucrats who had opposed him before 1933 were dealt with. Mayor Hermann Luppe was chased out of office and subjected to a series of petty harassments until he was killed in April 1945 by a bombing raid on Kiel. Luppe's replacement, an advancement-hungry Nazi named Willi Liebel, had learned how to live with Streicher. Meanwhile, Heinrich Himmler had taken temporary command of the Nuremberg police before appointing Johann Molsen-Ponikau police president. The new chief ran into immediate problems with Streicher, including a shouting match in Hitler's hearing, and soon left. His successor was unable to handle the job. The third man Himmler tried proved a better choice, Dr. Benno Martin, an extraordinarily capable administrator who had earned Streicher's respect before 1933 by handling relations between the NSDAP and the police. A shrewd man who knew how to run his department while keeping Streicher happy, he would later join with Mayor Liebel to drive Streicher from Nuremberg. But no one dared oppose Streicher at first. He had demonstrated his ability to survive challenges to his leadership in the years before 1933. With Hitler as chancellor, Streicher was even more formidable.[2]

And Hitler made it clear that he favored his old friend. In one of his first major appearances outside Berlin after January 30, the day he took power, Hitler spoke to an enormous mass meeting in Nuremberg on February 25, plain evidence of Streicher's favored position, for Hitler's speeches were usually rewards for faithful service. Hitler also decided that Nuremberg would remain the site of the annual party rally, held there from 1933 to 1938. The 1939 rally was canceled only at the last moment, with preparations quite complete, as the result of World War II. Hundreds of thousands of Nazis gathered each year in Julius Streicher's city, and his visibility was always high. Then there was November 9, the anniversary of Hitler's 1923 *Putsch,* the most sacred of the Nazi holidays. Each year a solemn procession of the surviving veterans of 1923 marched through Munich. Large smoking pylons lined the route, each bearing the name of one of the hundreds of Nazis who died during Hitler's battle for power. As the column reached each pylon, loudspeakers announced the name of a martyr. At the head of the procession marched Julius Streicher, immediately before the Blood Banner, the blood-soaked flag which had been carried by the saints of 1923.

Although Hitler made it plain that Streicher was in his good graces, it is interesting that the two were not really close friends. Streicher was one of the very few who used the intimate German pronoun *du* with Hitler, reserved for perhaps a half dozen Nazi leaders from the old days, but Hitler often avoided Streicher during his visits to Nuremberg. At dinner he preferred the company of better conversationalists, like Mayor Liebel or Police President Martin, men who could discuss intelligently such favorite Hitler topics as history and opera. Martin, indeed, would read up on an obscure piece of music before each of Hitler's visits. Streicher simply could not keep up his end of the conversation once things got off the Jewish question. At times Hitler even visited Nuremberg without letting Streicher know of his presence. But whenever anyone attacked Streicher for his crudeness, for his vehement attacks on the Jews, Hitler always defended him. "If I let Streicher fall and ban the *Stürmer,*" Hitler once said, "world Jewry would howl with glee. I will not give them the pleasure."[3] The *Stürmer,* Hitler was willing to say, was the only newspaper he regularly read from cover to cover. He was simply "on thorns" to see each new issue.

In the 1920s Streicher had told those who resisted his control of Nuremberg Nazism: "I am the locomotive and I pull the train." Now he pulled a long train indeed. He could act as he wished, for in a real sense he was the law. Many old enemies were fired or driven from Nuremberg with Mayor Luppe. Others went to Dachau. Sometimes he took personal vengeance. In June 1934 Hitler moved against his enemies in the Night of the Long Knives. Several hundred people were openly butchered. When word reached Nuremberg, a schoolteacher named Steinrück, sitting in a cafe, was heard to say that Streicher should have been among the victims. He was arrested, and word went to Streicher. Carrying the riding whip that was a trademark and in the company of two fellow Nazis, Streicher visited Steinrück's cell, where the three took turns beating the helpless prisoner. A lesser offender would have been punished, but the authorities realized prosecution was impossible and no action was taken against him. "I needed that," Streicher later said. "Now I feel released."[4]

Generally he used his power in ways that secured better public relations. As *Gauleiter* he controlled substantial resources. His newly founded daily newspaper, the *Fränkische Tageszeitung,* made sure that word of his charitable deeds reached a broad audience. Nurembergers saw pictures of their *Gauleiter* visiting the sick and poor, attending birthday parties for old party members, receiving visiting dignitaries. Streicher's annual Christmas dinner for former members of the Communist Party, now imprisoned at Dachau, even secured *New York Times* coverage.[5] At one such dinner he offered to pay the railroad fare of anyone who wanted to leave Germany for the Soviet Union. Streicher still took particular pleasure in speaking to school-children, before whom his simple and vivid presentation of anti-Semitism was invariably effective. By the mid-1930s he was a Nuremberg institution.

His personal life remained surprisingly modest by Nazi standards. The likes of Göring and Goebbels competed in the acquisition of wealth, and in its display, but Streicher was more comfortable in familiar surroundings. As *Gauleiter* he had the use of an impressive Nuremberg palace, but he preferred less ostentatious quarters. He was not poor—the revenues of his newspapers and the fringe benefits of being a *Gauleiter* made him wealthy by the end of the decade—but his tastes were more moderate than those of many of his Nazi brethren.

Despite his continual sexual affairs, his homelife too remained traditional. His long-suffering wife, who endured serious illnesses, kept in the background, rarely appearing in public with her husband. His two sons enjoyed the benefits of a powerful father. Lothar, the older son, saw service with the Nazi Condor Legion during the Spanish Civil War before returning to Germany in 1938 to work for his father's daily newspaper, also writing at times for the *Stürmer*. Elmar attended one of the party training schools for future leaders, also visiting England, where he got involved in a brawl between English Fascists and Communists.

Streicher's household included "Aunt Elia," an old family friend who had taught with him in the Nuremberg school system, and one of his sisters. Then there were a number of visiting English girls, some of whom lived with the family. The most notorious of these was Unity Mitford, a young Englishwoman from a bright but odd noble family. Captivated by the glitter of Nazism and oblivious to its evil, she attached herself to several leading Nazis, including the Führer himself. For some reason she found Streicher's anti-Semitic diatribes fascinating and regularly visited him in Nuremberg. In return, she served as a link between Streicher and British Fascism, and even threw a cocktail party for Lothar Streicher during his visit to London in 1938. Torn by the outbreak of the war, Unity Mitford attempted suicide in 1939 while in Germany. Eventually allowed to return to England, she died in 1948 as the result of meningitis stemming from her suicide attempt.[6]

There were many *Gauleiter* who in their realms exercised personal power equal to Streicher's. What made him stand out from his colleagues was a consuming anti-Semitism. His main energies after 1933 went into the Jew-baiting that would lead him to the gallows, but that first gained him international notoriety. From the first days of Hitler's regime Streicher's goals were plain. In February 1933 the *Stürmer* wrote: "We can be sure that National Socialism will take up the solution to the Jewish question with the same energy which led it to the chancellor's office." And in March, responding to worldwide uproar over Nazi policies: "The shrieks and hollers of Jews abroad will not stop the new Germany from its perfectly legal reckoning with its deadly enemies. No power on earth will hinder the cleansing of our foul, dishonored fatherland of deadly vermin."[7] Streicher had been preaching for ten years that the Jews were that deadly vermin.

He was soon at work. The first opportunity came when Hitler, seeking a way to occupy the Storm Troopers who, now victorious, were engaging in unauthorized anti-Jewish activity, decided on an organized anti-Jewish boycott, allegedly as a response to hostile foreign propaganda. What better person to direct the boycott than Julius Streicher, who Germans learned on March 28, 1933 was chairman of the Central Committee for the Defense Against Jewish Atrocity and Boycott Propaganda. Streicher announced a boycott that would begin on April 1 and continue until international Jewry ceased its anti-German propaganda. Hitler thought he had outwitted his coalition partners by making the matter a party affair, but their pressure forced him to restrict the action to a single day.

Streicher worked furiously in the few days he had before April 1, organizing a boycott that went surprisingly smoothly. In much of Germany uniformed Storm Troopers took up station outside Jewish shops and offices, discouraging customers from entering. The boycott failed to have much long-term impact on anti-Semitism—indeed, it was the kind of sudden measure that tended to promote sympathy for the Jews rather than hostility—but it did demonstrate the seriousness with which Hitler took Jew-baiting, and it made Julius Streicher's central role plain.

In Nuremberg Streicher as *Gauleiter* undertook immediate measures against the Jews. He intentionally refrained from associating himself with specific acts of violence against Jews. "I told the SA leaders that I would throw out of the party anyone who attacked a single Jew," he wrote Rudolf Hess in October 1933. "I told them they did not know what they would start, that a single beaten Jew could arouse the entire world against us."[8] Despite his reputation as the "Bloody Czar of Franconia," the physical lot of the Jews in Nuremberg was not much worse than elsewhere in Germany, which of course is not saying very much. Streicher implemented or encouraged every scheme he could devise to make the life of the Jews miserable. Nuremberg became a national leader in anti-Semitic policy.

The year 1935 demonstrated Streicher's position as the party's leading anti-Semite. It was the year of his fiftieth birthday, and Adolf Hitler himself attended the festivities. In August Streicher spoke to a huge Berlin mass meeting, his first major speech there since the Nazi takeover. In his customary 2½-hour speech he vividly summarized his ideas to an enthusiastic crowd. The pitch of Berlin anti-Semitism quickened noticeably. At the annual Nuremberg rally in September, Hitler announced the hastily drafted Nuremberg Laws. Sexual relations between Jews and other Germans were legally proscribed. No Gentile woman under forty-five could work as a maid for a Jew, an effort to keep the racial blood from corruption. Streicher long had called for such legislation, though to his annoyance he was not consulted while the laws were being written. To the world, however, it seemed that the Nuremberg Laws were Streicher's personal triumph. As he left the hall after Hitler's speech, surprised but delighted, the crowd of thousands cheered "Heil Streicher!" In November he again marched at the head of the procession commemorating the 1923 *Putsch.*

Der Stürmer was now selling five hundred thousand copies weekly, and his publishing house was putting out garishly illustrated children's books and pseudoscientific tomes on the "Jewish Question." To Germany and the rest of the world, Streicher was second only to Adolf Hitler as the enemy of the Jews. Indeed, some assumed Streicher was the driving force, urging Hitler on in the persecution of the Jews. Streicher retained a press clipping service to keep him abreast of what the world had to say about him. His files have hundreds of newspaper clippings from around the world, most naturally unfavorable. He was called "World Jew-baiter No. 1," "the high priest of stupidity," "the biggest bigot in the world," and "the shame of the century."

But his position was not as secure as it seemed. His enemies, chief among them Mayor Liebel and Police President Martin, were patiently building files of incriminating materials. Martin, particularly, was dangerous. The police guards he provided Streicher were also spies, giving Martin reports on Streicher's often unsavory activities. Martin installed electronic surveillance devices in Streicher's office and even secured Heinrich Himmler's permission to tap his telephone. Police photographers set up shop in a building across from a room where Streicher often took his mistresses for extramarital escapades. In the late 1930s Martin even sent anonymous letters to Nazi leaders denouncing Streicher and his associates. But Martin was also cautious. Streicher never realized what was up until it was too late. The police president kept smiling whenever his path crossed Streicher's, waiting for his opportunity.

The chance came on the evening of November 9–10, 1938, Crystal Night, a nationwide orgy of anti-Semitic violence that Goebbels organized after a Nazi diplomat in Paris had been shot and killed by a young Jew. Ironically, Streicher had no direct role in the evening's destruction. Roused from bed when violence began in Nuremberg, he said, "If Goebbels wants it, it's all right with me" and went back to sleep. Afterward, however, Streicher and his subordinates used the affair as an opportunity to secure millions of marks' worth of Jewish property at forced sale prices as low as 5 percent of the real value.

Such goings-on were not unusual—corruption was endemic to the Third Reich—but it gave Martin a chance to get at the formerly immovable Streicher. Gathering his impressive evidence, Martin went to Berlin to appeal for help. It was not the first time he had made such a trip, and as always the going was hard, since even though Streicher's defects were widely known, few among the party's leaders were willing to attack the demonstrably dangerous Streicher. Finally Martin saw Göring, whom Streicher had been saying was incapable of fathering a child. Göring's new daughter, Streicher had chuckled, was the result of artificial insemination. That warmed up Göring, whose sense of humor did not extend to his sexuality. Martin then gave his evidence of Streicher's other misdeeds, some of which involved the direct violation of Göring's orders. Moreover, much of that stolen Jewish property was supposed to have gone to Reich accounts that Göring controlled.

Göring appointed a top-secret special commission to investigate the events in Nuremberg. By fall 1939 a two-volume report was finished, containing an astonishing but well-documented list of abuses of power. Enormous irregularities in the disposition of formerly Jewish property were uncovered, many of which directly profited Streicher. But there was more. The commission looked into Streicher's general conduct as *Gauleiter*. Streicher's close collaborator Hans König, "the evil spirit of Franconia," committed suicide on Streicher's orders before the commission could interview him, but there was enough other damning evidence without him.

The commission even investigated Streicher's sexual life, greatly aided by the cooperation of a nervous mistress. Announcing that no proper man would wear a wedding ring, Streicher had collected those of his underlings to melt down into a jewelry box for his mistress Anni Seitz, who also received a regular salary for very limited duties from Streicher's *Fränkische Tageszeitung.* Other mistresses too received paychecks from surprising sources. A country house with a well-equipped bedroom had been built for Streicher's affairs. Further cases of the beatings of political opponents were uncovered, as were Streicher's detailed examinations of the sex lives of arrested juvenile delinquents and his boasts, in the presence of young people, of sexual prowess.

Concluding its report, the commission turned to Streicher's violent nature. In April 1938 he had told an associate: "You know, Fink, I would not be surprised at all if three or four police officers come by someday. I would go with them peacefully and answer all their questions politely. But when I came back I would take out a pistol, line up all the traitors, and shoot them." The Steinrück affair was reported in an unflattering manner.[9]

The report was devastating. There was no doubt that Streicher and his staff were corrupt and violent, unsuited for public or party office. Yet no one could act without Hitler's approval. It is uncertain if the Führer ever read the commission report. What is clear is that nothing, absolutely nothing, happened.

On February 12, 1939, now beginning to realize his danger, Streicher celebrated his fifty-fourth birthday in a style so grand it suggested nothing was amiss. Guests from all of Germany were present and the gifts were impressive. The city of Nuremberg gave him an old Jewish Torah scroll. Two towns made him an honorary citizen and a third gave a medieval door knocker with a caricature of a Jewish face so positioned that the nose got banged whenever the knocker was used. The widow of Houston Stewart Chamberlain, whose book *The Foundations of the Nineteenth Century* greatly contributed to German anti-Semitism, presented a book of her husband's letters. And Dr. Benno Martin, centrally engaged in driving Streicher from power, gave a bound volume of court decisions on the *Stürmer* between 1923 and 1933. Hitler sent a congratulatory telegram.[10]

Things were becoming clear to Streicher. By now he knew that Mayor Liebel was spreading stories about him, and he began to suspect Martin. In early August 1939 he wrote to Göring, denying that he had maligned his sexual abilities: "Anyone who knows me realizes that it is not my habit to slander or intentionally injure others," a startling statement given his long history of doing exactly that.[11] Meanwhile Streicher defended himself in a letter to Rudolf Hess, the party secretary, again denying any serious misbehavior. After attempting to refute the charges made against him, Streicher concluded: "If anyone had said to me twenty years ago that a time would come when I would be forced, as a *Gauleiter* of the NSDAP, to answer questions such as these I have answered at your request, I believe that I would not have had the strength or the courage to serve the party as I have done."[12]

War began on September 1, and Streicher immediately undertook a major speaking campaign to whip up enthusiasm for what was not initially a popular war. While speaking he made a final error, making comments about the conduct of the army during World War I that offended the military. And Mayor Liebel had been sending regular reports to Hitler that criticized Streicher's behavior. Hitler placed a ban on Streicher's speaking. Getting him to do more was, as Göring later put it, "a really tough job." But finally Hitler agreed to a party tribunal, consisting of six of Streicher's fellow *Gauleiter,* to look into his conduct. Even then Hitler carefully limited what could be considered. Only the most major charges were to be looked into. König's suicide was to be ignored. And the tribunal was not to render judgment, only an opinion. Hitler reserved final action to himself.

The tribunal began work on February 13, 1940, and its deliberations lasted four days. It reviewed the 1939 commission report and heard testimony from three men besides Streicher, one of whom was President Martin. Each was sworn to silence on penalty of death. Streicher defended himself with customary vigor. Outraged by Dr. Martin's ingratitude, Streicher accused him (rightly) of being responsible for the anonymous letters that had denounced him. Martin drew his pistol and threatened to shoot Streicher if he repeated the accusation. Martin and Liebel, incidentally, had previously agreed to shoot Streicher themselves if necessary. The startled chairman telephoned Göring, whose response was, "He should have done it." The tribunal concluded that Streicher was "unfit for human leadership." Now it was up to Hitler.[13]

The decision was not an easy one. Streicher was an old ally, one of the first, and there was no provision in the party rules for the removal of a *Gauleiter*. Finally Hitler decided to remove Streicher from Nuremberg without formally stripping him of his title. Streicher would retire to Pleikershof, his country estate outside Nuremberg, and he was banned from visiting the city. He could continue to publish the *Stürmer*. Hitler took care to be sure Streicher received the paper the *Stürmer* needed and the gasoline necessary to maintain a courier between his farm and the *Stürmer* office.

Even then the Führer felt guilty. Two years later, during one of his late-night monologues to his inner circle, Hitler said: "This Streicher affair is a tragedy. . . . Streicher is irreplaceable. . . . There's no question of his coming back, but I must do him justice. If one day I write my memoirs, I shall have to recognize that this man fought like a buffalo in our cause. . . . I can't help thinking that, in comparison with so many services, the reasons for Streicher's dismissal are really very slender." Speaking of the ways in which Streicher was deposed, Hitler attributed it to a plot among two Nuremberg women. Turning to the Machiavellian ways in which Streicher had been photographed, Hitler added: "Nobody has the right to photograph a man surprised in intimacy. . . . It was a disgusting way of behaving, and I've forbidden any use to be made of the photos. It's not fair to demand more of a man than he can give. Streicher has not the gifts of a great administrator."[14] The last surely was an understatement.

Obeying Hitler's orders, Streicher retired to Nuremberg. At first he made unauthorized visits to Nuremberg, but Martin made sure that Hitler's order was enforced. Though he forbade party officials to visit Streicher, Hitler saw to it that life for Streicher was comfortable. Streicher was assigned a number of French and Dutch POWs to work on his farm. In 1944 Robert Ley, the labor leader, and Goebbels secured permission to visit, though nothing seems to have resulted. In March 1945, however, as the end of the Third Reich approached, Streicher wrote to Hitler with the request that he be allowed to serve the fatherland in its desperate hour. Hitler instructed Goebbels to find something for Streicher to do. As Goebbels wrote in his diary: "At heart the Fuehrer is somewhat uncomfortable about Streicher since he was a man of stature who only once went off the rails."[15] Goebbels came up with an idea that Hitler approved, but the war ended before Streicher could be put to work.

As the American army neared Nuremberg, Streicher married his secretary, his first wife having died in 1943. The honeymooning couple left Pleikershof around April 21, shortly before the American army arrived. An English reporter, eager to investigate the lair of so notorious a figure, was not disappointed. Although Streicher's collection of riding whips had been looted by GI's looking for mementos, much of his collection of allegedly Jewish pornography remained, enough "to make a shady bookseller's fortune."[16]

The Streichers first planned to commit suicide as they wandered south toward Austria, but along the route Streicher overheard several German soldiers talking of how all the Nazi bigshots were killing themselves. He resolved to avoid the coward's way out. Disguised as a painter (painting was one of his hobbies), he and his new wife lived several weeks in a small Austrian village near Berchtesgaden. On May 23, 1945, a Major Plitt, the son of a Jewish mother, inadvertently captured Streicher. Meeting him by chance, Plitt intended to say, "You look so much like Julius Streicher I have a notion to take you," but his faulty German led Streicher to think he had been positively identified. Plitt became an immediate celebrity. Flown back to New York for Major Plitt Day, he helped sell war bonds.[17]

Streicher's fate was less pleasant. He later claimed to have been badly mistreated by Jews and blacks. In a note to his attorney he described his ordeal:

> Two niggers undressed me and tore my shirt in two. I kept only my pants. Being handcuffed I could not pull them up when they fell down. So now I was naked. Four days! On the fourth day I was so cold that my body was numb. I couldn't hear anything. Every 2–4 hours (even in the night!) niggers came along under command of a white man and hammered at me. Cigarette burns on the nipples. Fingers gouged into eye-sockets. Eyebrows and chest hair pulled out. Genitals beaten with an oxwhip. Testicles very swollen. Spat at. "Mouth open" and it was spat into. When I refused to open, my jaws were prised apart with a stick and my mouth spat into. Beaten with the whip—swollen, dark-blue weals all over the body. . . . Photographed naked! Jeered at wearing an old army greatcoat which they hung round me.[18]

The account continues at some length, and probably is at least partially accurate. During the summer of 1945 a photograph of a naked and beaten Streicher did circulate among American soldiers, complete with a sign: "Julius Streicher, King of the Jews."[19]

Finally Streicher was transferred to Mondorf prison in Luxembourg, the central gathering point for Nazi war criminals. Streicher was no newcomer to prison life, of course, but the Allies were less agreeable jailers than he had encountered in earlier years. When at Mondorf a Jewish soldier behaved kindly toward him while making it plain he was Jewish, Streicher's anti-Semitic confidence first crumbled into tears. "I am wrong," he told another soldier. "I have always said there were no good Jews, but that boy proved to me that I am wrong."[20] But not for long. Streicher was soon at work on his final political testament, finished on August 3, 1945, which reaffirmed all he had ever said about the Jews. "I would be a cowardly dog if, when in the power of my enemies, I abjured that which for twenty-five years had been known to be my conviction," he wrote.[21]

The Allies had wanted Streicher badly, but once they had him they had difficulty deciding what to do with him. He simply was not in the same class with defendants like Göring, Ribbentrop, and Speer, men who had had central roles in Hitler's war against the world. It became clear that Streicher was notorious more for his rhetoric than for any specific criminal acts. The major war criminals were charged under four counts: conspiracy to wage aggressive war, crimes against peace, crimes against war, and crimes against humanity. There was no sense in charging Streicher with crimes against peace or with war crimes, for he had no part in the German war effort. The Allies resolved to accuse him of being part of the Nazi conspiracy that planned war, and of crimes against humanity.

The Nazi leaders were moved to Nuremberg for the International Military Tribunal, an unprecedented and not entirely successful attempt to replace the rule of force with the rule of law. In the ruins of Julius Streicher's city, and in the same courtroom in which he had sometimes been tried during the Weimar period, the tribunal opened on November 20, 1945. The indictment of Streicher concluded that he had been "less directly involved in the physical commission of the crimes against Jews than were some of his coconspirators," but that his propaganda had prepared the way for genocide:

In the early days he was preaching persecution. As persecution took place he preached extermination and annihilation and, as millions of Jews were exterminated and annihilated, in the Ghettoes of the East, he cried out for more and more.

The crime of Streicher is that he made these crimes possible, which they never would have been had it not been for him and for those like him. Without Streicher and his propaganda, the Kaltenbrunners, the Himmlers, the General Stroops would have had nobody to do their orders.

In its extent Streicher's crime is probably greater and more far-reaching than that of any of the other defendants. The misery which they caused ceased with their capture. The effects of this man's crime, of the poison that he has poured into the minds of millions of young boys and girls goes on, for he concentrated upon the youth and childhood of Germany. He leaves behind him a legacy of almost a whole people poisoned with hate, sadism, and murder, and perverted by him. That people remain a problem and perhaps a menace to the rest of civilization for generations to come.[22]

The prosecution's case included anti-Semitic passages from Streicher's entire career; over fifty passages called for the annihilation of the Jews.

Streicher's defense was not easy to make, as his attorney, Hans Marx, soon learned. His unsavory client was uncooperative, fighting in court with his attorney. Repeatedly Streicher tried to launch into speeches from the stand, a behavior the Weimar courts often had permitted but that the Allies did not tolerate. Repeatedly Marx or the court were forced to silence him. The defense made two principle arguments. First, Marx argued that before 1933 Streicher was a local figure of limited national significance, and after 1933 only one of many Nazi Jew-baiters. Second, he argued that Streicher had no knowledge of the Holocaust, and indeed opposed violence against the Jews. Both Streicher's new wife and Ernst Hiemer, his *Stürmer* editor, testified that while Streicher at times made harsh anti-Jewish remarks under the pressure of outside events, he always advocated peaceful solutions to the Jewish problem when calm.

In a relentless cross-examination, Lieutenant Colonel M. C. Griffith-Jones of the United Kingdom confronted Streicher with article after article from the *Stürmer* that spoke of annihilation, extirpation, and death. He demonstrated that Streicher read a Jewish newspaper published in Switzerland and used material from it in his articles that regularly reported on the annihilation of European Jewry. Over and over Streicher claimed not to remember reading stories on the developing Holocaust: "I do not know [if I read it], and again I would not have believed it. To this day I do not believe that 5 million were killed. I consider it technically impossible that that could have happened. I do not believe it. I have not received proof of that up until now." But his denials sounded empty. Even his subordinate Ernst Hiemer testified that by mid-1944 Streicher knew of the ghastly fulfillment of his rhetoric.

During the trial Streicher continued his anti-Semitic activity, unmoved by the growing evidence of Nazi mass murder. For several months he was engaged in a study of the Old Testment with a view toward demonstrating that Jews condemned themselves even in their own writing. In an odd conversation toward the end of the trial Streicher announced to several fellow Nazis that he now was ready to fight on behalf of the Jews. Recent news reports of rioting in Palestine had convinced him that Jews had a fighting spirit after all: "I would be ready to join them now and help them in their fight!—No, I am not joking!" Several looked amused. Streicher continued:

> Absolutely! I am not joking!—And do you know why?—Because the democratic world is too weak and isn't fit to exist. I warned them for 25 years, but now I see that the Jews have determination and spunk.— They will still dominate the world, mark my word!—And I would be glad to help lead them to victory because they are strong and tenacious, and I know Jewry. I have spunk too! And I can stick to my guns!—And if the Jews would be willing to accept me as one of them, I would fight for them, because when I believe in a thing, I know how to fight!

By now his listeners were almost hysterical. Streicher continued: "I have studied them so long that I suppose I have adopted myself to their characteristics—at least I could lead a group in Palestine.—I am not joking.—I'll give it to you in writing.—I'll make a proposition. Let me address a gathering at Madison Square Garden in New York.—It will be a sensation."[23] That it would have been, but Streicher was probably not very serious.

In his surprisingly brief and coherent closing statement, Streicher claimed clean hands. The Holocaust, in which he had become a reluctant believer, had not been his work, rather Hitler's and Himmler's. "The executed mass killings I reject in the same way as they are being rejected by every decent German. . . . Neither in my capacity as Gauleiter nor as a political author have I committed a crime, and I therefore look toward your judgment with good conscience."[24]

The tribunal announced its verdicts on September 20, 1946. Streicher was acquitted of the first charge, conspiracy to wage aggressive war. There had been no evidence to support it. But the judges agreed that his long years of Jew-baiting constituted a crime against humanity. He would hang. On October 16, 1946, Streicher died on the gallows, a platform far different from those on which he had spoken so regularly since 1919.

Today Streicher is regularly dismissed as a crude, sadistic pornographer, not an entirely unjust description. Yet this man whose unpleasant personality so often made enemies of former friends and who was held in contempt even by many Nazis was attractive and persuasive at a distance to millions in a civilized nation. What sort of man was he?

Of his intellectual crudity there was never dispute. He boasted that he spoke the language of the masses, but that was not a language he assumed for tactical reasons. It was his own. Streicher was a man of limited intelligence; prison psychologists after the war found his intelligence to be almost exactly average, the lowest of any of the major war criminals tested. If Joseph Goebbels was one of the Nazi party's few intellectuals, Streicher was one of its far more numerous common men, and that was part of his appeal. He was one with the audiences to whom he spoke and for whom he wrote.

His arguments were simple, and he accepted evidence against the Jews regardless of its source. All men evaluate new information according to their existing attitudes, of course, and many like Streicher fail to apply any standards—but his gullibility was extreme. In 1929 a Jewish journalist reported on Streicher's behavior during the widely publicized "Talmud Trial," at which Streicher and a colleague were charged with spreading untrue stories about the Jews.

There he raised the most startling evidence. For Streicher, the reporter rightly argued:

> . . . the printed word possesses remarkable persuasive power. That which is found in some book or newspaper is irrefutable truth. Catholic legends presenting in fantastic ways the murder of Christian children by Jews are historical documents. Works of art portraying these fables in individual Catholic churches prove that what was written about really happened, indeed that the Catholic Church recognizes the reality of ritual murder. . . . "Gentlemen of the bench," exclaimed Streicher to the jurors again and again, "if it were not true it could not have been printed." Streicher had seen a painting by a famous painter in the city art gallery in Vienna which was an artistic representation of a so-called ritual murder. "Well, my dear jurors, would a great artist have painted it if it had not happened? And if the government hangs such a painting in its gallery, it must be convinced of the truth of the painting." That is almost verbatim from Streicher, said with a tone of deep conviction.[25]

In accusing Jews of slaughtering Christians to secure blood for religious purposes, for example, Streicher could with little difficulty believe a German translation of an Italian translation of a Greek translation of an early nineteenth-century Moldavian book by an embittered Jewish convert to Christianity. On the other hand, evidence favoring Jews, no matter how solid, he rejected. His tendency to see only evidence supporting his views is not unusual, but the extent to which he practiced it is.

If his evidence was shoddy, few doubted that he was totally convinced that Jews were evil. Rightly accused of many offenses during his career, even his enemies failed to accuse him of insincerity. The Weimar era courts that convicted him so regularly almost as regularly observed that he held his views with the force of religious conviction. After the war, psychologists like Douglas Kelly, who examined him, were equally convinced that Streicher firmly believed in Jewish depravity. That confidence was a major part of his appeal. Hitler had written that the masses preferred yes and no, black and white, not shades of gray. When Streicher spoke it was clear that there was no middle ground—a posture that ever finds followers.

Why he was so fervently anti-Semitic is difficult to know. Of the writing of books on anti-Semitism there is no end, but perhaps Streicher's own explanation of his Jew-baiting is the one we must rely on. As a child he had absorbed the prevailing suspicion of Jews. After World War I, it provided a clear and satisfying explanation for Germany's defeat and the world's difficulties. Anti-Semitism gave meaning and purpose to Streicher's whole existence, filling the vacuum left when the community of the trenches had been replaced by life in a disintegrating and defeated nation. The fanaticism of Julius Streicher is one with the fanaticism of every age.

Other explanations of his hatred of the Jews have been suggested. One writer reports the rumor that he had lost a girl to a Jew. Several make the interesting charge that Streicher himself may have had Jewish or Gypsy blood in his family tree. An early associate claims Streicher once said: "You have to have a good dose of Jewish blood in your veins to hate that race properly." And Streicher's official genealogy was missing what could have been an incriminating page by the mid-1930s. Streicher would not have been the first Jewish anti-Semite, but the claims do have a slender foundation.[26]

An interesting sidelight to Streicher's fanaticism was his conviction that he could identify Jews by their appearance—and not only those who met the physical stereotype. In a 1930 speech to the Bavarian legislature, for example, he said: "Representative Schaeffer is a baptized Catholic. To me, however, it is perfectly clear as to which race he belongs. His hand motions, which I have frequently observed in this room, appear to be so typically Jewish that there is no doubt that he is a Jewish bastard." He was never a welcome guest at a Munich hotel after he accused a visiting delegation of influential Greeks of being international Jews. In 1946 he thought three of his judges were Jewish: "I can recognize blood. I've been studying blood for 20 years." He then proposed his novel way of identifying them: "The Jewish behind is so feminine—so soft and feminine." His actual perceptiveness was less impressive. Besides those visiting Greeks he mistook for agents of the Jewish conspiracy, he complimented his Nuremberg interpreter on his fine Aryan appearance. But the interpreter was a Jew.[27]

Then there was sex, the element of Streicher's Jew-baiting career that contributed most to his notoriety. Even the citizens of the Third

Reich jokingly called him the *Reichspornograph,* the national pornographer. Later we shall look at how he used sexual allegations in the *Stürmer,* but his own conduct was hardly better than that he accused the Jews of. At the Nuremberg trial he boasted of having been a famous fornicator, and "even at the age of sixty-one, contended that the only true test of his physical health would be to make a young woman available to him." Substantial evidence supports his claim. As early as 1923 his enemies accused him of adultery. In 1932 he was apparently claiming that he could never give a powerful speech to a mass meeting unless he had had sexual relations with a young woman, a theory of public speaking not often proposed even in these liberated times. Baldur von Schirach, leader of the Hitler Youth, reported that Streicher once asked the Nuremberg Hitler Youth leader to supply two willing girls for a bicycle trip into the country. The Göring Commission report in 1939 detailed his sexual escapades in considerable detail.[28] The leering, sexually obsessed Jew he so often conjured up in order to attack was a reflection of his own conduct.

He was a violent man. His pictures during the Third Reich show a hard, combative man, uniformed, often with a whip. His hair was thin but he kept his head shaved bald. He took particular pleasure in accusing Jews of whipping German girls, yet in several instances he used his whips on helpless enemies. A good soldier, he had relished the political combat of the Weimar era. He missed the joy of battle when Hitler took power.

There were more normal sides to his personality, of course. He had the customary virtues and vices. A Swedish reporter who visited him in 1938 wrote: "Streicher the agitator is one man; Streicher the private citizen another. At the podium or behind the editorial desk he is a born fanatic, but in his favorite pub over a glass of beer, one meets an entirely different man, one whose spherical face laughs heartily over stories of soldiers and schools. There he is as comfortably middle class as any other German in a beer hall in the Third Reich."[29] He was a sparetime painter, mostly of landscapes, and even tried writing sentimental poetry.

He was, in short, a common man's fanatic. Hitler was distant, Goebbels too intellectual, but Streicher was a man of the people, easier to understand and identify with. He preached a terrible message with enormous fervor, and fervor is always convincing. That he was able to make so major a contribution to a dreadful cause is perhaps as much an indictment of the human character in general as it is of his in particular.

III

Der Stürmer: "A Fierce and Filthy Rag"

Der Stürmer is the most infamous newspaper in history. For twenty-two years every issue denounced Jews in crude, vicious, and vivid ways. Although Streicher employed a large staff by the end of the 1930s, he always had the final say. "Streicher and the *Stürmer*, they are one and the same," he would say proudly.

In its early years there was little to suggest the paper's future notoriety. Streicher began it during his first major battle for control of Nuremberg Nazism in 1923. Anti-Streicher forces had held an "Evening of Revelations" on April 14, 1923, at which Streicher was charged with being a liar and a coward, of having unsavory friends, of mistreating his wife, and of flirting with women, the kinds of accusations that would follow him throughout his career. Streicher's response was to begin a newspaper. Later he described how he chose the name *Stürmer*. Wandering through the woods on a fine spring day he thought about what to call his paper. While resting under a fir tree, inspiration struck. He jumped up and shouted, "I have it! Since the paper will storm the red fortress, it shall be called the *Stürmer*."[1] The story is most likely an afterthought, but the title he chose was typically Nazi. Other party organs had names like *Der Angriff* (the Attack) and *Die Flamme* (the Flame), names suggesting action and forcefulness.

The first issue appeared in early May (see figure 3). Most of it responded to the charges his opponents had made, and in reasonably persuasive style, but the Jews were not ignored. The issue concluded: "As long as the Jew is in the German household, we will be Jewish slaves. Therefore he must go. Who? *The Jew!*" The next issue carried a vehement attack on Mayor Luppe, an attack continued in the third and fourth issues. By the fourth issue too, Streicher was printing more general attacks on the Jews. The seventh issue, appearing in June, was headlined: "Walther Rathenau: Who he was. What he wanted. What he did." Rathenau, a leading Jewish politician assassinated the year before, had been a regular Nazi target. The *Stürmer* had become a private weapon in Streicher's war against the Jews.

The Nazi leadership in Munich worried over Streicher's new enterprise; they had already had difficulties enough with his independent ways. Max Amann, later director of the German press, wrote to Streicher in August 1923 asking him to cease publication since the intraparty feud that had spurred Streicher to begin the paper now was settled. "I do not know what opinion you have on this matter; however, Herr Streicher, I have no doubt that you will no longer consider it important for the *Stürmer* to appear when as much room as necessary will be made available for reports of the local group in the *Volkswille* [the official Nazi paper in Nuremberg]."[2] Streicher, however, did have larger plans, and his position was sufficiently strong to let him ignore Amann's wishes.

In appearance the early issues were unimpressive, four small pages with no illustrations and few advertisements. The paper ceased publication entirely for several months after the 1923 *Putsch,* but Streicher resurrected it in 1924. By 1925 the paper was from outward appearances healthier. More advertising was carried, and the pages now were tabloid size. Circulation had increased. The first issues sold several thousand copies at most, but by 1927 it was selling fourteen thousand copies weekly, most of them outside Nuremberg itself. As the circulation increased, Streicher broadened the *Stürmer's* coverage. At first he wrote mostly of the misdeeds of Jews and their friends in Nuremberg, chief of whom was Mayor Luppe. By 1930 Luppe rarely was the subject of the lead article. Streicher's changing view of his audience is suggested by a 1932 alteration in the paper's masthead slogan. Formerly it had been "A Nuremberg weekly in the struggle for truth." Now it became "A German weekly in the struggle for truth." The mainstay of the newspaper during the Weimar period was scandal. To maintain his readership Streicher had to provide a steady supply of interesting and fresh material, an enterprise in which he had surprising success. Early in 1924 he printed a notice that the paper's price was twenty pfennig, and that those newsdealers attempting to charge more should be reported to him. It was the spectacular that made it possible to scalp a weekly newspaper.

Most of the scandal at first was political. Mayor Luppe and his administration were accused of every manner of abuse of power. If there were problems with Nuremberg housing, it was the fault of Nuremberg Jewry. If there was unemployment, Jews were to blame. But Nuremberg politics was of limited interest to the growing numbers of readers outside Nuremberg, so Streicher turned to the standbys of sensational journalism, sex and crime, preferably together. Each new alleged case of Jewish rape or sexual criminality received eager attention from the *Stürmer's* staff. The sexual material naturally made it interesting to young people; the *Stürmer* became the Nuremberg equivalent to an American boy's clandestine copy of *Playboy*. In 1925 a gentleman who claimed to be neither Jewish nor one of Streicher's political opponents wrote to his own newspaper:

> Streicher always presents an attention-getting piece of news in his *Stürmer*. He always brings something rotten to the light of day. He wants to keep his readers in constant suspense. But what do his readers want? Sensation and filth. Streicher gives that to them. He floods his readers with tastelessness. And who are his readers? Mostly adolescents who are still wet behind the ears. Thanks to Streicher's "education," every lad is familiar with homosexuality and prostitution. One cannot blame Streicher for speaking about these matters. Every newspaper today does. The question is how one speaks of them. Streicher gives them great prominence. May not one be concerned when one sees the *Stürmer* not only in the hands of older students, but also in the possession of elementary school children?[3]

The *C. V. Zeitung,* a national Jewish monthly, made the same point in

1926, observing that many Nuremberg children read the *Stürmer*, and Mayor Luppe accused Streicher of publishing the "worst pornographic colportage literature."

Ironically, many early *Stürmer* readers seem to have been Jewish. After the war Streicher claimed Jews had given him valuable financial support by purchasing the paper. His statement is supported by an advertising circular from a Jewish newspaper in Nuremberg around 1925: "It is of great concern to the Licht Verlag that the *Stürmer* is very frequently read even in Jewish circles. We have found that large numbers of citizens of the Jewish faith buy the *Stürmer* and then take it home concealed in a copy of the *8 Uhr Blatt* or the *Morgenpresse*. THUS THE JEWS DIRECTLY SUPPORT THE *STÜRMER*."[4]

Where did Streicher's material come from? Each week there seemed to be a new scandal to report, and when there was nothing new, he would rehash an old one. Most material came from angry readers or dedicated Nazis. When the police raided the *Stürmer* office in 1927, they found that the paper received more material than it could use. Most readers, a later report concluded, were not seeking payment, but wanted to air their grievances publicly.[5] Nuremberg was a large city, and the surrounding countryside was well populated, so there was never a shortage of people out for revenge. Those who tried to sell information, in fact, were turned down. In 1926, for example, an anonymous correspondent offered to provide an incriminating letter from Mayor Luppe for five thousand marks, an offer the paper did not accept. Interestingly, Luppe received a similar offer of incriminating information about Streicher at about the same time.

What probably was typical of the source of much *Stürmer* material was later reported by Adolf Hitler:

> One must never forget the services rendered by the *Stürmer*. Without it the affair of the Jew Hirsch's perjury, at Nuremberg, would never have come out. And how many other scandals he exposed!
>
> One day a Nazi saw a Jew, in Nuremberg station, impatiently throw a letter into the waste-paper basket. He recovered the letter and, after having read it, took it to the *Stürmer*. It was a blackmailer's letter in which the recipient, the Jew Hirsch, was threatened that the game would be given away if he stopped coughing up. The *Stürmer*'s revelation provoked an inquiry. It thus became known that a country girl, who had a place in Nuremberg in the household of Herr Hirsch, had brought an

action against him for rape. Hirsch got the girl to swear in court that she had never had relations with other men—then produced numerous witnesses who all claimed to have had relations with her. The German judges did not understand that Jews have no scruples when it's a question of saving one of their compatriots. They therefore condemned the servant to one and a half years in prison. The letter thrown impatiently away by Hirsch was written by one of the false witnesses subborned by him—which witness considered that he could conveniently add blackmail to perjury.[6]

Since most material did not have to be paid for, editorial expenses were low. The Nuremberg police estimated that the *Stürmer* earned substantial profits, which were used to support other Nazi activities, a view common in Nuremberg at the time.

From its first issue, the *Stürmer* was directed to that lowest common denominator that Hitler thought the proper target of propaganda. Heinz Preiss, a young scholar who attached himself to Streicher after 1933, becoming his court historian, accurately described Streicher's intent:

Since he wanted to capture the masses, he had to write in a way that the masses could understand, in a style that was simple and easy to comprehend. He had recognized that the way to achieve the greatest effect on an audience was through simple sentences. Writing had to adopt the style of speaking if it were to have a similar effect. Streicher wrote in the *Stürmer* the way he talked. . . . The worker who came home late at night from the factory was neither willing nor able to read intellectual treatises. He was, however, willing to read what interested him and what he could understand. Streicher therefore took the content from daily life and the style from speech. He thus gave the *Stürmer* its style, a style which many intellectuals could not understand, but which fundamentally was nothing but the product of his own experience gained over the years.[7]

His sentences were in fact far shorter than the average for written German, and his vocabulary was elementary. There was never much doubt about what Streicher had to say—he avoided nearly every qualifier. As editor Ernst Hiemer put it in 1935: "The *Stürmer* is the paper of the people. Its language is simple, its sentences clear. Its words have one meaning. Its tone is rough. It has to be! The *Stürmer* is not a Sunday paper. The *Stürmer* fights for truth. A fight is not fought with kid gloves. And the truth is not smooth and slippery. It is rough and hard."[8]

Not only was what Streicher said simple and blunt, it also was repeated endlessly. A single issue might have half a dozen articles on the same theme. Major topics recurred so often that a reader had only to read a few issues before he encountered nearly all the arguments in Streicher's anti-Semitic arsenal. New evidence was always provided, but only rarely new arguments.

Streicher also realized the value of visual material. The message of a cartoon or photograph could be absorbed in seconds, not the minutes necessary even for the brief *Stürmer* articles. The first issues, it is true, carried no illustrations, but by 1925 he was running cartoons in nearly every issue, and in 1930 he added photographs.

The cartoons were certainly the most striking element in the *Stürmer.* Early in the publication of the paper Streicher discovered a cartoonist of outstanding crudity, Philippe Rupprecht, who under the pen name Fips became identified with the *Stürmer* almost as closely as Streicher. Immigrating to Argentina after World War I, Fips had worked as a cowboy on a cattle ranch. He returned to Nuremberg around 1924 and was hired by the *Fränkische Tagespost,* a newspaper affiliated with the Social Democrats. Sent to cover the second Luppe-Streicher trial with instructions to draw Streicher, he instead drew Luppe and a prominent Nuremberg Jew involved in the trial. The cartoons were published by the *Stürmer* in December 1925 (see figure 4), and Fips joined the staff. With the exception of the year 1927, he remained the *Stürmer*'s only regular cartoonist until 1945, drawing thousands of vivid and revolting anti-Jewish caricatures. His style changed over his career, but the essential characteristics of a Fips Jew remained constant. He was short, fat, ugly, unshaven, drooling, sexually perverted, bent-nosed, with piglike eyes, a visual embodiment of the message of the *Stürmer*'s articles.

Though Streicher came to have a large staff, he retained control of what appeared in the *Stürmer.* Many of the lead editorials carried his name after 1933, when it was safe to claim credit, and interior articles often were written according to his instructions. He would read much material on the Jews, underlining in red what he thought useful for

Stürmer articles. Lesser writers could then recast the indicated material into proper form.

When Hitler took power the *Stürmer* was already one of the most popular Nazi publications, selling about twenty-five thousand copies weekly. Curiously, Streicher did not yet own the paper. Legal arrangements had never been written out, and when his printer died in 1934, the widow claimed ownership. To avoid legal proceedings, Streicher purchased all rights for forty thousand marks, not a bad price since the *Stürmer* soon made him wealthy. By the mid-1930s it was selling hundreds of thousands of copies weekly. Precise figures are hard to determine, but the circulation guaranteed advertisers climbed rapidly, particularly after Streicher hired a capable circulation manager in 1934, reaching about five hundred thousand in 1935. The print run then seems to have been around seven hundred thousand.

TABLE 2

Der Stürmer Circulation: 1927–38

Issue/Year	Circulation
1927	14,000
1933	25,000
No. 6 (1934)	47,000
No. 13 (1934)	49,000
No. 17 (1934)	50,000
No. 19 (1934)	60,000
No. 33 (1934)	80,000
No. 35 (1934)	94,114
No. 42 (1934)	113,800
No. 6 (1935)	132,897
No. 19 (1935)	202,600
No. 29 (1935)	244,600
No. 32 (1935)	286,400
No. 36 (1935)	410,600
No. 40 (1935)	486,000
No. 5 (1938)	473,000

The circulation growth after 1934 was assisted by enthusiastic promotion. Robert Ley, the Nazi labor leader, pushed the *Stürmer* on his membership. Various party affiliates conducted circulation drives. In 1937, for example, a Nazi district farmer's organization leader wrote his subordinates ordering them to attend to the *Stürmer* when conducting anti-Jewish agitation. "No educational material is better there than the old anti-Semitic fighting paper of the *Gauleiter* of Franconia, Julius Streicher, the *Stürmer*. With blunt plainness he reveals the crimes of the Jewish race from the beginning to the present."[9] All subordinates were to subscribe, and were to inform him that they had done so. No excuses would be accepted.

Nine special editions also were published after 1933, often timed to appear at the annual Nuremberg rally. These had themes such as ritual murder, Jewish criminality, the world Jewish conspiracy, Jewish sex crimes, and the Jews of Austria and Czechoslovakia. Print runs were as high as 2,000,000, and extensive national advertising was conducted.

The readership of the *Stürmer* was even larger than the circulation figures suggest, for thousands of elaborate display cases were built by loyal readers throughout Germany that displayed each week's issue. A journalism handbook published during the Nazi era claimed that such display cases were to be found everywhere in Germany, giving the paper an unprecedented readership. These cases, built in areas where many people passed by, were often elaborate structures (see figure 5). Usually they were graced with slogans from the *Stürmer* such as "The Jews are our misfortune" or "German women and girls: the Jews are your destruction." The *Stürmer* regularly urged readers to keep the display cases well maintained and uncluttered. A 1936 notice to readers, for example, instructed readers to keep only the latest issue of the newspaper and *Stürmer* publishing house literature on display. "It is especially important that *Stürmer* display cases do not adversely affect the local scenery."[10] Many issues of the paper carried photographs of particularly impressive display cases, and most issues in the 1930s carried long lists of newly erected ones.

Showcases were built in places where people naturally congregated—bus stops, factory canteens, public squares, parks, and busy streets. A passerby could, within a few seconds, pause to see the latest Fips cartoon, or devote the several minutes necessary to read any of the generally brief articles. The showcases became part of everyday life in the Third Reich.

The enormous circulation of the *Stürmer* was in itself evidence of its official popularity, but there was more. Adolf Hitler himself praised it. Hermann Rauschning, summarizing a conversation with Hitler, reports the Führer's admiration for Streicher's work:

> Anti-Semitism . . . was beyond question the most important weapon in his propagandist arsenal, and almost everywhere it was of deadly efficiency. That was why he had allowed Streicher, for example, a free hand. The man's stuff, too, was amusing, and very cleverly done. Wherever, he wondered, did Streicher get his constant supply of new material? He, Hitler, was simply on thorns to see each new issue of the *Stürmer*. It was the one periodical that he always read with pleasure, from the first page to the last.[11]

Streicher regularly cited Hitler's praise, which does not have to be strictly true, of course. But the fact that Hitler was willing to make such a statement gave the *Stürmer* considerable force.

Other leading figures of the party wrote letters praising the *Stürmer*, apparently in response to a request from the paper. Victor Lutze, chief of the Storm Troopers, wrote in 1937: "The *Stürmer* has an essential role in seeing that each German today views the Jewish question as the crucial question of the nation, and the honor of having put racial thought in popular language." Albert Forster, *Gauleiter* of Danzig, wrote:

> With pleasure I say that the *Stürmer*, more than any other daily or weekly newspaper, has made clear to the people in simple ways the danger of Jewry.
>
> Without Julius Streicher and his *Stürmer*, the importance of a solution to the Jewish question would not be seen to be as critical as it actually is by many citizens.
>
> It is therefore to be hoped that those who want to learn the unvarnished truth about the Jewish question will read the *Stürmer*.[12]

Similar letters came from Heinrich Himmler, Robert Ley, Max Amann, and other prominent Nazis.

The success of the *Stürmer* allowed Streicher to broaden his activity by publishing anti-Semitic books. Two garishly illustrated children's readers were published after 1936, along with a third storybook with lurid tales comparing Jews to unpleasant animals. His early speeches and editorials were published in collections edited by Heinz Preiss. Streicher's collaborator Fritz Fink wrote a guide to anti-Semitic education, copies of which were conveniently available in Braille. A series of pseudoscholarly works appeared, including a study of court Jews, a collection of anti-Jewish proverbs, and a brief work on Bismarck's treaty with Russia. Streicher also produced a series of illustrated books on the Nuremberg rallies and even put out a short-lived anti-Semitic medical journal.

Another major project was the *Stürmer* archive, first mentioned in 1933. This grew to a sizable collection of anti-Semitica, including thousands of books in Hebrew and Aramaic (languages few staff members could read) and many more in German and other languages. There were many Jewish and Gentile periodicals and a large collection of Fips cartoons and photographs, along with assorted Jewish paraphernalia such as Torah scrolls and the tools of ritual circumcisers. The most notorious part of the collection was its large holding of pornography, which Streicher claimed was for scientific research into the Jewish question.

Much of the material was sent in by readers, to whom the paper often appealed for such items; more came from seized Jewish property. The Gestapo supplied considerable information, particularly on the theme of Jewish criminality. The Gestapo was usually cooperative, but when some offices were recalcitrant Streicher complained and as usual got action. A 1937 Gestapo memo instructs local offices to turn over to the *Stürmer* whatever it requested. And a 1940 *Stürmer* letter to the Düsseldorf Gestapo office asked particularly for material relevant to Jews and pornography, requesting all pornography in any way connected with Jews—if Jews had written, printed, published, or sold it, the *Stürmer* wanted it.[13]

Over three hundred people worked for Streicher by 1939, including, remarkably enough, a Jew named Jonas Wolk, who under the pen name Fritz Brand wrote particularly dreadful *Stürmer* articles. The Göring report noted that, while Streicher paid Wolk a good salary, he refused to shake hands with him. A 1939 letter from Vienna came from a Jew who also wanted to have his material printed by the *Stürmer*[14]. The bulk of the staff, of less puzzling background, helped Streicher conduct an operation that reached the entire German-speaking world. Copies went to the United States, Canada, Brazil, Argentina, and other countries with large German populations. The world press regularly reported Streicher's doings, viewing him as a major force in Nazi Jew-baiting.

In Germany, even though the *Stürmer* lacked status as an official party paper, it had semi-official status. As a Berlin court that rejected the suit of the victim of a *Stürmer* attack stated:

> The *Stürmer* has the task of spreading and deepening the understanding of racial matters among the people, as well as supporting the movement in its vital struggle against international Jewry. Thus it is quite proper for the *Stürmer* and others to be critical of the relationships between individual citizens and the Jews. This is done not to slander the individual, rather to show the whole of Germany how each individual conducts himself with respect to Jewry. The individual has no right to complain about such criticism of his behavior, as long as it is reported objectively, since that would unreasonably hamper or even endanger the necessary work of the *Stürmer*[15]

Elsewhere in Germany, citizens were arrested for criticizing Streicher or disparaging his *Stürmer*.

As such a court case suggests, however, even the official anti-Semitism of the Third Reich failed to make Streicher's work popular with many Germans. All sorts of protests from German citizens occurred. The most common involved the sexual element in many *Stürmer* stories. Editor Ernst Hiemer responded vehemently to such complaints: "You may survey the entire thirteen volumes of the *Stürmer* and note every passage which you think endangers the youth. But we will then take the holy books and do the same." It was better to have a youth educated in the sexual threat of Jewry than one ruined through ignorance. A later issue spoke of "perfumed women with delicate nerves and men of the same sort" who objected to the *Stürmer*'s frank treatment. When Streicher attacked the Old Testament (see Chapter V), angry Christians around the nation protested vigorously. Doctors, upset when Streicher's anti-Semitic medical journal argued that vaccinations were part of the Jewish plot, denounced his idiocy.[16]

Streicher also received many anonymous letters, which he turned over to the police for investigation. *Stürmer* display cases often were vandalized. The *Stürmer* regularly attacked its critics. One Fritz Eckart earned space in the paper in 1936, for example, when he walked into his barber shop only to leave when he found a copy of the *Stürmer* on display. Thereafter he would say: "I am a Center Party man and will remain so, come what may."[17] The sixty businessmen in another town who attended a Jewish funeral were attacked, without, however, suffering adverse consequences.

Even leading Nazis sometimes worked up the courage to attack Streicher and the *Stürmer*. Otto Dietrich, the press secretary, tried to persuade Hitler to ban the *Stürmer* on several occasions, only to have Hitler respond that Streicher's "primitive methods" were most valuable in reaching the average man. Hans Lammers, Hermann Göring, Joseph Goebbels, and a number of other top party figures also tried to do something about Streicher at one time or another, with the most limited success.[18]

When Streicher did get into trouble, he could always turn to Hitler for help. In 1934, for example, the ritual-murder special edition produced international uproar, including protests from the Archbishop of Canterbury. Hitler finally permitted it to be banned, only after most copies had already been distributed, on the pretext that Streicher's comparison of the Christian sacrament of communion to Jewish ritual murder was an affront to Christians. Later that year, the *Stürmer*'s ill-advised attack on a Czechoslovakian statesman got in the way of German diplomacy, resulting in a two-week ban. In 1935 the paper attacked Hans Lammers, and a three-month ban was imposed. But Streicher visited Hitler and secured his order allowing him to resume publication. Hitler revoked another ban in 1938, once again after Streicher made a personal appeal.

By 1940 such difficulties had lessened. With the general tightening of censorship that accompanied the war, proofs of each *Stürmer* issue were sent to Berlin before publication. In November 1940, for example, the censor instructed the paper to hold back an article on Jews in Turkey, to omit an article on Switzerland, and to alter parts of other stories.[19] These changes were not critical of the anti-Jewish tone—the worst stories passed untouched—but attempts to avoid diplomatic difficulties.

After 1940 the *Stürmer*'s circulation dropped sharply, in part due to war time paper shortages, though Hitler assured enough paper for Streicher to keep going. A more important reason was the disappearance of Jews from everyday life within Germany. In the 1920s and 1930s each issue of the paper had been filled with charges that Jews were about nefarious deeds everywhere in Germany, posing an immediate threat to each reader. But by the war years, most Jews who had not emigrated had been removed to the East, where under the ministrations of the SS and out of public view, they were annihilated in growing numbers. Lacking the element of immediate threat, large numbers of Germans lost whatever interest they had had in the Jewish question. The *Stürmer* was left a journal of international affairs, not the scandal sheet that had made it notorious. Without the appeal of immediate scandal, the circulation soon dropped to under two hundred thousand. By mid-1944, paper shortages had reduced it from its high of sixteen pages to the four pages it had had in 1923. Yet Streicher continued to the end, his final issue appearing in February 1945. Denouncing the invading Allies as tools of the international Jewish conspiracy, the issue had a limited audience.

The *Stürmer* was published for twenty-two years. Never before or since was there a newspaper that so crudely proclaimed racial hatred to so many people. Even today, the *Stürmer*'s message is available in anti-Semitic literature published the world over. Indeed, in 1976 the New Christian Crusade Church, a very right-wing organization in Louisiana, printed "The Julius Streicher Memorial Edition" of the 1934 ritual murder special edition (see figure 16). According to the introductory material: "Julius Streicher, German educator, writer, and politician, in whose memory this paper was printed, was a victim of the horrible Talmudic Blood Rite known as the Nuremberg Trials. . . . We now proudly present to you, the reader, for the first time in English, this new edition of Julius Stricher's [sic] most famous issue of *Der Sturmer*." The English-language version has, apparently, sold well.

IV

The German
Anti-Semitic Tradition

"I have not met a German yet who was well disposed toward the Jews; and however unconditionally all the cautious and politically-minded repudiate real anti-Semitism, even this caution and policy are not directed against the species of this feeling itself but only against its dangerous immoderation. . . ."[1] So Friedrich Nietzsche wrote in 1886. Heinrich von Treitschke, one of the leading historians of the day, said much the same in a widely read series of essays in 1879. He saw the rising tide of anti-Jewish feelings as the natural reaction of the Germanic race to those whom they perceived as an invading foreign element: "Even in the most educated circles, among men who reject any thought of religious intolerance or national arrogance, one hears as if from a single mouth: The Jews are our misfortune."[2] Von Treitschke's words, echoing similar comments of Martin Luther three centuries earlier, were to become Julius Streicher's motto, gracing the bottom of nearly every front page of the *Stürmer*.

Anti-Semitism is more than a Nazi aberration. The Holocaust rests comfortably in the traditions not only of Germany, but also of all mankind. Never has there been a time when one group of people did not hate another enough to kill. The Holocaust is unique not because of the millions who died in it, but because it was an attempt by a civilized society to kill a group of fellow human beings solely because of their genetic makeup, as opposed to the customary motivations of greed, envy, or aggrandizement.

Why were the Jews so despised in Germany, indeed in all Europe? The question is a large one that has to be surveyed here briefly if Streicher's remarkable success at Jew-baiting is to be understood.[3] Jews are seen as the eternal outsiders in Western society. With traditions more ancient than those of the developing nations of Europe and a religion that, though much the same, was also very different, Jews were distinct from other Europeans in ancestry, religion, and culture. Any of these is sufficient to call up the darker side of the human spirit; together they made of Jews the most evident minority on the Continent.

By the Middle Ages an astonishing variety of wild tales about Jews were part of everyone's common knowledge. In the plays, the arts, the popular fables of the day, the Jew was a stereotype, already more a "Jew" than an individual. It was not in fact clear to the medieval mind that a Jew was a person. Christians believed that although Jews had longed for the coming of the Messiah, they rejected and crucified him. Christians believed that Christ himself had said of the Jews that their father was the Devil. So evident was the Christian consensus that many could see no reason but perverse stubbornness for the Jewish failure to move from circumcision to baptism, a stubbornness that could only be the work of the Devil himself.

The belief that the Devil and the Jews made common cause was virtually undisputed among Christians. A very popular legend, precursor to the Faust story, is found nearly everywhere in Europe in some form. A ruined clergyman successfully turns to the Jews for assistance in selling his soul to Satan. Another story has a Jew appear magically before an impoverished Christian who has called upon the Devil for succor. Much later, Shakespeare, always a shrewd judge of the popular mind, has a character in "The Merchant of Venice" say: "Certainly the Jew is the very devil incarnal." If Christ was God made flesh, the Jew, almost, was the human incarnation of Satan, the enemy of all that was good.

It is not surprising, then, that stories of Jewish women giving birth to pigs were believed. And, people confidently asserted, the distinctive nature of the Jews was indicated by their foul odor, though generally it was thought that baptism cleansed both physically and spiritually, since baptized Jews no longer stank (at least to Christians— commonly, baptized Jews were thought to smell to their former coreligionists). The fact that regular thorough bathing was manda- tory Jewish ritual at a time when Christians habitually shrank from the touch of water made no difference.

Confident of an alliance between the Devil and the Jews, the medieval mind expected to find Jews about every manner of their father's business and, as is so often the case, it found what it looked for. Since magic and witchcraft were Satan's work, Jews were thought particularly adept at the arcane arts. Even Christian sorcerers gener- ally resorted to Hebrew in their incantations. Stories were told of Jewish sorcerers who magically raised a person into the air, chopped him into his constituent parts, and then reassembled the sundered parts, leaving the subject hale. In a day when thousands of witches were burned, often confessing to their deviltry only after severe tor- ture, the evidence for Jewish necromancy was almost unquestioned.

Other ghastly charges were raised, charges of Jewish ritual murder and of the use of Christian blood in Jewish life. Ritual murder is the claim that Jews need the blood of freshly slaughtered Gentiles to use in religious rituals. The accusation dates to before the Christian era, but it achieved widest circulation after 1300. The first recorded case in Germany was in 1334. Exactly what Jews did with Christian blood was disputed. Some thought they used it in perverse Easter observ- ances, though later sentiment held that Passover was a likelier occa- sion. Parallel to ritual murder was the blood libel, which held that Jews used Christian blood for other purposes, an easy assumption to make since it was believed that blood had magical properties. The best blood was innocent blood, explaining why Jews allegedly attempted to kill young children whenever possible. Once secured, the blood could be used for medicinal purposes—for example, to heal the wounds of circumcision or to relieve menstrual bleeding, from which both Jewish men and women were thought to suffer.

Then there were volumes of charges that Jews were guilty of more ordinary crimes. Since Christians were to avoid moneylending, Jews served in that ever unpopular role, at times only as fronts for Chris- tians, yet taking all the blame. Jews were deemed treacherous, dealers in shoddy merchandise, blasphemers, desecrators of the host, traitors.

Medieval Christians believed that no manner of evil was beyond the ken of so wicked a people.

Central to medieval anti-Semitism was religion. Jews who converted to Christianity found general approval among Christians. They after all testified to the truth of the Christian consensus and made plain what was already widely believed: that Jews who failed to convert were stubbornly blind.

The Reformation, clearing away large parts of the medieval legacy, failed to reform the European image of the Jew. Martin Luther, it is true, early in his career urged tolerance for the Jews and condemned persecution of them. But later, perhaps deciding that Jews would not use the toleration he proposed for the purpose he intended—conversion—he turned against them in some of the most vitriolic language in the long, malevolent history of anti-Semitism. Jews, he wrote in 1543, "are nothing but thieves and robbers who daily eat no morsel and wear no thread of clothing which they have not stolen and pilfered from us by means of their accursed usury. . . . Such a desperate, thoroughly evil, poisonous, and devilish lot are these Jews, who for these fourteen hundred years have been and still are our plague, our pestilence, and our misfortune."[4] Luther proposed that Jews be treated harshly. Their synagogues should be burned, their houses razed, their holy books seized, their legal protections abolished, their rabbis banned. They might even be expelled entirely from Germany, following the example of other European nations. His words were the delight of later, and lesser, German Jew-baiters.

In the two hundred years after Luther, the lot of German Jews improved, unevenly and slowly to be sure, but the gradual modernization of society did not leave Jews untouched. The Protestant-Catholic wars of the seventeenth century left the combatants too concerned with each other to worry much about Jews. Indeed, the princes of the many German states found their court Jews valuable advisers and business associates, and the most prominent of these privileged Jews were able to help their people in many ways.

The hold of anti-Jewish feelings remained clear—the legacy of hundreds of years was not easily vanquished. The strength of the enduring anti-Semitic tradition is suggested by Johann Andreas Eisenmenger's monumental *Endecktes Judenthum (Judaism Uncovered)*, published in 1700, though legal challenges delayed its wide distribution for ten years. Eisenmenger, an accomplished scholar fluent in the source languages, provided 2,120 pages of material documenting what he alleged to be the depravity of Judaism, in the hope that his work would persuade Jews to leave their sinful faith for the Gospel of Christ. Contrary to a frequent accusation, Eisenmenger did not mistranslate or forge his material, taken from the Talmud and other Jewish writings. Indeed, he provided his evidence in lengthy quotations in the original Hebrew and Aramaic languages and in German translation. His argument was that Jews had distorted God's nature. Their laws were wicked or foolish, he said, and contrary to the teachings of Christ. The evidence he gathered was the foundation of much later German anti-Semitism, though most of his successors lacked his abilities with the source languages and were less careful to maintain context.

The problem with Eisenmenger's work is not that it is mistranslated or forged, but that he began his work with the conviction that Jews were evil, and he looked for evidence to support his preconceived ideas. A person convinced that Dutchmen were an evil lot would, with little trouble, find a profusion of evidence to support his case. Eisenmenger likewise allowed his conclusions to determine his evidence, not his evidence to guide his selection of conclusions. What he found was a small portion of the Jewish tradition which, when read literally, seemed to lend itself to his preconceptions, and to him it overshadowed the far more prominent ethical core.

By the early nineteenth century the progress toward Jewish emancipation was obvious. French Jews benefited from the grant of civil equality, the result of the Revolution of 1790–91, and Napoleon brought the French code to much of what would later become Germany in 1796–1808. Even Prussia broadened Jewish rights in 1812. Anti-Semitism was certainly not a relict; the "hep-hep" riots of 1819 (so-called as that was the common mob chant) demonstrated that many Germans would still take to the streets to fight Jews, but anti-Semitism was retreating. The leaders of the Revolution of 1848 called for complete emancipation of the Jews, but their defeat had no major anti-Jewish consequences, evidence that Jews were becoming more acceptable. By 1871, year one of the Second Reich, the German constitution gave Jews full rights as citizens. In the confident days at the end of the century, it seemed plain that with time Jews were certainly to become integrated fully into the larger society and that the legacy of the Middle Ages would inevitably fade.

But now a new and ominous movement developed which, while holding to the medieval stereotype of the Jew, found for it a more dangerous foundation. So-called scientific or racial anti-Semitism based its mistrust of the Jews on nonreligious grounds. The argument varied. For some, Jews were a more primitive product of evolution. Others thought Jews to be the product of their environment, a dry, desert, intellectually shallow people. Their primitive desert religion was said to lack the refinement of Christianity. Whatever the reason, the problem now was one of "race" or ancestry, not religion, a problem that could in no way be remedied by so simple a solution as baptism. The combination of religious and racial anti-Semitism was to revive the power of the medieval stereotype, giving it a foundation more acceptable to an age that liked to think of itself as scientific. A landmark year was 1879, the year von Treitschke wrote his widely read essays, the year a Berlin preacher named Adolf Stöcker found that preaching against Jews drew larger crowds than preaching Christ, the year Wilhelm Marr coined the term anti-Semitism, a word suggesting the racial grounds of the new Jew-baiters.

The rise of modern anti-Semitism is plain in retrospect in the years before 1879. All Europe was intrigued by what now look to be very odd racial theories. Darwin's theory of evolution suggested to many that Jews might deserve their lowly estate. Pseudosciences like phrenology gained startling popularity. Even the popular fiction of the day demonstrates the enduring hold of anti-Semitism. Gustav Freytag's *Debit and Credit* (1855), which influenced millions of Germans over the years, contrasted Jews and Germans. Jews were pictured as ugly, ill-dressed, dirty, rootless, corrupt. The book said that Germans, holding to racial traditions far superior to those of the Jews, were noble and upright. In 1868 Hermann Goedsche, writing under the pen name Sir John Retcliffe, published his novel *Biarritz* in which, in the Jewish cemetery in Prague, thirteen elders of Zion plot world takeover. These and similar novels enjoyed wide sales, a significant testimony to popular suspicion of the Jews, for a novelist not only shapes popular attitudes, he is even more shaped by them. Had an American novel published in 1942 had as its hero a Japanese Army officer doing good and noble service for his country, sales would not have been high. German anti-Jewish novels sold well in part because they affirmed popular attitudes. Despite legal emancipation imposed from above, to many Germans the Devil and the Jews were still close kin. Jews were different, and the different is always unpleasant. Curiously, Jews were beginning to be seen as exemplars both of ancient and of modern evil. Aside from the traditional baggage of anti-Semitism, the Jews also were identified with the ills of developing modern society, with cities and industrialization, and the consequent social changes. They were to blame for the decay of old-fashioned life.

A new flood of anti-Semitic literature appeared. August Rohlfing, professor at the German University at Prague, published his *Talmud-Jude (Talmud Jew)* in 1871. It saw many editions. Rohlfing essentially relied on Eisenmenger's earlier work, though he was far less scrupulous in his selection of material, often omitting the context that Eisenmenger had provided. That Rohlfing failed to defend himself in several lawsuits did little to reduce his credibility.

In 1887 Theodor Fritsch published his *Antisemitischen-Katechismus,* later to become the *Handbuch der Judenfrage* which Julius Streicher read in 1919. Selling seventy-five thousand copies by 1930, Fritsch's work was a compendium of anti-Semitic arguments throughout the ages. It began with a discussion of the distinctiveness of the Jewish "race," followed by an unflattering summary of the impact of the Jews on world history. Turning to the Talmud, Fritsch paraded the well-known and generally unreliable passages from the Jewish religious writings. Jews, Fritsch claimed, were to rob and steal whenever possible. Non-Jewish women could be raped any time past the age of three, ritual murder was a holy obligation. All these and more were supported by alarming, if implausible, citations. Fritsch then turned to the role of Jewish organizations and political parties, claiming that Jews dominated the churches, the press, economic life, and the arts. A lengthy section at the end gave an anti-Jewish dictionary of quotations from leading Gentiles down the ages, followed by compromising statements from Jews.

What was to be done to the Jews? Fritsch's solution was straightforward. They were to be evicted. "Where shall they go? That is their problem. They did not ask where the farmers and workers they evicted were to go. Certainly they have enough money to buy land somewhere to live on—perhaps in Australia or Africa."[5] Fritsch's book seems to have been a standby in the *Stürmer* offices.

Then there was Houston Stewart Chamberlain, an Englishman who adopted Germany. In 1899 he published his *Foundations of the Nineteenth Century,* a book that sold one hundred thousand copies by 1918 and that had a deep influence on Adolf Hitler. A work of pseudoscience, it saw history as a battle between Jews and Aryans, an egocentric view of history that understandably found favor in Germany. Kaiser Wilhelm II became a leading advocate.

Despite the outpouring of such books and pamphlets, German anti-Semites were unable to form a united movement, for reasons that in part are simple enough. All agreed on the depravity of the Jews, but there was little agreement on philosophy or tactics. Some Catholic anti-Semites were still willing to grant baptized Jews status as human beings, while the more radical anti-Semites often attacked the Old Testament roots of Christianity along with the Jews. The more intellectual in the movement rejected their cruder brethren. A series of attempts at anti-Semitic political parties failed, though in Austria men like Karl Lueger, lord mayor of Vienna from 1897 to 1910, demonstrated the popular appeal Jew-baiting could have. Hitler drew the conclusion from watching Lueger's policies that there was a future in Jew-baiting, though he later complained that Lueger's anti-Semitism was more political than applied, suggested by the mayor's well-known statement: "I decide who is a Jew."

Then came 1914, and with it the collapse of the grand illusions of a proud generation. As ever in trying times, the power of anti-Semitism rose. In 1916 the German army held a census to see if it were true that Jews were not serving in the front lines in proportion to their numbers in the general population, a result of anti-Semitic agitation. The war brought with it a new emphasis on heroism and camaraderie, images of brotherhood from which Jews easily were excluded. Had Germany won the war these might have passed into history as temporary aberrations of a nation at war, small roadblocks on the road to emancipation.

But Germany lost the war, and what is more, lost it with Russia defeated and German armies still deep in France. Defeat carried with it the need for explanation, it brought social chaos, a new and imposed form of government, economic collapse. In astonishing numbers, Germans turned to anti-Semitism for some of the answers. Germany, General Ludendorff claimed, had been stabbed in the back, not defeated on the battlefield. Soon it was widely believed the traitors had been Jewish. And as thousands of Eastern European Jews immigrated to Germany after 1918, carrying with them customs and traditions visibly different from those of the largely assimilated German Jews, the Jewish presence suddenly became more evident.

Many anti-Semitic groups were established, the largest of which was the Schutz und Trutz Bund, which Julius Streicher joined for a time in 1919. By 1922 it had 530 local groups and 200,000 members. German student fraternities agitated for limits on the admission of Jewish students to the universities and refused to admit Jews as members. Radical groups like Hitler's Nazis and Streicher's Nuremberg groups found growing numbers of adherents, harkening to a past when Jews had not been citizens.

The anti-Semitic revival took on a clearly racial tone. Artur Dinter's novel *The Sin Against the Blood* (1918) told of a woman, ruined by a Jew, who married a German only to bear children who still bore signs of Jewish blood. She had been ruined forever. A total of 235,000 copies of Dinter's remarkable book were in print by 1927; realizing he had a good thing, he wrote several similar novels. The theme was one Julius Streicher would use throughout his career. Then there was the 1920 German translation of the *Protocols of the Learned Elders of Zion,* allegedly the minutes of a secret meeting of the hidden rulers of the world, the Elders of Zion, held to discuss their dreadful schemes to seize total control of the world. A demonstrable forgery originating in Russia in 1903, a total of 120,000 copies quickly sold.

By 1923, one recent German scholar writes, "one large part of the population hated and despised the Jews, the other, just barely the majority, had either inwardly given them up or displayed no inclination to get involved on their behalf.[6] George L. Mosse argues convincingly that Nazism was successful because of rather than despite anti-Semitism, and even if his argument is too strong it is certainly clear that anti-Semitism was a respectable political philosophy in Germany. Major political parties and leading public men stood for it. Even those who were themselves not anti-Semites generally accepted it as a reasonable part of the political spectrum, not an aberration, just as many in the American South who themselves were not white supremacists nonetheless accepted those who were.

What distinguished Nazism, then, was not that it attacked the Jews, but the fervor with which Hitler preached and the centrality Jew-baiting had in his convoluted thinking. *Mein Kampf* devotes an astonishing amount of space to the matter. From the preface, which speaks of "the evil legends created about my person by the Jewish press" to the conclusion, which maintains "A State which, in the epoch of race poisoning, dedicates itself to the cherishing of its best racial elements, must someday be master of the world," Hitler ties the most disparate themes into the racial question.

According to Hitler's racial theory, race was the critical factor in world history. In a familiar passage he wrote: "All that is not race in this world is trash." There had been, he thought, an original race of which the Aryan race was the offspring, a race that was responsible for every advance in human civilization. All great art and culture, every grand thought and invention had been the product of this admirable race. The remarkable advances in the United States were to be attributed to the presence of so many of Aryan ancestry, and even in Asia, the progress of the Japanese was only a reflection of Aryan progress. The Aryan was self-sacrificing, willing to suffer personal loss to advance the race, idealistic, hardworking, virtuous.

In contrast, the Jew lacked idealism, the will to sacrifice, and the true creativity that flowed from those elements. Jews would not sacrifice for the common good. When they did cooperate, it was only because outside forces made it necessary. Left to themselves, Hitler was sure Jews would begin quickly to squabble among themselves, for the Jew "is led by nothing but pure egoism on the part of the individual."

Since Jews were by nature incapable of constructing or creating anything on their own, they of necessity had to live parasitically among others. The Jew "is and remains the typical parasite, a sponger who, like a harmful bacillus, spreads out more and more only if a favorable medium invites him to do so." Hitler saw a consistent pattern to Jewish parasitism. When they first entered a nation, Jews settled openly as shopkeepers or tradesman, becoming intermediaries, not the true creators of wealth. Moneylending thus became the perfect Jewish occupation, creating money for the Jews in nonproductive ways, ways that initially might even be welcomed by the host people. As the yoke of usury tightened, there would be resistance, riots, and pogroms. In response Jews would coddle up to the leaders of the nation, making themselves useful, ingratiating themselves, until they became the power behind the throne. Now Jews pushed for citizenship, even permitting themselves to be baptized, becoming "Germans" or "Frenchmen," becoming emancipated.

Once citizens, Jews became proponents of liberalism, of modernity. They fostered religious toleration, universal suffrage, the equality of all men. They took control of the press, the labor unions, capital, even the churches, using all to persuade the masses that men were the same regardless of race. The final Jewish goal, according to Hitler, is democracy, "because it eliminates the personality—and in its place it puts the majority of stupidity, incapacity, and last, but not least, cowardice." With the Jews in control of opinion, democracy becomes only a tool of Jewish self-interest.

As part of the general drive for power, Jews had to destroy the racial purity of those who opposed them, "for a racially pure people, conscious of its blood, can never be enslaved by the Jew. It will forever only be the master of the bastards in this world." Since Jews can rule only when others have been brought down to their level, Hitler argued that they engaged in a gigantic conspiracy to poison the blood of superior races. He wrote about "the black-haired Jew boy, diabolic joy in his face," who "waits in ambush for the unsuspecting girl whom he defiles with his blood and thus robs her from her people." "The loss of purity of the blood destroys the inner happiness forever; it eternally lowers man, and never again can its consequences be removed from body and mind." Earlier, Hitler claimed: *"The sin against the blood and the degradation of the race are the hereditary sin of this world and the end of a mankind surrendering to them."*

Thus Hitler thought Jews were responsible for Germany's decline, but more even than that. They had caused the fall of Greece and Rome, the decline of every great civilization. The most terrible example of the effects of the Jews on a nation Hitler saw in Russia, where they had "killed or starved about thirty million people with a truly diabolic ferocity, under inhuman tortures, in order to secure to a crowd of Jewish scribblers and stock exchange robbers the rulership over a great people."

Yet the victory of the Jews was also their defeat, Hitler observed. For in seizing control of a nation, the inability of the Jews to create anything new becomes deadly. Just as the death of a host kills the parasite, so Jewish success ultimately kills them. "With the death of the victim, this peoples' vampire will also die sooner or later."

To Hitler, the Jewish question was the connecting link of all history. Lacking a proper understanding of the Jews, a person could never come to a satisfactory theory of history, art, or politics. In battling the Jews, Hitler was engaged in the noblest possible human struggle. As he put it: "By warding off the Jews I am fighting for the Lord's work." And in *Mein Kampf* he made his ultimate solution to the Jewish question clear. Germany would never have lost World War I, he explained, if at its beginning "12,000 to 15,000 Hebrew corrupters of the people" had been executed with poison gas.

As over the years Julius Streicher went about the work of Jew-baiting, he was not a crackpot. He was in a tradition of ancient familiarity. He was, it is true, more intent, more single-minded than most Germans, but his ideas were fundamentally respectable to them. And in National Socialism, he had found a party guided by a man smarter and more capable than he, to whom his radical views were welcome.

1. Julius Streicher in the 1930s.

2. Streicher speaking in Munich during the 1923 Beer Hall *Putsch*.

Der Stürmer

Sonderblatt zum Kampfe um die Wahrheit.

Nr. 1   Weitere Ausgaben erscheinen nach Bedarf.   **1925.**

Streicher's
Antwort
an die
Verleumder und Verräter!

Die „Fränkische Tagespost" vom 15. August 1913 führt Bebel's Worte aus dem Jahre 1903 an. Diese lauten:

„Wenn bei uns (Sozialdemokraten) ein **Eitergeschwür** auftritt, dann operieren wir **vor aller Welt**; wenn wir **schwarze Wäsche** zu waschen haben, dann waschen wir **vor aller Welt**. Das ist ja gerade das **Großartige** in unserer Partei, daß wir diese Wäsche **vor der ganzen Welt** waschen und doch keinen Schaden dadurch erleiden, sondern nach **erfolgter Wäsche größer dastehen, als je zuvor**".

Wir Nationalsozialisten machen das gleiche.

Wer sie sind!

1. Ferdinand Bürger.

Im Oktober 1922 gründete ich die Ortsgruppe Nürnberg der „Nationalsozialistischen Deutschen Arbeiterpartei". Von den zur Gründung Erschienenen wurde **Ferdinand Bürger** einstimmig zum 2. Vorsitzenden gewählt. Bürger erbot sich, die parteigeschäftlichen Arbeiten **ehrenamtlich** zu übernehmen. Da die neugegründete O.-Gr. ohne Geldmittel war und heute noch nur von den Mitglieder-Beiträgen und Sammel-Geldern ihre Notwendigkeiten bestreitet und da Geldmittel in größerem Maße nicht zu erwarten waren, erklärte ich Bürger, daß wir ihm für seine Arbeit eine Vergütung zukommen lassen würden, sobald dies möglich sei. Gelegentlich frug ich Bürger, der sich anfangs eifrig der ihm anvertrauten Sache annahm, wovon er lebe, da er ja neben der Partei-Arbeit keinen anderen Beruf nachgehen könne. **Bürger erklärte mir, er lebe mit seiner Mutter zusammen, die durch Näharbeiten genügend verdiene und ihn mitversorgt.** Bürger erschien mir als anderen als Idealist, dem die Bewegung, der er sich verschrieb, über alles gehe. Ich war beglückt, einen solch uneigennützigen Mitarbeiter in Bürger gefunden zu haben und nahm wiederholt die Gelegenheit wahr, auf die Opferbereitschaft Bürgers in Mitglieder- und Sprechabenden hinzuweisen. **Bürger genoß meinerseits volles Vertrauen und auch das Vertrauen fast aller Mitglieder**, die ihn auch bei der Neuwahl der Vorstandschaft einstimmig wiederwählten. Nach Bürgers Rückkehr aus Rumänien, wohin er sich im Dezember zu privaten Zwecken begeben hatte, stiegen innerhalb der Mitgliedschaft Zweifel über Bürgers Ehrenhaftigkeit und Ehrlichkeit auf. Es wurde berichtet, daß Bürger viel Bier trinke und für andere bezahle. **Seine Lebensführung machte immer mehr den Eindruck, als hätte man es mit einem Mann zu tun,** der über außerordentliche Geldmittel verfüge. Ich machte Bürger auf die aufsteigenden Zweifel aufmerksam und bat ihn, alles zu vermeiden, was den Glauben an die persönliche Ehrenhaftigkeit des 2. Vorsitzenden und des ehrenamtlichen Geschäftsführers erschüttern könnte. Bürger versicherte mir wiederholt, daß er sogar Mittags kalt esse und sich äußerst einschränke. Ich mußte bald darauf erfahren, daß Bürgers Angaben zur Verdunkelung bereits vorhandener Schäden und daß er sein Gewissen schon längst belastet fühlte. Obwohl nach den Angaben Bürgers die Ausgaben für die Partei die Einnahmen weit überschritten, gestattete ich nun Bürger, sich kleine Beträge als Entlohnung aus der Kasse zu nehmen. Ende Januar gab mir Bürger auf meine Anfrage zur Antwort, er habe sich für diesen Monat 85000 Mk. entnommen. Von einem ähnlichen Betrag sprach er im Februar. Bürgers Angaben bestärkten mich auf's Neue im Glauben, es mit einem ehrlichen, nur aus Idealismus der Bewegung dienenden Mann zu tun zu haben. Um zugleich alle gegen Bürger schon gewordenen Zweifel zu zerstreuen, ordnete ich an, daß zwei von der Mitgliederversammlung ernannte sachkundige Prüfer die von Bürger geführten Bücher durchsehen sollten. **Bürger hintertrieb diese Nachschau.**

Mitte März wurden in einer Mitgliederversammlung 66000 Mk. gesammelt mit der ausdrücklichen Bestimmung, daß ich persönlich das Gesammelte in Raten an hilfesuchende Ruhrflüchtlinge verausgaben solle. Bürger, dem das Geld zur Parteistelle zu bringen hatte, erklärte tags darauf, er habe nur noch 21000 Mk., es sei ihm über Nacht das Uebrige gestohlen worden. Bürger versicherte mir auf die Aeußerung meiner Zweifel hin, er dürfe umfallen und tod sein und sein Leben lang kein Glück mehr haben, wenn ihm das Geld nicht gestohlen worden sei.

Im Augenblicke dieses eigenartigen Schwures empfand ich den ersten Ekel vor Ferdinand Bürger, das Vertrauen war erschüttert, der Glaube an seine Ehrenhaftigkeit vernichtet. Auch die übrigen Vorstandsmitglieder berichteten, sich von Bürger für betrogen. Eine bald darauf einberufene

---

3. The first issue of the *Stürmer*.

Der Stürmer

Nürnberger Wochenblatt zum Kampfe um die Wahrheit

HERAUSGEBER : JULIUS STREICHER

| Nummer 50 | Einzelverkaufspreis 20 Pfennig. Bezugspreis unter Kreuzband monatlich 90 Pfennig. — Postscheckkonto Nürnberg 165. | Nürnberg, im Dezember 1925 | Wegen Aufgabe von Anzeigen wende man sich an den Verlag Nürnberg, Menschelstr. 70, Fernruf 4972 | 3. Jahr 1925 |

Bis auf die Knochen blamiert

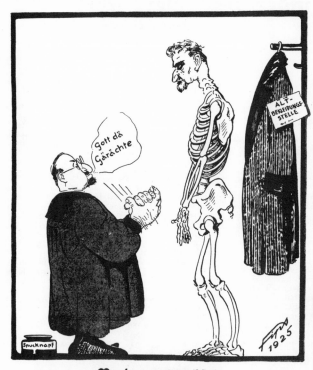

Regierungswechsel

Unsere Reichsregierung ist wieder einmal zurückgetreten. Wir sind neugierig, wer jetzt „dran" ist. Die Schaffung der „Koalition" soll die ganze nächste Woche in Anspruch nehmen. Das kann wieder ein blutiges Geraufe geben. Praktisch hat es ja doch keine Bedeutung. Man läßt die Maschine einfach laufen. Nur daß sich heute der, morgen jener Lokomotivführer nennt.

Abwärts geht's nun schon einmal und drum ist schließlich alles wurscht.

Die Zeitungen aber bringen den Regierungswechsel fett gedruckt. Auf den Gang der Weltgeschichte aber hat diese Mitteilung absolut keinen größeren Einfluß, als wenn der Herr Bierdimpfl von morgen ab statt seines braunen wiederum den grünen Hut aufsetzt.

Der Giro-Zentrale Merkel wieder im Amt

Die Millionen sind kaput. — Die Stellung ist gerettet.

Der frühere Nürnberger Finanzminister, Stadtrat Dr. Merkel, ist seit längerer Zeit wieder im Amt. Er war einer der heftigsten Gegner der Nationalsozialisten. Bei der Entlassung unseres Pg. Holz war Dr. Merkel der treibende Keil. Wenn es galt, gegen die Nationalsozialisten-Front zu machen, dann war Dr. Merkel der große Wortführer.

„Die Nationalsozialisten untergraben das Ansehen der Stadt, sie entleiden den Stadtrat seiner Würde, es ist unmöglich unter solchen Umständen weiter zu arbeiten u.s.w. usw." So könnte dieser Herr Finanzreferent stundenlang zetern und schreien.

Bis dann der Skandal in der Girozentrale kam. Bis dann bekannt wurde, daß Stadtrat Dr. Merkel in seiner Eigenschaft als Finanzreferent einen großen Teil der städtischen Gelder der Girozentrale zur Verfügung gestellt hatte. Es waren etwa 10 Millionen Goldmark, die aus der Nürnberger Bevölkerung durch Erhöhung von Steuern und Abgaben herausgeholt waren.

Dr. Merkel war aber nicht nur für die Verwaltung der städtischen Gelder, sondern auch für richtige Verwendung derselben in der Girozentrale verantwortlich. Denn er war dort Vorstandsmitglied.

Während damals in Nürnberg der Mittelstand langsam zusammenbrach, weil die Stadt sich weigerte, den erforderlichen Kredit zur Verfügung zu stellen, verlieh Stadtrat Dr. Merkel die zum größten Teil aus dem Mittelstand herausgeholten Gelder an eine Schwindelgesellschaft.

Dadurch erlitt die Stadt Nürnberg einen Verlust von mehreren Millionen Goldmark.

Dieser Verlust muß selbstverständlich wieder gedeckt werden. Anstatt nun den verantwortlichen Finanzreferenten zum Ersatz des Schadens heranzuziehen, holt man das Geld wiederum aus der Bevölkerung in Form von Steuern usw. heraus.

Der Herr Finanzreferent Dr. Merkel aber erlaubte sich noch mehr:

Er ließ sich von den Geldern, die ihm zur Verwaltung übergeben waren, einen Kredit von 40 000 Mk. gewähren und zahlte dafür etwa 5°/₀ Zinsen.

Die Nürnberger Bürgerschaft aber, aus der dieses Geld herausgeholt war, zahlte zu derselben Zeit für jeden Kredit vierzig bis sechzig Prozent Zinsen.

Dr. Merkel baute sich um dieses Geld eine luxuriös eingerichtete Villa.

Aus dem Inhalt:

4. The first Fips cartoon.

5. A *Stürmer* display case, one of thousands (No. 8 [1935]).

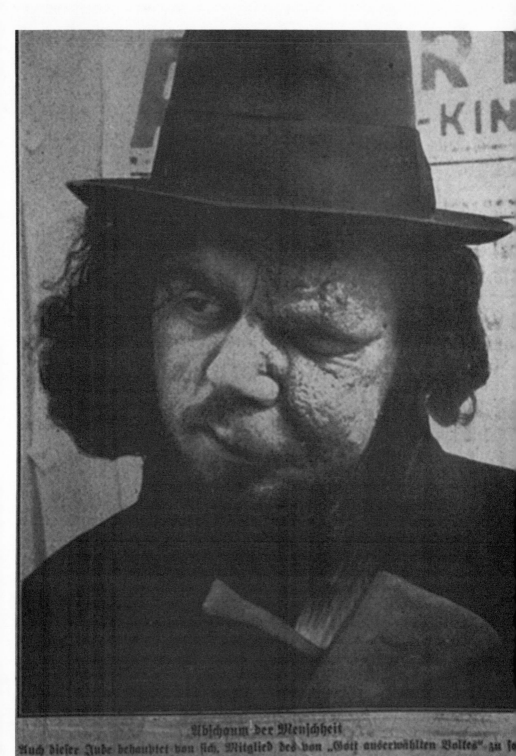

Abschaum der Menschheit
Auch dieser Jude behauptet von sich, Mitglied des von „Gott auserwählten Volkes" zu fe

6. A typical *Stürmer* photograph of a Jew. "The scum of humanity. This Jew says that he is a member of God's chosen people.' " (No. 7 [1943]).

7. A retouched *Stürmer* photograph of a Hollywood screen test (*Sondernummer* 8 [1938]).

. An Aryan girl and a Jewish girl. "What natural nobility speaks from the face of this Aryan girl! How horribly this face reflects Jewish depravity!" (No. 1 [1943]).

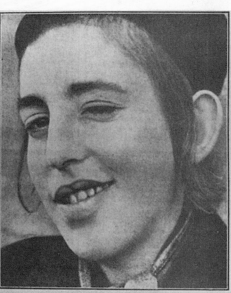

Welch natürlicher Adel spricht aus dem
Antlitz dieses arischen Mädchens!

Wie abscheulich spiegelt sich in diesem Gesicht
die jüdische Verworfenheit!

Der Vampyr

Vom Teufel in die Welt gesetzt er stets die Völker quält und het

9. The Jew as vampire (No. 31 [1934]).

Jm Talmud steht geschrieben: ,Nur der Jude allein ist Mensch. Die nichtjüdischen Völker werden nicht Menschen genannt, sie werden als Vieh bezeichnet.' Und weil wir Juden den Nichtjuden als Vieh betrachten, sagen wir zu ihm nur Goi."

10. A Jewish pupil, under the guidance of his rabbi, studies the Talmud in a picture from *The Poisonous Mushroom*.

Auf diesem Bilde sehen wir achtzehn Juden. Von ihnen sind vier katholisch und drei protestantisch getauft. Es gibt Leute, die behaupten, getaufte Juden seien keine Juden mehr sondern Christen. Wer der Stürmerschriftleitung die getauften Juden durch An-kreuzen bezeichnen kann, erhält einen Preis

11. "A Contest." Readers were offered a prize if they could determine which Jews in the drawing had been baptized (No. 31 [1935]).

12. Four Jewish faces (No. 7 [1934]).

13. A Jewish butcher grinds a rat to make hash (No. 7 [1935]).

14. A Jew cheats a farmer in *Don't Trust a Fox on His Heath or a Jew on His Oath.*

15. A Jewish lawyer cheats a farming couple in *Don't Trust a Fox on His Heath or a Jew on His Oath.*

Preis 30 Pfennig

Ritualmord-Nummer

Der Stürmer

Deutsches Wochenblatt zum Kampfe um die Wahrheit

HERAUSGEBER: JULIUS STREICHER

| Sonder-nummer 1 | ... | Nürnberg, im Mai 1934 | ... | 12. Jahr 1934 |

TRANSLATED FROM THE GERMAN BY EVA-MARIA HOOD   EDITED BY L. CRAIG FRASER AND THOMAS E. O'BRIEN

JEWISH MURDER PLAN
AGAINST GENTILE HUMANITY EXPOSED

THE MURDEROUS PEOPLE

The Jews are under a terrible suspicion the world over. Who does not know this, does not understand the Jewish problem. Anyone who merely sees the Jews, as Henrich Heine (Chaim Bueckburg) described them, "a tribe which secures its existence with exchange and old trousers, and whose uniforms are the long noses", is being misled. But anyone who knows the monstrous accusation which has been raised against the Jews since the beginning of time, will view these people in a different light. He will begin to see not only a peculiar, strangely fascinating nation; but criminals, murderers, and devils in human form. He will be filled with holy anger and hatred against these people.

The suspicion under which the Jews are held is murder. They are charged with enticing Gentile children and Gentile adults, butchering them, and draining their blood. They are charged with mixing this blood into their masses (unleaven bread) and using it to practice superstitious magic. They are charged with torturing their victims, especially the children; and during this torture they shout threats, curses, and cast spells against the Gentiles. This systematic murder has a special name, it is called

RITUAL MURDER

The knowledge of Jewish ritual murder is thousands of years old. It is as old as the Jews themselves. The Gentiles have passed the knowledge of it from generation to generation, and it has been passed down to us through writings. It is known of throughout the nation. Knowledge of ritual murder can be found in even the most secluded rural villages. The grandfather told his grandchildren, who passed it on to his children, and his children's children, until we have inherited the knowledge today.

It is also befalling other nations. The accusation is loudly raised immediately, anywhere in the world, where a body is found which bears the marks of ritual murder. This

VICTIMS OF JEWS

In secret rites for thousands of years, the Jew has spilled human blood. And still today the devil is persecuting us, it is up to you to clean out the hellish crew.

THE JEWS ARE OUR MISFORTUNE!

---

16. The 1976 English-language translation of the 1934 ritual-murder special edition, republished by an American anti- Semitic organization.

Preis 20 Pf

Der Stürmer
Sonder-Nummer
...sches Wochenblatt zum Kampfe um die Wahrhei...
HERAUSGEBER: JULIUS STREICHER

Sonder-nummer 5   Nürnberg, Reichsparteitag 1936   14. Ju... 193...

Weltverschwörer
Die enthüllten Geheimnisse der Weisen von Zio...

Das große Rätsel

Der Reichsparteitag 1936 findet in einer Zeit statt, die gekennzeichnet ist durch Unruhen, Revolutionen und blutige Bürgerkriege. Eine gewaltige Erschütterung geht durch die Welt. Verschwörungen haben sich in allen Ländern gebildet. Ihre Kanäle reichen bis in die höchsten Stellen der Politik und der Wirtschaft. Politische Drahtzieher sind heimlich tätig und peitschen die Massen auf. Ein großer Teil der Weltpresse steht geheimen Richtlinien bekommen zu haben. Er trauert aller oder verflucht auf ein bestimmtes Ziel los. Dieses Ziel heißt: Durch die Weltrevolution zum Weltkommunismus.

Das auserwählte Volk

Den Satan, der die Menschheit quält / Hat nur der Teufel auserwäh...

Deutscher Volksgenosse!

Was hat es für eine Bewandtnis mit den Geheimnissen der Weisen von Zion? Woher kommen die Sorgen, die Revolutionen, die Kriege in der Welt? Wer sind die Drahtzieher des

Massenmordens in Spanien?

Hast Du die Sonder-Nummer und Du bist Millionen geworden, hilf mit an der Aufklärung! Gieb diese Sondernummer weiter! Schicke sie denen, die die Anleitungen noch nicht kennen! Es soll das ganze deutsche Volk lesend werden. Es soll auch der letzte deutsche Volksgenosse wissen, worum es geht. Sorge noch Du dafür, daß vieles große Ziel erreicht wird!

Der Stürmer

Die Juden sind unser Unglück

Im Jahwe-Zeichen

Der Traum des Juden ist die Welt,
Die ihm, als Herrscher, unterstellt,
Drum schlug er sie in Mord und Grauen,
Den Thron im Chaos sich zu bauen.

18. Jews controlling Russia, England, and the United States. "The dream of the Jew is to rule the world. Therefore he throws it into murder and horror, to build his throne in chaos."

Der Juden Kriegsgott

Er trägt kein Schwert womit er Schlachten schlüge,
Denn seine Waffen sind Gemeinheit, Trug und Lüge

19. "The Jewish War God. He carries no sword with which to fight his battles, for his weapons are dirty trick fraud and lies." (No. 27 [1934]).

Der Stürmer

Deutsches Wochenblatt zum Kampfe um die Wahrheit

HERAUSGEBER: JULIUS STREICHER

| Nummer 14 | Verlag: „Der Stürmer", Julius Streicher, Nürnberg, Fürtherstraße 25/II. Postscheckkonto: Amt Nürnberg Nr. 105. Geschäftsstelle 21830. Schriftleitung: Nürnberg. Einzelnummer-Ausgabe 791. Schriftleitungssekretär: Ferling (nachm.). Fernsprecher: 21827. Brieffanschrift: Nürnberg 2, Schließfach 235. | Nürnberg, 6. April 1944 | Erscheint wöchentlich. Einzel-Nr. 10 Pfg. Bezugspreis monatlich 64 Pfg. zuzüglich Postbestellgeld. Bestellungen bei den Briefträgern oder der zuständigen Postanstalt. Nachbestellungen an den Verlag. Schluß der Anzeigenannahme 8 Wochen vor Erscheinen. Preis für Gelegenheits-Anz.: Die ca. 31 mm breite, 1 mm hohe Raum-Zeile im Anzeigenteil laut Preisliste. | 22. Jahr 1944 |

Hilfskolonnen

Eine interessante Meldung aus Palästina

Was wir dazu sagen

Der britisch-amerikanische Nachrichtendienst „Exchange Telegraph" meldet aus Jerusalem:

„In Palästina sind jüdische „Hilfskolonnen" gebildet worden. Sie sollen sobald wie möglich im Gefolge der anglo-amerikanischen Truppen in Marsch gesetzt werden und in Europa eindringen."

Jeder, der diese Meldung hört, wird sich fragen:

„Zu welchen Zwecke wollen diese jüdischen „Hilfskolonnen" in Europa einmarschieren, und welche Aufgabe haben sie dort zu erfüllen?"

Wenn man von „Kolonnen" hört, denkt man natürlich an Soldaten. Und wenn man sobald berichten vom Judenkolonnen spricht, so liegt die Vermutung nahe, daß es einer Armee von Judensoldaten vorbehalten ist, zusammen mit anglo-amerikanischen Truppen in die Schlacht zu marschieren und Europa zu „befreien".

Wie ist es nun in Wirklichkeit?

Seit Jahren faseln die Judenzeitungen der Welt von einer großen gewaltigen Judenarmee. Einmal schreiben sie, die Judenarmee sei schon gebildet, ein andermal berichten sie kleinlaut, die Aufstellung des Judenheeres leide noch an großen Schwierigkeiten. Einmal schrei-

ben sie, die Judenarmee sei bereits so organisiert, daß sie jeden Tag zu ihrem großen Schlage ausholen könne, ein andermal aber üben sie Kritik an den wehrfähigen Juden, die leider nur wenig Verständnis für die große Sache der Judenarmee hätten.

Einmal schreiben sie so und ein andermal so! Die Wahrheit ist, daß die Juden gar nicht daran denken, eine Armee jüdischer Soldaten an die Front zu schicken. Zum ehrlichen Kampf von Mann gegen Mann fühlt sich der Jude nicht geboren. Dafür sind die Nichtjuden da! Sie sollen sich gegenseitig töten, damit der Jude dann als lachender Dritter ihr Erbe antreten kann. Und deshalb gibt ja der Talmud den Rat, als Letzte in den Krieg zu ziehen, damit sie als Erste wieder zu Hause sind, um dort „ernten" zu können. Es ist also Tatsache: Der Jude denkt gar nicht daran, seine „Hilfskolonnen" als kämpfende Soldaten in Europa einmarschieren zu lassen.

Worin aber besteht dann die Aufgabe der jüdischen „Hilfskolonnen?"

Die Antwort auf diese Frage geben uns die jüngsten Geschehnisse in Süditalien. Nach dem feigen Verrate italienischer Judenknechte war es den anglo-amerikanischen Truppen möglich geworden, in Italien Fuß zu fassen und einen Teil des Landes zu besetzen. Die Armeen der

Judensklaven

Sie sind durch den Juden versklavt und verkommen.
Man hat ihnen Freude und Seele genommen.
Sie schielen nach Deutschland, wo die Arbeit geehrt,
Wo jeder im Volke erkennt seinen Wert.

Die Juden sind unser Unglück!

20. "Jewish slave colonies."

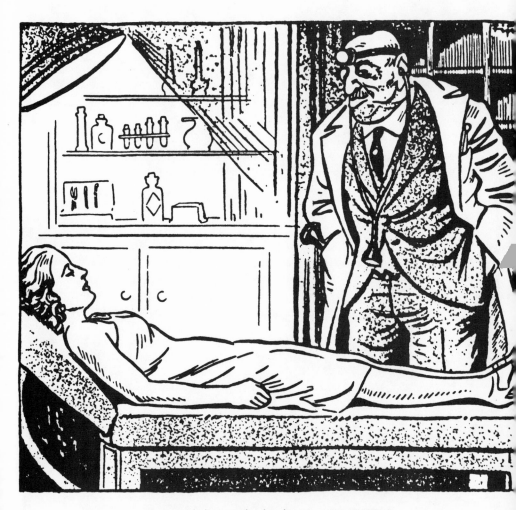

21. A Jewish doctor with a female patient (No. 17 [1935]).

Hinter den Brillengläsern funkeln zwei Verbrecheraugen und um die wulstigen Lippen spielt ein Grinsen.

22. A girl visits a Jewish doctor in *The Poisonous Mushroom.*

23. A Jew attacks a girl (No. 53 [1925]).

24. A girl being seduced by a Jew in *Don't Trust a Fox on His Heath or a Jew on His Oath.*

25. "The spider. Many victims are trapped in the web, caught by flattering words. Rip the web of deceit and free the German youth." (No. 26 [1934]).

Die Spinne

Manch Opfer blieb im Netze hangen / Von Schmeicheltönen eingefangen
Zerreißt das Netz der Heuchelei / Ihr macht die deutsche Jugend frei

"Fort mit der Kultur! Her mit der Hure Unnatur!"

26. "Down with culture! Up with the whore of unnaturalness!" (No. 21 [1929]).

27. "Revenge. Go where you wanted me to be, you evil spirit," a cartoon published shortly after Hitler took power (No. 22 [1933]).

Vergeltung

Fahre hin, wohin Du mich haben wolltest, Du Ungeist

Sieg

Der Spuk ist zu Ende   **Der Tag ist erwacht**

The *Stürmer's* response to Hitler's chancellorship. "Victory. The nightmare is over, the day has dawned." (No. 10 [1933]).

29. Jewish children being mocked in *Don't Trust a Fox on His Heath or a Jew on His Oath.*

Der Stürmer

Deutsches Wochenblatt zum Kampfe um die Wahrheit

HERAUSGEBER: JULIUS STREICHER

Nummer 18

Verlag: „Der Stürmer", Julius Streicher, Nürnberg, Zöberleinstraße 1011. Postscheckkonto: Amt Nürnberg Nr. 106. Fernsprecher: 21396. Schriftleitung: Nürnberg, Pfannenschmiedsgasse 1911. Schriftleitungsschluß: Freitag (nachm.). Fernsprecher: 21672. Briefanschrift: Nürnberg 2, Schließfach 268.

Nürnberg, 29. April 1943

Erscheint wöchentlich. Einzel-Nr. 20 Pfg. Bezugspreis monatlich 84 Pfg., zuzüglich Postbestellgeld. Bestellungen bei dem Briefträger oder der zuständigen Postanstalt. Nachbestellungen an den Verlag. Schluß der Anzeigenannahme 8 Tage vor Erscheinen. Preis für Geschäftsanzeigen. 2 ½ cm. 22 mm breite, 1 mm hohe Raum-Zeile im Anzeigenteil 1,00 Reichsmark.

21. Jahr
1943

Der heilige Haß

Wer die Geschichte der Juden, wie sie in ungekürzten und ungefälschten Übersetzungen des Alten Testamentes aufgezeichnet ist, aufmerksam liest, den überkommt ein Grauen. Ein Grauen über die beispiellose Verkommenheit der Juden, ein Grauen über die von den Juden begangenen Verbrechen, ein Grauen über den teuflischen Haß, mit dem die Juden von Anfang an alle jene verfolgten, die sich nicht dem Joche Alljudas beugen wollten! Dieses Grauen aber steigert sich zum Entsetzen, wenn man gar das talmudische Schrifttum zur Hand nimmt und von den jüdischen Mutausbrüchen liest, wie sie im Talmud-Schulchan-Aruch niedergelegt sind. Es steht geschrieben:

Vom Berg Sinai:

„Was bedeutet Sinai? Sinai ist ein Berg, auf dem sich Moses von Gott Jahwe die jüdischen Gesetze geben ließ. Von diesem Berg hat sich der Haß der Juden über alle Völker der Welt ausgebreitet."

(Schabbath, Fol. 89 a).

„Jeder Jude hat die Pflicht, danach zu trachten, daß die christlichen Kirchen verbrannt und ausgerottet werden. Die Heiligen müssen mit Schimpfnamen belegt und die Geistlichkeit muß getötet werden."

(Schulchan Aruch, Jore dea, § 146, 14.)

„Der Nichtjude ist dem Menschenkot gleichzuachten, er wirkt ebenso wie dieser verunreinigend."

(Orach Chajim, § 55, 20.)

So also steht in den „Heiligen" Büchern des Judentums geschrieben. Und jeder Jude, ganz gleich, ob er in Deutschland lebt oder in Amerika, ob er russisch spricht oder spanisch, ob er im Ghetto haust oder an der Wallstreet in Neuyork residiert, denkt, fühlt und handelt so, wie es der Talmud ihm gebietet. Die abgrundtiefe Abneigung der Juden gegen die Nichtjuden hat mit dem Worte „alttestamentarischer Haß" ihre Prägung gefunden. Trotz seiner beispiellosen Minderwertigkeit konnte sich das Judentum Jahrtausende hindurch behaupten, weil es durch einen satanischen Haß gegen alles Nichtjüdische geeint und damit ungeheuer stark gemacht wurde.

Der Haß des Juden ist aber auch heute noch der gleiche geblieben wie jener in der grauen Vorzeit. Wer sich nicht dem Juden unterwirft, ist sein Feind. Und diesen Feind haßt er mit allen Fasern seines Herzens und von der ganzen Kraft seiner Teufelsseele. Es sei nur daran erinnert, mit welch verbissener Wut sich die Judenheit zu allen Zeiten auf jene Wissenden stürzte, die den Versuch machten, den Juden als Teufel in Menschengestalt zu entlarven und die nichtjüdische Welt zum Kampf gegen ihren Todfeind aufzurufen. Nach einem bewährten Rezepte wurden diese Männer im Zug niedergekämpft und schließlich kurzerhand beseitigt. Durch planmäßig in die Welt gesetzte üble Gerüchte nahm man ihnen die Ehre, raubte ihnen dann durch raffinierte Schachzüge Hab und Gut und ließ sie plötzlich eines „natürlichen Todes" sterben. Es muß einer künftigen Geschichtsschreibung überlassen bleiben, die „Herzschläge", „Selbstmorde" und sonstigen Todesursachen zahlreicher Judengegner eingehend zu ergründen und als Werk des ewigen jüdischen Hasses zu entschleiern. Es werden da —

Unsere Aufgabe

Der „Stürmer" muß den Juden zeigen,
Damit ein jeder ihn erkennt.
Verbrechen wäre, zu verschweigen,
Warum ein Volk ins Unglück rennt.
Wir müssen auch die Sprache sprechen,
Die jedermann im Volk versteht.
Furchtbar müßt' sich in Judern rächen,
Wenn es um Sein und Nichtsein geht.

Aus dem Inhalt

Die Juden sind unser Unglück

30. "The Holy Hate" (No. 18 [1943]).

V

Children of the Devil: Streicher's Image of the Jew

In 1937 Streicher published a book explaining to teachers how children were to be taught to hate Jews:

> Our children must know that Jews remain Jews, despite baptism, despite the fact that they have lived in Germany for hundreds of years, despite the fact that they dress as we do and have given themselves German names. They never take on our way of thinking. They remain Jews, hucksters, usurers, swindlers, criminals, because language, baptism, and domicile do not change the blood.[1]

The unrelenting crudity with which Streicher preached that message was to his mind essential if Germans were to come to hate their Jewish fellow citizens. Germans needed to be convinced that Jews were different from themselves, both in race and religion, that these differences made Jews dangerous, and that something ought to be done to protect Germany from the Jewish menace. This required the creation of a thoroughly unsavory image of the Jew.

To persuade his countrymen that Jews were different, Streicher relied on a crude version of an already crude racial theory. There were, he thought, three pure races: the black African, the yellow Oriental, and the white Aryan. The Aryan race, of course, was the highest, but blacks and Orientals, lower though they were in the racial hierarchy, still were as pure races entitled to their portion of the planet. But Jews were a mixed race, the product of intermingling the blood of the pure races. Like Hitler, Streicher argued that the consequences of race mixing were necessarily deleterious. Jews were bad because, in mixing the races, all the bad characteristics and none of the good ones came to expression.

These odd theories hardly were self-evident, so Streicher needed ways to reach his generally ill-educated audience with his arguments. Using a familiar rhetorical tactic, he turned to areas with which his audience was already familiar to find examples. A 1934 cover cartoon, for example, showed a German holding two well-bred dogs. Two unpleasant Jews are conversing with him, one of whom is saying that although one must know the race and ancestry of a dog, all men, to the contrary, are equal. In another article Streicher suggested that just as one is not surprised to find differences in nature between rocks and plants, so too one ought to expect differences between human beings.[2] Such reasoning superficially makes sense, and those used to more critical thinking were not likely to be regular *Stürmer* readers.

Making the same point, Streicher used ridicule and humor. In his 1935 Berlin speech he told of an Englishman he had met during the 1920s who maintained that all men were equal during the discussion period of a public meeting. Streicher replied: "Wait a minute. You say that everyone who has a human face is the same. Very well. Yesterday I was in Koblenz and Mainz and I looked into the barracks [of the French occupation troops]. There, in Germany, I saw black Negroes and yellow Siamese in French uniforms. Now, you come up here to the podium and bring along in your imagination a black Negro, and then say that everyone who has a human face is the same." The Englishman, according to Streicher, sprang up, shouting: "That is impudent. I will not tolerate such slander." In the same speech Streicher told of a German whom he called Dr. So-and-So. The doctor for some reason decided he wanted to be a Jew. Visiting a rabbi, he requested circumcision. The astonished rabbi complied, and the next day the doctor proudly told his colleagues that something about him had changed, which however they were quite unable to detect. Finally he explained that, having been circumcised, he was now a Jew. A Nazi replied: "What? You let yourself be circumcised? You are an ass. You look just like you did before. You had a German father and a German mother, so you are German. The fact that you let yourself be circumcised shows only that you are stupid, as stupid as a pig."[3] The *Stürmer* regularly carried jokes along similar lines, and of similar quality. Crude they were, but that has never stopped a joke from drawing snickers.

Hundreds of articles over the years repeated the racial argument. Many times the point was made in passing in other articles whose main theme was along different lines. The most prominent Jewish organization during the Weimar period, for example, was the Central Union of German Citizens of the Jewish Faith, which the *Stürmer* often remarked would more properly be called the "Central Union of German Citizens of the Jewish Race." Streicher regularly used such terms as *Judenanwalt, Judenartzt,* and *Judentenor* (literally Jew-lawyer, Jew-doctor and Jew-tenor, respectively, as if somehow a Jewish tenor sounded quite different from his Aryan colleague). Each issue of the *Stürmer* pointed out many times that Jews and Germans were racially separate.

The argument that Jews were of a different and lesser race is a version of an ancient and ever-popular argument. To make the jump from believing that a Thoroughbred horse is of greater value than a nag to the belief that the same is true with people is both superficially plausible and personally satisfying, provided of course one believes oneself of pure ancestry. That Streicher's defective arguments met wide popular acceptance is not surprising; more intellectually persuasive ones of the same sort had, after all, secured wide support in educated circles during the preceding century. And it is the stuff of which wars and crusades have ever been made.

The argument of course did not stop with inherent genetic inferiority. That inferiority led to every manner of ill effect. Mixed blood was bad blood. As Streicher put it: "The blood is the seat of the spirit. If the blood is bad, the soul will not be good. That blood which is bad comes from the blood of different races." Later, he extended the argument: "Racial science has incontrovertibly proven that the bastard, the halfbreed, receives only the bad characteristics of the races from which he stems, not the good spiritual or physical characteristics. Therefore, the Jew possesses the lust of the Negro, the craftiness of the Mongol, and the criminal drives of all the races which have combined to produce his blood." There was no way, obviously, for a Jew to improve. His Jewishness was inherent. A Fips cartoon titled "The Curse in the Blood" illustrated the point. A drawing of an ugly Jewish baby was captioned: "Every Jewish child becomes a Jew."[4]

The results of bad blood began with the physical. *Stürmer* Jews were wretched, deformed creatures. Fips's cartoons are the most obvious examples. His Jews were generally fat, unattractive, half-shaven, protruding-lipped, bent-nosed, slouching creatures. Fips did not invent the familiar caricature of the Jew but certainly gave it far greater circulation. The *Stürmer* took particular pleasure in letters from readers who claimed to have seen Jews looking just like the ones Fips drew— letters that testified that the caricatures were not imaginary creatures but the unvarnished truth.

Photographs were another form of evidence used to demonstrate Jewish ugliness. The *Stürmer* archive collected thousands of unflattering photographs of Jews and was constantly appealing to readers for assistance in building the collection. Favorite shots were sometimes repeated, but the *Stürmer* seemingly had an inexhaustible supply of ugly Jews to present to the readers (see figure 6). A 1934 special edition served up a full-page photograph of an old bearded Jew with open mouth and closed eyes. In 1938 there were fifteen photographs of bearded Jews in one issue, and the *Stürmer* claimed "the depravity of their race is evident in their horrible faces."[5] Regularly in the late 1930s there were full-page collections of photographs of unpleasant-looking Jews on such themes as Jewish criminality, Jews in Czechoslovakia, or Jewish rabbis. On a similar theme, the paper maintained that even Jews thought themselves ugly. Several rather graphic treatments of plastic surgery to straighten Jewish noses were carried. And Streicher suggested one reason for the alleged Jewish interest in German women was that their own were ugly.

The outbreak of World War II provided Streicher with a potent source of new photographs. As German soldiers marched through Poland, they came across many conservative Eastern Jews, no longer visible in Germany. One soldier wrote that he had often been amused by what he thought to be the exaggerations in Fips's cartoons, but having seen thousands of such Jews in the flesh in Poland he was now a convert.[6] A German soldier in 1939 had considerable credibility with the *Stürmer*'s audience, and the many letters from the troops that Streicher printed suggested his eagerness for fresh evidence.

When photographs were insufficiently ugly, the *Stürmer* resorted to retouching. A careful look at *Stürmer* pictures sometimes reveals the signs of tampering. Noses are changed to make them look more "Jewish," expressions are altered to appear less attractive, clothes are removed from women in the company of Jews. A favorite photograph depicts a Hollywood screen test, for example. A scantily clad young woman dances before a group of particularly ugly Jews. The signs of retouching are obvious (see figure 7).[7] A surviving memo from Ernst Hiemer includes his instructions to the editorial staff to retouch a photograph of a distinguished-looking Jew "so that he looks worse."[8] Too attractive a Jew, after all, would weaken the stereotype.

Ugly Jews were sometimes contrasted to attractive Gentiles. Two adjacent photographs in 1943 compared a beautiful young German girl with a Jewish girl in the midst of a distorted expression (see figure 8). Another pair of photographs contrasted a tall, marble Grecian statue, apparently the typical Aryan, with a hairy, slouching Jew. Not only did Jews look worse than Aryans, but also Jews were at times compared with animals. A 1937 issue of the *Stürmer* borrowed *Life*'s fisheye shot of Jimmy Durante's nose, comparing it to a long-nosed monkey in an adjacent photograph.[9] Durante's ancestry, however, was solidly Italian—not the only time the *Stürmer* would make such an error.

Comparisons to animals were better made in cartoons, however. Over the years Fips depicted Jews as toads, vampires, vultures, horned monsters, insects, spiders, bacteria, and toadstools (see figures 9 and 25). Ernst Hiemer wrote a book of children's stories titled *The Poodlepugdachshundpinscher*, which compared Jews to mongrel dogs, chameleons, locusts, bedbugs, tapeworms, poisonous snakes, drones, hyenas, coo-coos, and sparrows. The title story told of a mongrel dog of uncertain ancestry who wandered about town causing every manner of mischief. The story explained how, just as the Poodlepugdachshundpinscher's defects were the consequence of his mixed ancestry, so too Jewish depravity was the result of mixed blood:

There are bastards among the animals and among people. The Jews are bastards. They show the racial characteristics of the white, yellow and black peoples. Their curly hair and protruding lower lip remind one of the Negro. Typical characteristics of the Jews also include their crooked legs and flat feet. Many Jews have a nose which is bent at the point and jughandle ears. Their revolting body odor also brands them as a foreign race. Their sneaky gait and posture suggest the apes. Many Jews have a small, receding forehead and a skull like a gorilla. As the Poodlepugdachshundpinscher is a bastard among the dogs, so the Jew is a bastard among the peoples.[10]

These kinds of comparisons were an important part of Streicher's strategy. First, of course, the unpleasant associations of unpopular forms of animal life were transferred to the Jews. To compare a Jew to a tapeworm is to make all kinds of unstated accusations, accusations the audience will itself fill in. And the comparison renders the Jew less human, perhaps not human at all. It is hard to kill a human being, but we step on spiders without a second thought. To dehumanize Jews was a first step on the road to Auschwitz.

Jews were dehumanized in yet another way. Streicher presented them as such evil creatures that it was difficult to allow them a place in the natural creation. In a throwback to medieval legends, Jews again became unnatural, supernatural. Jews were unnatural in that they acted contrary to normal human behavior. An early Fips cartoon titled "The Natural and the Unnatural" depicted in one frame a happy German couple enjoying an afternoon in the country, while in the second frame a Jew and his German victim watched a pornographic film. Streicher later argued that Jews were incapable of ordinary human laughter. A full page of photographs titled "When Jews Laugh" depicted a variety of Jews captured in distorted mirth, incapable of "laughing in a free and open manner."[11]

The source of Jewish unnaturalness became an even more prominent theme—the Devil himself. Just as God battled Satan in the heavenly realms, so on earth their respective allies joined battle. In 1934 a *Stürmer* writer asserted: "We know that the Jew is the eternal, natural, and sworn enemy of Germany. We know that this is true of all Jews. The Jews living in Germany are no exception; indeed, it is even more true of them."[12] To be the eternal enemy meant that Jews needed outside help, and that help had to be satanic. The precise nature of the relationship between the Devil and the Jews was not entirely clear. A 1935 article signed by Streicher was titled "The Devil." It argued that the battle against the Jews had to be continued, since the Nazi takeover had hurt but not destroyed the Jewish cause. The same year Ernst Hiemer wrote that "the Jew has the Devil in his blood," rather a stronger relationship.

The airship *Hindenburg* exploded in New Jersey in 1937. In the classic photograph of the disaster a *Stürmer* reader thought he saw the outline of a Jewish face in the smoke, and the *Stürmer* agreed: "Nature has here shown clearly and with absolute correctness the Devil in human form." Another lead article was headlined: "Light against Darkness: The German Struggle for Freedom Against the World Devil." The world Devil was of course the Jew.[13] Fips regularly drew on the ancient identification of the serpent with the Devil, drawing, for example, a cartoon titled "The Satanic Serpent Judah."

But individual Jews as well as the race were identified with the Devil. A 1928 Fips cartoon titled "Satan" showed a Jew lurking behind a German girl. The thoughts running through his mind were pictured in the background: drinking, dancing, and disrobing. In one of the few absences of a Fips cover cartoon, there was instead a large photograph of an old bearded Jew captioned simply "Satan."[14] Individually and collectively, then, Jews were the Devil. Such an image drew on centuries of prejudice, reinforcing what Germans had long heard. It transcended the real Jew, who for all practical purposes ceased to exist. Instead he became only a facade, behind which was concealed horrible depravity.

So much for the physical nature of the Jew. Mixed blood made Jews more than ugly, however—it made them morally inferior, inheriting as they did the base drives of all mankind. Jews were, to begin with, dirty. Fips's cartoons displayed filthy Jews, a point reinforced by many articles. When, for example, in 1936 the last Jews were driven from the town of Roth, the townspeople explored the now-deserted synagogue. According to a *Stürmer* reporter they were revolted by their discoveries. "The dirt on the floors and windowsills was half an inch deep. Papers, bottles, boxes, bedsteads, rats, and rubbish covered the floor. A foul odor came from the furniture. Just a few weeks before, the Jews held their 'worship services' in these rooms." A *Stürmer* reporter in Vienna found "clouds of dust" upon entering a deserted Jewish apartment. Conditions were "beyond words. . . . Even in a pigsty one does not find such disorder." When the former Jewish inhabitants had gone out they had looked clean and well dressed, but that was illusion, for their true character was shown by the way they had lived when out of public eye.[15] A month later the paper provided a full page of photographs from another filthy Jewish house. Letters from German soldiers in Poland testified to piles of filth there. And Streicher typically referred to Jewish women as "filthy Talmud wives."

It followed that if Jews were physically dirty, they were also morally soiled. The strong and clean, like the beautiful or handsome, have ever been inclined to do good, as the list of the heroes of Western civilization makes clear. Cleanliness is rooted in our traditions. The ritual cleanliness of the Old Testament and the later Christian emphasis on being "washed clean" are two of many examples. Since cleanliness is next to godliness, filthiness is evil. Pornography is described as "filthy," a shady action is a "dirty" trick. It was to be expected, then, that a dirty Jew would be morally filthy as well. The jump here is important. Individuals may be physically dirty without endangering the community, but moral depravity is seen as socially dangerous. And that is the argument Streicher would build and that we will look at in later chapters.

Another unpleasant personality trait Jews supposedly displayed was laziness, a particularly dreadful failing given the well-known German propensity to work hard. Streicher accused Jews of being do-nothings, spongers who lived off the work of others. They avoided physical labor, seeing that as shameful work suitable only for Gentiles. In Vienna, the *Stürmer* charged, 85.5 percent of the lawyers were Jews, as were 75 percent of the bankers and 51.6 percent of the doctors, but there were no Jewish street cleaners, no Jewish manual laborers. In all of Poland, a later article asserted, there were no Jewish farmers, masons, or factory workers.[16] In Germany too, Streicher claimed, Jews avoided physical labor, sticking to the professions and low trades. The argument was not that it was dishonorable to be a professional, rather it was a question of intent. Streicher thought a German doctor took up his profession from love of his people and a desire to serve. The Jewish doctor entered medicine for quite contrary reasons, one of which was a hatred of common physical labor. It was possible, in short, to imagine a German doctor as a factory worker, but never a Jewish doctor as a common laborer. The point was made by a Fips cartoon titled "Jewish Nightmare." The Jews, having formed their own state, are horrified to learn that there is no longer anyone to do their work for them.[17]

As the moral opposite of the German, it could hardly be expected that the Jew would make a good soldier. In 1932, for example, Streicher asserted that Jews had avoided the front lines during World War I, a demonstrably false statement, and asked readers to send in their accounts of what Jews did during the war, an appeal that met practically no response. He later wrote: "Jews were never soldiers and will never be able to become soldiers. Their physical and spiritual qualities make them unsuited for military service." A 1937 article on a Jew accused of sex crimes noted in passing, "naturally he was not a soldier."[18] Even the Jews admitted as much, Streicher thought, citing a favorite Talmud passage that advised: "When you go to war, be the last to go rather than the first, so that you may also be the first to return home." Out of context, the passage certainly supported his argument, but a more careful examination, the kind his readers were most unlikely to do, in fact gave evidence for the contrary argument. The saying is reported as one of the "Jerusalem people," thought by other Jews to be frivolous. It is cited unfavorably by the Talmud. Furthermore, it was those same Jerusalem people who put up bitter armed resistance to the Romans, culminating in the destruction of the Temple in A.D. 70.[19]

Jews were also portrayed as money-loving, scheming, and sexually perverted, though these carried an element of threat and will be treated in later chapters. The whole matter of the Jewish character is summarized in a remarkable passage from *Mein Kampf,* with which Streicher was in perfect agreement: "If the Jews were alone in this world, they would suffocate as much in dirt and filth, as they would carry on a detestable struggle to cheat and ruin each other, although the complete lack of the will to sacrifice, expressed in their cowardice, would also in this instance make the fight a comedy." The argument in short was that Jews were an entirely different sort of being.

But there remained several problems. One would expect a devilish people to have a depraved religion, yet Judaism shared better than half the Bible with Christianity. Streicher therefore revived the old charges that Judaism was a perverted faith with reprehensible teach-ings, charges dating back to Eisenmenger's *Judaism Uncovered* and before. Since neither Streicher nor his close collaborators could read Hebrew, they had to rely on such dubious scholars as Rohlfing and Fritsch, whose compendiums of anti-Semitic quotations from Jewish sources were mistranslated, taken out of context, or not infrequently simply invented. Jewish law allegedly permitted—indeed, com-manded—every manner of crime against Gentiles. Raping young girls, robbing elderly widows, selling shoddy goods, murdering inno-cent children, all were said to be the holy obligation of the Talmud Jew. That few Jews had much to do with the Talmud, which runs to sixty volumes in a Hebrew-English edition, and that even fewer were familiar with the less common Jewish religious writings, was to Streicher irrelevant. According to a 1928 *Stürmer* article, the Talmud was "the Jewish spirit set down on paper," and ten years later an article asserted that "the Jew is the Talmud made flesh."[20] One of the children's books includes a story describing how a young Jewish boy is guided through the mysteries of the Talmud, happily absorbing its horrible commands (see figure 10 and Appendix II).

Since the Jew was the Talmud and the Talmud was the Jew, it was entirely unnecessary for the Jew to be familiar with the physical volumes—the Talmud was engraved in his soul. The *Stürmer* claimed that "the entire life of the Jew is ruled by the Talmud. In every situation he asks himself, 'What is written in the Talmud? What must I do to be a genuine Talmud Jew?' Every Jew thinks like this."[21] If so, Streicher had little to worry about. The best efforts of the anti-Semites produced perhaps two hundred alarming citations. Meanwhile thousands of pages of high moral character were passed over. But Streicher's readers were unlikely to search out a full edition of the Talmud, a rather difficult set of books for a novice to use anyway—and those passages Streicher cited certainly were alarming.

So far we have the traditional anti-Semitism, anti-Semitism that in the past could be relieved by conversion and that accepted the Old Testament as God's word. But Nazi anti-Semitism went farther, for Nazism could not grant any good to the Jews. Now, this was a trickier matter, since many Germans, among them *Stürmer* readers, had been raised on the Old Testament and were convinced that a baptized Jew was as good a Christian as anyone else.

Sreicher had to argue that Jews could not be Christians, but that left him with thousands of baptized Jews to explain. The response was simple enough: He denied they were Christians. The clearest example of his approach came in a 1935 Fips cartoon titled "A Contest." The cartoon showed eighteen typical *Stürmer* Jews. The caption said that four were baptized Catholics and three were baptized Protestants. "There are people who maintain that baptized Jews are no longer Jews, rather Christians. A prize will be awarded to anyone who can pick out the baptized Jews" (see figure 11). Two weeks later it was reported that some readers actually had tried to pick out the baptized Jews, thereby showing that they completely misapprehended the nature of the *Stürmer*'s allegations, since baptism changed a Jew not at all.[22] One of the children's books showed a fat Jewish couple leaving a Christian church. Two Nazi girls in the background, looking at the man, comment: "Baptism didn't make a Gentile out of him!"

Then Streicher relied on Jews to testify on the point. His editor Ernst Hiemer, who specialized in attending Jewish sex-crimes trials, interviewed the Jewish defendant at one such trial as to the effects baptism had had on him. The reply was that there had been no effect: "I have remained a Jew. Baptism did nothing to me." This "confession," Hiemer exclaimed, was just what the *Stürmer* had been saying for years.[23] The testimony of one Jew became evidence for the attitude of all Jews.

Why were Jews unsuited to Christianity? Their defective racial makeup rendered them incapable of accepting the high moral teachings of Christ. Jews lacked the ability to sacrifice for the good of the whole, to put others first, which was essential to true Christianity. When Jews were baptized, it was only as a means of concealing their devilish nature, of deceiving trusting Christians.

That was the easier problem, since even in the churches many were uncomfortable with Jewish Christians. The much harder problem was the plain fact that the roots of Christianity were Jewish—indeed, that Christ himself had been a Jew. It was one thing to persuade Church members that Jews could not accept the high ethical nature of Christianity, quite another to convince them that the Old Testament was part of the Jewish plot. For years, Streicher proceeded cautiously. Passing comments criticized the Old Testament or suggested that Christ really had not been a Jew.

By 1936 Streicher decided the time had come for a frontal assault. In September a lead article argued that the Old Testament was not Christian. There was a problem in education, the author explained. Nazi teachers told their pupils the truth about Jews, whereas priests and pastors taught the same children from the Old Testament, presenting stories in which Jews were heroes. Thus children learned "more about the history of the Jews than of their own people." The article made a vehement attack on the moral teachings of the Old Testament, concluding that it had no proper part in the Christian faith.[24] As Fritz Fink later put it in the *Stürmer* guide to anti-Semitic teaching:

> Jehovah is unjust. He divides the peoples into the chosen and the outcasts. He is horrible. He demands the annihilation of non-Jewish peoples. He gives his love only to one people, indeed choosing the worst and the most corrupt. . . . The god of the Jews is not our God. What Jehovah promises the Jews cannot be said by God. These promises contradict the nature of God. It is a great error to identify the Jewish god Jehovah with our God. The assertion that the Jews are the "chosen people" chosen from the world for salvation is a Jewish supposition and a slander thousands of years old against Gentile humanity.[25]

These arguments were not new—but never before had they achieved such widespread semi-official distribution.

The reaction was vehement. As one letter writer put it, the first issue "hit like a bomb." Outraged Christians protested throughout Germany, and the *Stürmer* received many letters, a fact that troubled it not at all. A provincial bishop wrote that the article displayed "a painful lack of expert knowledge," while a Berlin pastor thought that Christianity needed "the mirror of the Old Testament" to understand God better. The *Stürmer* replied that "a healthy man sees a thousand grinning Jewish faces in that mirror."[26]

The battle opened, Streicher continued to address the theme. Early in 1937 he published a special edition on the topic "Jewry against Christianity," which argued that Christianity was radically distinct from Judaism. It had not grown out of Judaism, rather was a response by the Aryans of Palestine to Jewish exploitation. Christ, it seems, was a revolutionary protonordic leader fighting Jewish domination. His movement had come "from the depths of his Nordic soul," and the

Jews had crucified him because he dared openly to oppose them. Had he not said of the Jews that their father was the Devil?

Several years later a *Stürmer* writer maintained that those who said Christ was Jewish made a terrible error. Such people proved that they knew "nothing about the great racial laws to which every man on earth is subject.... One of these laws says: 'A teaching which does not come from Nordic blood and which does not incorporate the Nordic spirit cannot spread among the Nordic peoples.'" Since Christianity had in fact spread in northern Europe, it could not have had Jewish origins. Too, anyone who maintained Christ was a Jew "thereby maintains that the Jewish race is able to show grand spiritual heroism, enormous courage, a love of truth, intelligence and far-sightedness." Such a person had "no understanding either of the Jewish or the racial question. The Jew is not in the least capable of these things."[27]

At Nuremberg after the war, Streicher had an interesting conversation recorded by G. M. Gilbert in which he discussed another argument he often used—the charge that Jews viewed Christ as the offspring of a whore:

> "Do you know what the Talmud says about Christ? It says he was born on a dungheap—yes—and it says he was the son of a whore." His ugly face broadened into a lascivious grin. "Sure—that is right.—She was not married, and that story about getting the child from God. Now you know, if we have to be perfectly honest about it—it is true that according to that story she must have been a whore." His leer expanded into a laugh of self-satisfaction as he continued. "I agree with that myself—but naturally, when I used that for propaganda, I didn't say that. I just said, 'You see, Christians, what the Jews say about the Immaculate Conception.'"[28]

Arguments on similar lines, however cynically made, were certain to arouse the concern of faithful if gullible Christians.

Streicher's attacks on the Bible made plain the Nazi antipathy to traditional Christianity. The furor eventually proved uncomfortable to the Nazi regime. In May 1938 the Propaganda Ministry, in a secret press directive, instructed journalists to stop discussing Christ's ancestry. "The problem is two thousand years old and no longer resolvable, and extensive handling of it will only intensify religious tensions."[29]

But the issue is one that Streicher would have returned to had the war ended differently. And he would have had the support of Goebbels, who was looking forward to a reckoning with the churches.

The image of the Jew that Streicher presented was most unpleasant. The Jew was physically ugly, morally weak, and had a depraved religion. An astonishing amount of "evidence" buttressed his conclusions. But he had a final problem—to move from the general to the specific. That is, were one to accept his evidence one would be compelled to accept the conclusion that Jews were in general a bad lot. The problem was that many were willing to grant that proposition and yet maintain that they knew "decent Jews," neighbors, friends, or shopkeepers who were exceptions, who displayed none of the unfortunate traits common to the run of Jewry as pictured in the *Stürmer*. Widespread belief in the existence of "decent Jews" militated against drastic anti-Semitism. If Jews are in general a bad lot, one of course keeps closer watch on them than on others, but the fact that some are innocent means that only those actually apprehended in criminal activity should be punished. Yet Streicher, like Hitler, thought of the Jewish question as one requiring a total solution, alternating in his mind between deportation and annihilation. How were such plans to be accomplished if every German knew decent Jews?

In response Streicher was forced to argue that there were no decent Jews, that every Jew was depraved and dangerous. He held the position from his earliest days, but it took time to formalize it. In 1926, for example, he printed a statement by a Jewish leader who rejected the "decent Jews" argument since it accepted in essence the racial argument, implying that such Jews were the minority. Streicher seized the statement, writing that the argument "that there are also decent Jews is a moral death sentence for Jews," as no one thought it necessary to argue that there were also decent Germans.[30] The problem with such an argument is that it grants the possibility of upright Jews, leaving the audience free to conclude that their Jewish friends are among that minority. That probably is why Streicher dropped it. For the remainder of his career he consistently argued that the concept of a decent Jew was contradictory.

In 1935, for example, he wrote: "It is hard to believe that there are still Germans, among them even some so-called National Socialists, who say that there are also decent Jews."[31] In one of the children's books, a mother takes her son mushroom gathering. When the son brings to his mother a toadstool, confusing it with an edible mushroom, she uses the occasion for a lesson in racial biology. Just as some toadstools look safe but are nonetheless deadly, so some Jews seem at first innocent. But each and every Jew, she explains, like each and every toadstool, is deadly poison.

To persuade those who thought they knew good Jews of their error, Streicher first preferred the use of the singular term the Jew (*der Jude*) to the plural the Jews *(die Juden),* even when referring of all Jews. The term made all Jews into one enormous, corrupt body, the individual Jew being part of the larger entity, so much like his racial brethren that it was not worth the effort to distinguish him as a person. The bacteria metaphor, so often used, was particularly appropriate on these lines. The character of an individual bacterium is irrelevant; what is important is that it can multiply rapidly and infect an entire organism, just as a few Jews could undermine an entire nation. The Jews work together. Each is implicated in the crime of every other. The individual is guilty of the crimes of the race, and the crimes of the race in turn are the responsibility of the individual, a convenient simplification that makes each piece of evidence support two arguments.

A second strategy was to detect allegedly "decent Jews" in assorted mischief. In 1929, for example, a *Stürmer* article spoke of two "respected and decent" Jews in a small town, who it turned out were implicated in a major agricultural scandal. In 1935 the *Stürmer* told of a Jewish doctor, respected by everyone in his town, who drugged and raped his female patients. Or Streicher told of a Jewish family, thought the very model of respectability—but the whole family was involved in a huge tax-evasion scheme. Ernst Hiemer warned parents to keep their children from playing with Jewish children no matter how pleasant they seemed. "Just as one rotten apple can spoil the bushel, a single Jewish child can destroy a whole crowd of Gentile children, and can lead them down the path from which there is no return."[32] Hundreds of similar stories were printed over the years. The point was always the same: Jews could never be decent.

The last major article on the theme ran in 1943. Streicher signed the lead, titled "Decent Jews?" He recalled the days when Nazi orators faced hostile crowds who claimed "I also know decent Jews." He remarked: "Does not that little word 'also' express the belief of Jewry's defenders that decent Jews are the minority and the indecent the majority?" That was the argument he had used in 1926, but now he went on. "Are there really decent Jews!" It was not a question. He gave examples of Jews who had been thought decent. There was, for example, "a Jew who gave a professor the money necessary to proclaim from his desk or in a public meeting teachings somehow useful for the Jews—he was a decent Jew!" All those who were thought decent were really about Jewry's business, Streicher wrote. Decency was only a façade. Their blood and ancestry rendered them unable to behave morally. To say there are decent Jews "is and remains a revelation of stupidity or of criminal lack of character."[33] By then there were few Jews at large in Germany.

Streicher in summary was attempting to build a universal stereotype of the Jew, the persuasive advantages of which are plain. A soldier in war develops a stereotype of the enemy—he is to be shot on sight. Streicher's goal was along a similar line. Germans were to hate Jews automatically, regardless of personal differences. Such a stereotype makes thinking unnecessary. If one believes all Jews are bad, knowing someone is a Jew is all one needs to know about him. And the process works both ways. That is, when one sees or hears of a Jew performing some nefarious deed, the action transcends the individual Jew—it is typical. Just what one would expect a Jew to do. The kind of reaction Streicher's mother had had so many years before.

Since Streicher's image of the Jews was so unflattering, it is amazing to find that Hitler accused him of *underestimating* Jewish depravity. "Streicher is reproached for his *Stürmer*," Hitler told his inner circle. "The truth is the opposite of what people say. He idealized the Jew. The Jew is baser, fiercer, more diabolical than Streicher depicted him."[34] What Hitler probably meant is that Streicher's caricature of the Jew was adequate only for the broad masses. Streicher assailed the visible Jew, the one who approached the stereotype, while the deadlier foe was the Jew who blended in, who could carry out his evil undetected. The higher SS leaders also held to a more "bloodless anti-Semitism," more refined, less vulgar, but also more deadly. For the masses to whom Streicher appealed, his rhetoric was appropriate. Those who rejected his brand of anti-Semitism could if they wished find less blatant Jew-baiters in the Third Reich.

The creation of an unfavorable image of Jews was a first step. The second step was to persuade Germans that Jews were more than unpleasant. They were dangerous, posing a direct and immediate threat to each individual German as well as to the existence of the German nation as a whole. To that argument we now turn.

VI

Fraud, Conspiracy, and Murder

A consistent strain in anti-Semitic thought is the notion that Jews are engaged in a sinister and deadly conspiracy to rule the world. As the *Stürmer* put it: "Today as before, individual Jews willingly submit to their rabbi. The education of young Jews is entirely in the hands of these learned and racially conscious Talmud scholars. Thus, they are instilled with racial pride and entrusted with the plans of world Jewry. Each Jew therefore becomes a fighter for the Jewish world goals. The rabbis are subordinate to the Elders of Zion (the highest Jewish council), at whose head is the King of the Jews." And what were those plans? As another issue claimed: "The greatest desire of the Jews is to rule the world. From the beginning their primary aim has been to destroy Gentile states and to gain control of them through a world revolution."[1]

Belief in gigantic and improbable conspiracies is the intellectual weakness not only of anti-Semites. Richard Hofstadter's illuminating essay "The Paranoid Style in American Politics" outlines the characteristics common to most conspiratorialists:

> The central image is that of a vast and sinister conspiracy, a gigantic and yet subtle machinery of influence set in motion to undermine and

119

destroy a way of life. . . . The distinguishing thing about the paranoid style is not that its exponents see conspiracies here and there in history, but that they see a "vast" or "gigantic" conspiracy as *the motive force* in historical events. History *is* a conspiracy, set in motion by demonic forces of almost transcendent power, and what is felt to be needed to defeat it is not the usual methods of political give-and-take, but an all-out crusade. The paranoid spokesman sees the fate of this conspiracy in apocalyptic terms—he traffics in the birth and death of whole worlds, whole political orders, whole systems of human values.

To the ardent conspiratorialist, the conflict is one of good versus evil. The enemy is "the perfect model of malice, a kind of amoral super-man; sinister, ubiquitous, powerful, cruel, sensual, luxury-loving." The paranoid style requires masses of data to support the arguments, but as Hofstadter observes, there is always "a curious leap an imagina-tion" that is made during the argument. The enormous mass of data does not compel the conspiratorialist's conclusion.[2] Thick books have been written to demonstrate that Catholics or Masons or Commu-nists or imperialists control the world from behind the scenes. At first glance the thickness is impressive, but the paranoid exponent is not convinced by logic. The data have been gathered to support existing conclusions.

The idea of conspiracy fits together well with stereotyping. Just as a stereotype allows one to "know" a great deal about a Jew without ever having met him, so a conspiracy has great explanatory power. If a single Jew is implicated in a scandal or a war, the anti-Semite has sufficient proof that it is part of the general conspiracy. Every individ-ual Jewish misdeed confirms individual depravity, racial depravity, and the existence of that vast, evil plot.

But how could Jews cooperate so effectively? Having argued that Jews were morally deficient and incapable of noble action, Streicher needed to explain how they could work together at all. The driving mechanism of the conspiracy seemed to be common interest. Although Jews were a depraved race, they had to be loyal to their own race in order to survive. As a minority, their only hope was to stick together, lest their individual evil bring about collective doom. The conspiracy was the result of pragmatic considerations. Streicher as well as Hitler thought that the Jewish conspiracy depended on the existence of Gentiles. Were the Jews ever to attain their goals, civilization would collapse.

To visualize such an improbable conspiracy is difficult, yet Streicher knew his readers had to feel the immediacy of the threat if they were to hate Jews. A conspiracy a thousand miles away is not frightening; only when there is a local outpost do conspiratorialists feel most threatened. A person reading a newspaper story about the death of thousands of people in an earthquake on a far continent is less moved by mass death than by the death of a single friend, or even by the loss of a pet dog. This is, of course, fortunate; otherwise, reading each evening's newspaper would be a dreadful experience. But it also says something about persuasion. If Streicher were to get Germans to hate Jews, they had to feel directly threatened. He therefore grounded his allegations of Jewish world conspiracy not on goings-on in Berlin or London, but in alleged outbreaks of Jewish criminality in every part of Germany.

Die Juden sind unser Unglück (The Jews are our misfortune), Streicher's motto for twenty years, graced the bottom of nearly every front page of the *Stürmer*. It summarized Streicher's contention that Jews were responsible for nearly every ill that affected Germany and its people. Jews were to blame for children who stayed out late and got into mischief, for tainted sausages, for agricultural scandals, for economic depressions, for world war. The conspiracy reached every German in every part of his life. The center of Streicher's anti-Semitism was the contention that Jews were more than unpleasant. They also were dangerous.

Until the late 1930s, when the disappearance of Jews from within Germany made it harder to find them carrying out evil deeds, every issue of the *Stürmer* contained numerous allegations of Jewish crimes. Of the thousands of examples, a few are sufficient to suggest the range of Streicher's interest. In 1929 the *Stürmer* carried a story about a Nuremberg woman who had bought a nightgown at a Jewish shop. Supposedly the regular price of the garment was 5.50 marks, but it had been reduced 10 percent, to 4.95 marks. The happy woman soon encountered a friend, who informed her that the item regularly sold for 4.50 marks.[3] A similar point was made in the paper's occasional humor column:

> The Jew Katz visits his friend Drach in astonishment.
>
> "Is what I've heard true? You're declaring bankruptcy and are giving your creditors only 40 percent? You scoundrel, how can you do that to me?
>
> The Jew Drach laughed and clapped the other genially on the shoulder. "Don't get excited. You are my racial comrade, and won't suffer any loss. Your goods are not part of the bankruptcy estate. You can have them all back."
>
> At this the Jew Katz turned pale. "Good God, do you want to cheat me? Give me the 40 percent!"[4]

Besides suggesting that Jews sold inferior merchandise, the joke also emphasized that they stuck together.

Jewish goods, Streicher claimed, were not only overpriced, they could also be dangerous. In 1931 he told of a Jewish baker's daughter who urinated in the trough used to make bread. Such an event, he thought, should not surprise anyone familiar with the Jewish question. "Jews by themselves are unclean and swinish. To Gentiles, however, they are two or three times as bad."[5] The assertion that the whole world knows the truth of the anti-Semitic line is striking—such statements, common to the *Stürmer*, are variants of the bandwagon technique. The pleasures of being in the majority are always great, and such claims, founded or unfounded, carry force.

In 1935 a Fips cartoon had a Jewish butcher grinding up a rat to make hash. "We don't need a cat," he says to his unsightly wife. "Catch the rats in a trap and make hash from them. The *goy* will slop up anything if it's cheap enough" (see figure 13). A children's book showed the interior of a filthy Jewish butcher shop. In revolting color stood a dirty Jew in a bloodstained apron, feet firmly planted on a steak, his cigar ashes falling on other cuts, while in the background a grimy cat prowled. The text accompanying the picture emphasized Jewish evil:

> Here Isaac Blumenfeld we see;
> As butcher he makes good money.
> But take a closer look, look closely,
> A rogue this Yid is mostly.
> Isaac sells you meat, 'tis said,

But he gives you filth instead.
See that piece upon the floor,
Another the cat has in its paw.
The Jewish butcher never fails;
Dirty meat weighs more on the scales.
And—please just keep this in your mind—
He does not eat it, nor his kind.
Only Jews, to their dire shame,
Could play you such a dirty game!

The general argument was that buying from Jews was unsafe, a point reinforced by stories like one in 1935 that claimed thirty-two people had become ill as a consequence of eating bad meat sold by a Jew.[6]

The persuasive power of such stories should not be discounted. The committed anti-Semite naturally would not buy from a Jew under any circumstances. The wavering German was a far more likely victim. Even if a woman did not entirely accept Streicher's argument, she would be reluctant to buy from a Jewish butcher if she had the slightest suspicion that the sickening stories might be true. Too, the charge was irrefutable. Jews would be expected to deny the charge, since anyone dastardly enough to sell hash made of ground rats would also be dastardly enough to deny it. When recently an American hamburger chain was rumored to include ground earthworms in its product, the company's energetic efforts to refute the rumor were not always believed—and in this case the rest of the media were not working to reinforce the rumor. It is not surprising that many Germans decided to play it safe, to avoid the Jewish tradesmen, about whom so much had been heard. But that was to take the first step in anti-Semitism, a step that would make it easier in the future to follow Streicher's injunctions.

Farmers were another regular *Stürmer* topic. There were few Jewish farmers, but there were many Jewish livestock dealers and merchants with whom farmers dealt. In 1929 Streicher told of a farmer who had been ruined by the Jews. Beginning with a dubious Talmud citation that asserted that "the property of Gentiles is ownerless property, and any Jew can take it," the story explained how a farmer had borrowed money from a Jew that he had been unable to repay. The Jew came to collect, offering a ridiculous sum for the farmer's best cow. Somehow "overcome and hypnotized" by the Jew, the farmer sold his best cow and her calf for half their proper value.[7] A children's book describes how a Jew robbed a farmer of his livestock for a few marks (see figure 14).

Stürmer stories often took on a *True Confessions* style. Letters from readers explained how they, through ignorance, had run afoul of Jewish corruption. A typical example from 1935 came from a farmer who had bought a horse from a Jew. "The Jew demanded 800 marks for the nag. If I had heeded the many warnings I received to avoid the deal, I and my family would have been spared enormous trouble. The Jew Bildstein, who immediately saw that I lacked the necessary experience to make a deal, realized I was a perfect mark. Not only did he pawn off as a six-year-old a nag of at least fifteen, he also swindled me out of 550 marks." That sum apparently was due to a bank to pay off a loan on the horse. To simplify the transaction, the farmer gave the entire sum to the Jew with the understanding that the bank would be paid off. However, "the Jew did not tell the bank he had received the money. A lawsuit resulted. The Jew Bildstein had to pay back the 550 marks and cover the legal costs. He appealed. The second trial reached the same verdict. Now the Jew, who wanted to ruin me, came at the matter from another direction. He sued me for perjury." Inconsistencies in the farmer's testimony led to a one-year jail term. Now recently released, the farmer continued: "I swear to God and man that I have not wanted to do anything wrong. Ten days ago I left jail, broken in body and soul. Since I was not home to do the work, my wife overexerted herself and had to spend two long stretches in the hospital. Things went rapidly downhill with my property. My release saved us from the worst, and at least postponed the end. I will do all I can to save my farm." To this sad story the *Stürmer* appended an edifying commentary: "The tragedy of a German farmer! Repeated hundreds and thousands of times in Germany. He who deals with the Jews is ruined. When the Jew enters a house, he brings a curse. Many believe that only when it is too late."[8]

Such stories were *Stürmer* mainstays. Time and again an ignorant German was ruined after thinking he could deal with Jews. Generally the story suggested that the immediate case was typical, that the same thing happened everywhere in Germany. And the persuasive force of a vivid story is remarkable. A single touching tale convinces most people more effectively than a statistic based on thousands of cases that supports an opposite conclusion. The individual can be identified with, numbers cannot. And the hundreds of individual cases Streicher presented, however unrepresentative, supplied by eager readers from every part of Germany, made it easy for readers to believe the worst of German Jews.

Jewish professionals were a particular target of Streicher's ire. Hundreds of *Stürmer* articles urged Germans to avoid Jewish doctors and lawyers, as did stories in the children's books. One children's story had two frames. In the first, a fat and prosperous farming couple visit a Jewish lawyer. The second frame, months later, shows the same couple, thin and poor, visiting their now prosperous lawyer. They had won their case but been ruined by the legal fees (see figure 15). The accompanying story gave the whole sad tale:

> Just as children have their fights,
> Grown-ups have their quarrels, too.
> Parents judge in children's squabbles,
> Judges settle grown-ups' disputes.
> A good lawyer must before the judge
> Lay bare all the details of the case
> When the trial once begins.
> The lawyer gets his money.
> So it is in the whole wide world. . . .
> Our farmer Michael goes to town.
> He's got a date with the sharp attorney.
> See him in the sketch I've drawn,
> With handsome wife in fine attire.
> Next to them the lawyer may be seen,
> He's looking very poor and mean.
> Just now his trade is very slack,
> From farmer Michael he expects a whack!
> To the farmer he makes a plea:
> "Dear rich Michael be kind to me.
> Couldn't you bring me butter, wine,
> Flour and eggs? That would be fine!
> Just give me time with this tricky suit;
> We'll win the case and money to boot!"

Here's good prospect, I surmise,
But all he said was a pack of lies.
The peasant folk from Dummelsbrumm
Believe it all: they are so dumb!
They bring him every kind of food
And, Boy! that lawyer's feeling good.
The end is sad to this long tale:
The farmer had to go to court,
So long the Jewish lawyer fought,
Primed with the farmer's butter and eggs.
Now round and plump and plump and round.
The Jew lawyer weighs 240 pound.
Only when there was nothing left
Did, strangely enough, the trial end.
The farmer, true, had won the case;
Now he wonders with long face
Who his goods and money took.
They were stolen all by the Jewish crook.[9]

And German women were told that Jewish doctors regularly drugged and raped their female patients (see Appendix II).

Jews were said to commit every other manner of local misdeed. In 1929 a *Stürmer* writer thought that just as Jews had inspired the medieval Children's Crusade, they were behind the current campaign to get Nuremberg children to stay out late and cause trouble. The Gentile servant of a Jewish family, a later issue reported, had been held captive and mistreated for eight years. In 1934 an elderly women lost her life savings to a Jew. Two years after Hitler's takeover, a Fips cartoon commented on the large number of Jews being arrested. In a jailyard filled with Jews, one says to a neighbor: "If things go on like this, soon every prison will be a synagogue."[10] And a 1937 special edition was given over to the theme "Jewish Criminality." In short, the average German seemed in immediate danger from every manner of scheming Jews. There seemed an avalanche of Jewish criminality.

But the average German had worse to fear than the crooked dealings we have so far considered. Jews according to Streicher were about even more horrible plans. As part of the international Jewish conspiracy they were engaged in a widespread plot to murder innocent Germans and rape German women. The sexual theme we shall consider in the next chapter; here we shall examine Streicher's revival of medieval legends of ritual murder, a topic that even many other Nazis were reluctant at first to raise. The charge was that Jews needed the blood of freshly slaughtered Christians for nefarious purposes.

The sources for so wild a charge were even thinner than Streicher's usual sources. When accusing Jews of more ordinary crimes, he could at least find individual Jews in fact guilty of assorted crimes, but it simply was not possible to find real cases of ritual murder. Thus Streicher depended on outlandish evidence. A regular pillar of his case, for example, was a book written in 1803 by a Jewish convert to Christianity in Moldavia, then translated into Greek, then into Italian, and finally into German. The author claimed that he had been initiated into the knowledge of ritual murder by his rabbi father. Jews were to kill Christians at Purim and Passover, healthy adults to be chosen in the former case, young children in the latter. The children "must not be over seven years old and must die in agony." Once the fresh blood had been secured, small amounts were mixed with the wine and bread and the head of the household was to pray to God as it was served that the same fate should be visited on all Gentiles. Leftover blood could be used by pregnant women or the elderly, or administered to newlyweds. "The ritual murder and the Blood Mystery are acknowledged by all Talmudic Jews, and are practiced whenever possible."[11]

The charge's very absurdity added to its credibility. Hitler had observed that large lies are more readily believed than small ones, since they are harder to disprove. The reader, who had already demonstrated his lack of critical facilities by reading the *Stürmer*, could easily accept such stories, particularly since the rest of the propaganda apparatus gradually came to join Streicher in making them.

Such horrifying Jewish ceremonies were certainly outside the experience of Streicher's readers, despite claims that thousands of ritual murders had occurred. To bridge the gap, Streicher first argued that Jewish ritual slaughter of animals was proof that they treated Gentiles in the same way. The argument was based on a Talmud citation that allegedly compared Gentiles to animals, taken grossly from its context. Streicher found other passages from Jewish literature denouncing Gentiles. Although Streicher did not think the calumnies Martin Luther had raised against the Catholics evidence that Lutherans despised them, he easily assumed that hostile statements by Jews about Gentiles, often made under extreme persecution, were characteristic of what all Jews thought.

How, then, did Jews treat animals? In dreadful ways. He presented kosher slaughter practices in gory detail. A 1936 article, for example, had this to say about the death of a cow in a Jewish slaughterhouse:

> The animal's legs are roped together. The rope is tightened with a winch. The pressure pulls the legs of the animal together. The animal cannot keep its balance. It falls. It senses that its life is at stake. In its fear of death it tries to rise again, lurching here and there, half succeeding. But the bonds do not break. It falls once more to the ground with a thud. Its head hits the floor. It knows the end is near.
>
> The Jewish butcher approaches. He has a good sharp knife in his hand. He grasps the animal's neck with his hand and tightens the muscles. With three cuts he slices open the neck. The cut is over two feet long! An arc of blood springs from the wound. In its death agonies, in terrible pain, the animal tries to escape. It tears at its bonds with all its strength. Repeatedly it rears up, struggling to free itself. Terrible cries well out. The butcher grasps the gaping wound. He cuts a second time, a third time. The animal must be fully conscious of the pain it endures! Often, ten minutes pass before the animal is bled dry.[12]

A children's book told how two young boys secretly peered in the window of the town's Jewish slaughterhouse and saw a bloody scene of animal misery. They leave, shaken and convinced that all they have heard about the Jews is true. A 1939 issue had a full page of photographs from the Vienna fish market, claiming that Jews showed up there to watch live fish being killed for the customers, and another photograph, captioned "Joy in Murder," allegedly depicted two grinning Jews watching an animal being slaughtered. Such an argument is unlikely to convince the skeptic, but its vivid nature certainly left an impression on less critical readers.

The second strategy was to present repeatedly every case of alleged ritual murder in the anti-Semitic canon. These were generally of extraordinarily dubious ancestry, most lacking any foundation at all outside the imaginations of anti-Semites. Nonetheless they sounded ghastly. A favorite *Stürmer* example was the murder of Simon of Trent in 1475:

> It was at this time that the Jew Tobias approached the child, who was not quite 30 months old, and while speaking kindly, picked him up and carried him at once to the house of the Jew Samuel. When night fell, the brothers Saligman and Samuel, with Tobias, Vitalis (Veitel), Moses, Israel and Mayr, undressed the little boy and mercilessly butchered him. While Moses strangled him with a handkerchief as he lay across Samuel's knee, pieces of his flesh from his neck were cut with a knife and the blood collected in a bowl. At the same time, they punctured the naked offering with needles and murmured Hebrew curses. Then they cut pieces of flesh from the boy's arms and legs and collected the blood in pots. Finally, the torturers imitated the crucifixion by holding the twitching body upside down and the arms outstretched, and during this horrible act they spoke the following: "Take this, crucified Jesus. Just as our fathers once did, so may all Christians by land and sea perish." Then they rushed to their meal. When the child had died they threw his body into the river which flowed by their house. After this, they joyously celebrated the Passover.[13]

That repellent story is not unusual; over the years many similar allegations were presented in detail. During the early 1920s Streicher had claimed that several children disappeared annually from the Nuremberg area, victims of the Jews. Child murders during the Weimar period were seized on as examples of ritual murder. In 1925 Streicher reported on a bloodflecked Jewish scroll, which he thought must have resulted from a case of ritual murder. A Fips cartoon showed three Jews who, having bound a woman to the ground, were drinking her blood. Cartoons were supplemented by medieval wood-cuts of ritual murders, in which Streicher put full credence. Even humor of a sort was used. In a ghoulish series of fake Jewish adver-tisements, Streicher promoted "Holy Synagogue Wine," slightly tinged with human blood.[14] Even during the war, ritual murder remained a regular theme. A lengthy article series began in 1943, for example. After a general survey of the topic, it presented a single case in detail.

Although the 1934 ritual-murder special edition claimed that "thousands, yes, perhaps hundreds of thousands" of cases of ritual murder remained undiscovered, it could list only 131 cases (see figure 16). A 1938 issue spoke of the "countless ritual murders of the Jews," and a 1939 special edition confidently asserted that hundreds of thousands had occurred.[15] But the same cases were repeated every time. Streicher's explanation was the one we have encountered before: The fact that so few cases came to light was evidence that Jews had successfully covered up the others. Lack of evidence, paradoxically, becomes evidence.

The whole argument had a certain perverse internal consistency: if one believed Jews were evil to begin with, everything else followed. The point is that one does not come to hate Jews because one is convinced ritual murders occur. Rather, one first hates Jews and then accepts such otherwise unbelievable tales.

These individual criminal acts on the part of Jews were local manifestations of an even broader problem—an international Jewish conspiracy intent on world conquest. The notion of such a conspiracy dates back at least to the French Revolution, but only after World War I did it secure broad acceptance. A major cause was the appearance of the *Protocols of the Learned Elders of Zion,* one of those crazy books that somehow wins multitudes of adherents. The *Protocols* first appeared in Russia in 1903, their broadest distribution coming with the 1905 edition prepared by the Russian Orthodox priest Sergey Nilus. The first German and English translations appeared in 1920, reaching a world made gullible by four years of horrible war.[16]

Supposedly the *Protocols* are the minutes of a meeting of world Jewish leaders, though devotees of the work have never been able to agree on when and where the covert meeting transpired. The discussion centered on the status of the Jewish campaign for world revolution. In a passage that could almost be from *Mein Kampf,* the nature of the masses is described:

> Is it possible for any sound logical mind to hope with any success to guide crowds by aid of reasonable counsels and arguments, when any objection or contradiction, senseless though it may be, can be made and when such objection may find more favor with the people, whose powers of reasoning are superficial? Men in masses and the men of the masses, being guided solely by petty passions, paltry beliefs, customs,

traditions and sentimental theories, fall a prey to party dissension, which hinders any kind of agreement even on the basis of a perfectly reasonable argument. . . . The political has nothing in common with the moral. The ruler who is governed by the moral is not a skillful politician, and is therefore unstable on his throne. He who wishes to rule must have recourse both to cunning and make-believe.

Later the *Protocols* explain that the Jews are on the brink of conquest. The mass media, the banks and other financial institutions, education, even the churches follow their bidding. Things are being arranged such that society will crumble and the Jews will be able to take over in a single world-wide revolution. "We shall so wear down the GOYIM that they will be compelled to offer us international power of a nature that by its position will enable us without any violence gradually to absorb all the State forces of the world and to form a Super-Government."[17] Should existing governments resist, explosives were being placed in the subway tunnels being constructed under all major world cities.

The *Protocols* are a curious combination of traditional and modern anti-Semitism. Jews are exemplars both of ancient vices and modern evils. That they are forged has been demonstrated repeatedly. A fifth of them are taken almost verbatim from an obscure 1870 French attack on Napoleon III. Other sections clearly were written to appeal to the Russian aristocracy, who are told they are the last bulwark against Judaism. And the plot to blow up the world's cities is not the only absurdity they contain. That such demonstrable nonsense has enjoyed such wide acceptance says much for the appeal of anti-Semitism.

In the 1920s they won remarkable acceptance. *The Times* of London shortly after their appearance in 1920 wrote:

What are these "protocols"? Are they authentic? If so, what malevolent assembly concocted these plans, and gloated over their exposition? Are they a forgery? If so whence comes the uncanny note of prophecy, prophecy in parts fulfilled, in parts far gone in the way of fulfillment? Have we been struggling these tragic years to blow up and extirpate the secret organization of German world domination only to find beneath it another, more dangerous because more secret?[18]

In the United States, Henry Ford was much taken with the *Protocols,* running the text in his *Dearborn Independent.* "The only statement I care to make about the PROTOCOLS is that they fit what is going on," he wrote. "They are sixteen years old, and they have fitted the world situation up to this time. THEY FIT IT NOW."[19]

The *Times* recanted its comments the next year, and Henry Ford was recovering from his attack of anti-Semitism by 1927, but in Germany the *Protocols* remained a lasting sensation. Hundreds of thousands of copies were in print by 1930, and the anti-Semites who nearly annihilated European Jewry read them avidly. Alfred Rosenberg, Nazism's muddleheaded theorist, promoted them with enthusiasm. And Adolf Hitler wrote: "They are supposed to be a 'forgery' the *Frankfurter Zeitung* moans and cries out to the world once a week; the best proof that they are genuine after all. What many Jews may do unconsciously is here exposed consciously. It makes no difference from the head of which Jew these disclosures come, but decisive it is that they demonstrate, with a truly horrifying certainty, the nature and activity of the Jewish people and expose them in their inner connection as well as in their ultimate final aim." Even those Nazis who realized the forgery still promoted them as true since they thought them an accurate summary of Jewry's plans. One popular illustrated Nazi anti-Semitic tome, for example, asserted: "Whether or not the *Protocols* are genuine does not concern us, rather whether that which is in them corresponds to reality. He who knows them must affirm that it does."[20]

Julius Streicher, not gifted with a critical mind, was one who accepted the *Protocols* in their entirety. As early as 1921 he wrote: "Seldom has a book aroused so much excitement as the *Protocols of the Elders of Zion,* in which the campaign plan of Pan-Jewry for the enslavement of Gentile humanity is laid out."[21] In 1924 the *Stürmer* carried excerpts from the *Protocols.* A 1936 special edition on the Jewish world conspiracy, timed to appear during the Nuremberg rally, used the *Protocols* as a foundation to explain what the Jews were about (see figure 17). The issue opened with a remarkable passage:

> The Reich Party Congress is occurring at a time which is marked by unrest, revolution and bloody civil wars. Powerful convulsions shake

the world. Conspiracies have formed in every nation. They reach to the highest positions in politics and the economy. Political agitators are feverishly active, whipping up the masses. The greater part of the world press seems to have received secret directives. Whether overtly or covertly, everything is moving toward a certain goal. That goal is: World communism through world revolution.

The issue then printed parts of the *Protocols,* accompanied by evidence that they were being fulfilled. The mysterious documents, the *Stürmer* concluded, were "already hundreds, perhaps thousands of years old." Generations of Jews had been at work perfecting the outline of world conquest. The form of the *Protocols* was modern, but they were rooted in the demonic Talmudic Jewish spirit.[22]

If Streicher's favorite slogan was "The Jews are our misfortune," his second probably was a line from one of Disraeli's novels: "The racial question is the key to world history," a statement cited in nearly every issue. Streicher took the clearly forged *Protocols* as irrefutable evidence of Jewish conspiracy.

Before 1933, his major interest had been in the operation of that conspiracy within Germany, since his primary goal was to secure political power. Streicher joined the rest of Nazism in denouncing the Weimar Republic as a Jewish republic, instituted and controlled by them. From the anti-Semitic perspective, there fortunately had been a number of prominent Jews involved in the transition from empire to republic, and Jews like Walther Rathenau, assassinated in 1922, had had important positions. Having gained control of Germany, Streicher thought Jews were working hard to keep power. The Treaty of Versailles, of course, was part of Jewry's plans, as were the various efforts to deal with war reparations, notably the Dawes Plan and the Young Plan. A 1931 Fips cartoon titled "Young Plan Germany" depicted a German up against a wall named Versailles. A spike labeled "Locarno" (after another treaty) is driven through one hand and an ax labeled "foreign policy" is sunk into his leg. The unfortunate German hangs from a rope labeled "Dawes" and is weighed down by a ball and chain named "Young." A pole labeled "unemployment" is rammed through his stomach. Various knives carrying labels like "brotherly hatred" are sticking out from the wall. And a Jew, standing on boxes bearing the names of German political parties, is bleeding the German's arm into a pail labeled reparations, already nearly full.[23] The cartoon graphically portrayed Streicher's contention that Jews were the cause of Germany's difficulties.

But Jews ran Germany economically as well as politically, he said. In 1922 Streicher told a public meeting that Jews ran the German press. "It is incomprehensible and unbelievable that a nation of sixty million people is not able to call its press its own. The whole German press is in Jewish hands, either directly or indirectly."[24] Jewish control of the press explained why Jewish crimes were not exposed more often. The stock exchange, department stores, major industries, the courts, all these too followed the dictates of the learned Elders of Zion.

And if Jewish control of German politics and economics was not bad enough, Streicher went on to argue that Jews were even trying to evict Germans from their own land. Jews favored abortion reform, for example, as a way of reducing the German population. Germans who committed suicide were victims of the same plot. A 1929 Fips cartoon had a fat Jew walking over the bodies of Germans who had killed themselves. The caption read: "20,000 Germans are driven to death each year by the impoverishment of the German people brought about by the Dawes Jews." A grim future was portrayed in another cartoon. A solitary man walked through the deserted streets of Nuremberg. "For Rent" signs filled every window.[25]

Germany's every problem then was the result of the Jews. That such a view is both oversimplified and distorted is certainly true, but that was precisely the appeal Nazism had. Its answers were simple, black and white, good and evil. The unemployed worker, the strained farmer, the confused war veteran were interested less in complicated explanations for their misery than in clarity. And a particular virtue of Nazism was that it took all the responsibility for Germany's difficulties from the shoulders of the Germans—whatever the problem, it was the Jews who were guilty.

The 1933 takeover forced an abrupt change in strategy. With Hitler in power, many Germans thought the Jewish problem to be settled. Surely Hitler would keep them in their place. In 1934 a *Stürmer* writer responded to those who thought along such lines: "There are still many Germans who are of the opinion that Jews are no longer any danger to Germany. Their power is broken and one should leave them alone." But that was false, since the Jews were as active as before, only more cautious. "Therefore we have to fight as fanatically as before."[26]

The problem Streicher faced was common to the whole Nazi anti-Semitic campaign. A 1934 report to Heinrich Himmler found that "since the boycott of April 1933 and the subsequent anti-Jewish legislation, a significant portion of even the Nazi-oriented public felt the Jewish question to be settled. The armchair anti-Semite who was satisfied to see the Jews made a little more modest could view that aim as having been accomplished."[27] That kind of attitude would not do. Partial victory was hardly enough for Streicher and Hitler; for them it was even worse than defeat, for in defeat one could at least fall no lower, whereas to leave the Jews half defeated was to risk their later resurgence and the destruction of all that had been won. Thus Streicher argued after 1933 that world Jewry had now made Germany its primary target. The threat was greater than ever.

As the number of Jews in Germany decreased, Streicher came to depend more and more on the alleged crimes of foreign Jews. Indeed, by the 1940s it was difficult to find a Jewish criminal of any kind in Germany, a problem that resulted in major changes in the *Stürmer*. A typical 1929 issue, for example, carried articles that claimed Jews were trying to hasten the end of the German race by encouraging abortion, that the Communist Party was using a public hall to honor leading Marxists, and that Jews were behind difficulties in the Nuremberg housing office. Three trials were covered in which Jews were involved, and a reader wrote that Jews were still selling hops improperly. A brief item applauded the death by lynching of an American Negro accused of raping a white woman, but little else was said of the broader world.

In contrast, a typical 1940 issue urged that a world court be established to pass judgment on the Jews. Another story dealt with a Jewish broadcaster on English radio. The attack on the Old Testament continued, with a discussion of its ethics. Part of an article series on the Jews and World War I made a variety of charges, and dozens of brief articles described Jewish misdeeds in Holland, Poland, Hungary, Canada, England, and the United States. Hardly anything was said of Jewish crimes in Germany.[28] Indeed, not long after, a number of readers suggested that the slogan "The Jews are our misfortune" be changed to "The Jews were our misfortune," since Jews were no longer able to cause mischief in Germany. The suggestion was not in order, the paper replied, for all the misery Germany was suffering as the result of World War II was the consequence of the international Jewish plot. Jewish power had indeed been broken within Germany, but now world Jewry, recognizing the danger National Socialist Germany represented, was attempting to smash it utterly.

All sorts of odd evidence over the years purported to document that worldwide Jewish conspiracy. In 1928, for example, Streicher printed alarming news from the United States. Between 1910 and 1920, the number of people giving Yiddish as their mother tongue had risen from 1,057,767 to 1,091,767. And in the previous twelve years, the New York Public Library had increased its collection of Jewish books by 18.8 percent. A 1934 *Stürmer* article explained that the Jews controlled the major American cities on the Atlantic coast, including New York, Boston, and Chicago, a statement displaying if nothing else an interesting view of geography.[29] An article series in the 1940s found the United States to be almost completely run by the Jews. They held important positions, ran the press, and controlled industry and finance.

Other countries too were endangered. In 1938, just before Hitler absorbed Austria, the *Stürmer* claimed: "Vienna today is the finest and greatest Jewish paradise in Europe. The Jews control on the average 80 to 90 percent of industry and commerce." By 1940, London had become "the modern Jewish paradise." A series titled "Paradise of the Plutocrats" demonstrated how England was under Jewish rule.[30] Then there was France, a country ruined by the Jews. A series on France's fall ended in 1941. It attributed France's decline to the Jews. France, for example, was suffering from *Volkstod*, a declining population. In 1935, a total of 20,000 more Frenchmen died than were born, while in Germany that year 500,000 more were born than died. Moreover, many French children were inferior, the product of mixed marriages fostered by the Jews as part of their plan to weaken France's racial purity. The Jewish ideas of the French Revolution had had unfortunate results, proving that "whatever comes from the Jews is poison for Gentile peoples." These and other problems were brought on by the Jews, just as they had attempted similar depredations in Germany—but ironically it was the Nazis who benefited from the weakened France.[31] The other countries that fell to Hitler's armies received like treatment.

The capitalist West, however, was only part of Judaism's schemes; the Soviet Union, and Marxism generally, were also involved. Since Marxism was to the Nazi mind Jewish (had not Marx himself been a Jew?), communism was a deadly threat. As Streicher told a public meeting in 1926: "One can see what the dictatorship of the proletariat means by looking at Russia. It is the dictatorship of the Jews." Later a *Stürmer* writer found that "Judaism and Marxism are blood relations." Given the emphasis on the importance of blood, a closer relationship would be hard to imagine.[32]

During the Weimar period, Marxism was an immediate threat to the Nazis, since both movements competed for radical votes. Hitler's seizure of power ended the direct Communist threat within Germany but left an enormous danger beyond Germany's borders. Streicher claimed that fifty to sixty million people had been killed in Russia.[33] Those who remained alive were scarcely more fortunate. Several representative headlines from the 1930s suggest the approach Streicher took: "Soviet Russian Hell," "The Truth: A Factual Report on Soviet Russia," "Overgrown Graves: A German Pastor Remembers the Soviet Hell," and "Satan's Deed: The Soviet Jews Test Poison Gas on the Russian People." The last story was credited to a Viennese newspaper, which had taken it from a Manchurian paper, which relied on the tale of a former White Russian general who had traveled through Siberia on a secret mission.[34]

A ten-part article series in 1936–37 reported the experiences of "a simple German worker" who went to Russia convinced of Marxism's truth but left horrified by the hell he had seen. His concluding appeal to the readers announced: "I have only one wish. May every German citizen read my report. May every German citizen draw the proper conclusion. *The Jew is our deadly enemy!* His single goal is to destroy us and rule the whole world. As *Julius Streicher* says, Bolshevism is nothing more than radical *Jewish domination.*"[35]

For most of the 1930s the *Stürmer* advocated violent ways of facing the Soviet Union. In the spring of 1939, for example, an editorial suggested: "A punishment expedition must reach the Jews in Russia. A punishment expedition prepared to mete out the end which has to be expected by every murderer and criminal. The death penalty, execution! The Jews in Russia must be killed. They must be exterminated root and branch. Then the world will see that the end of the Jews is also the end of Bolshevism."[36] Most issues of the paper until summer 1939 carried Streicher's banner slogan: "Bolshevism is radical Jewish domination."

The German-Soviet treaty of August 1939 left Streicher bewildered. There had been few attacks on Russia in the preceding months, as Streicher had received a Propaganda Ministry directive in May that said: "Effective immediately all polemics against the Soviet Union and Bolshevism are to stop."[37] Generally, Streicher ignored the treaty, probably the best thing to do under the circumstances. A single Fips cartoon approved the signing. In September an article noted that the Jews were greatly upset by the treaty, a puzzling development for the careful reader who only recently had been told the Jews completely controlled the Soviet Union. Although readers with long memories or files of the paper may have been momentarily disturbed, the internal structure of anti-Semitism was sufficiently flexible to contain contradictions. And as Jacques Ellul observes, the resistance of the individual is fragmentary and sporadic when compared to the continuous assault of modern propaganda.

Streicher said very little about the Soviet Union or Marxism during the two years the treaty was in force. He did praise Hitler's genius in negotiating it in 1940. And Streicher's loyal scholar Peter Deeg, author of several *Stürmer* Press tomes, produced a pamphlet titled *Fifty Years Ago: For and Against the Treaty with Russia,* a study of Bismarck's earlier diplomatic efforts. In a full-page announcement of Deeg's pamphlet, Streicher wrote: "Bismarck is dead, Bismarck has come again."[38] Streicher printed very few attacks on Marxism during the period, all aimed at countries other than the Soviet Union.

Hitler's attack on Russia in 1941 must have been a relief to Streicher. In a lead article titled "Battle in the East," he claimed that the 1939 treaty had been no more than a tactical move.[39] Now the struggle to free Russia, the first nation to fall under total Jewish control, had begun. For the remainder of the war Marxism once again was a central theme.

But how could both capitalism and communism be part of the Jewish plot? To Streicher the answer was simple. Jews pulled the strings from behind the scenes in both cases, creating the illusion of conflict when in fact there was none. The clearest proof was World War II itself. Were not both Russia and England cooperating to defeat Germany (see figure 18)? As early as 1934 Streicher was running articles accusing the Jews of attempting to lead a holy war against Germany (see figure 19). An article that year titled "World Jewry's Plans: Germany Must Be Annihilated" was typical of what he considered evidence. Based on an article in a Romanian Jewish newspaper that argued that Germany ought to be deprived of colonies and urged "every Jew in the world" to join the fight against Germany, to Streicher it was not the product of an obscure writer for an insignificant newspaper, but the product of an agent of world conspiracy.[40] A 1939 article headlined "Jews Cry Revenge" was based on an intercepted letter from a Palestinian Jew who was pleased with the recent assassination of a German diplomat in Paris and wished disaster on Germany. This, the *Stürmer* thought, proved that all Jews thought in like manner.[41] Many similar examples could be given. If a single Jew in an isolated corner of the world said bad things about Germany, Streicher was convinced he was representative of every Jew.

In September 1938 Streicher accused the Jews of planning a new world war. "Who is the inciter of this second world war?" His answer was, of course, the Jews. The first *Stürmer* lead after the war actually began was based on a letter from a London Jew that claimed that the war was Jewry's work and prophesied that it would end with the destruction of everything German. German men would be castrated and German women sterilized, guaranteeing the end of the race. "We are fighting not only for our National Socialist world view, but also for our people, our nation, our children, and our future," Ernst Hiemer wrote. The same issue had a Fips cartoon depicting a Jew setting Europe on fire.[42]

When by January 1942 Germany was at war with most of the world, Streicher wrote a lead article reviewing the world situation. "This second world war is a fight to the finish! A fight to the finish between good and evil, between light and darkness. It is a struggle with the Devil, a struggle for life and death." To prove that it was all the fault of the Jews, he quoted a Jewish newspaper in the Netherlands that in 1939 had written: "The millions of Jews in America,

England and France, in North and South Africa, not to mention Palestine, are resolved to carry out our struggle to annihilate Germany to the end. We Jews find ourselves in a clearer position in this powerful world conflict than in 1914. . . . We know that the fight to the finish has come."[43] What clearer evidence could there be? Cover cartoons regularly showed Jews controlling the Allies and enslaving the world (see figure 20).

Streicher took particular pleasure in stories alleging that Jews were earning enormous profits while Gentile peoples were bleeding on the battlefields of the world. A Fips cartoon titled "The Bloodbath" showed a sack of Jewish war profits floating in a sea of blood, a common theme. In 1944 Streicher cited a 1917 speech by Isaac Marcosson, an American Jewish journalist. The section of his remarks that Streicher used, taken from *The Times* of London, sounded most alarming: "The war was a gigantic business proposition, and the merchandise it dealt with were not safety-razors, soap and trousers, but human blood and lives." But Streicher failed to print what Marcosson went on to say: that those earning profits from the war should remember that those profits were "drawn from the blood and sweat and agony of the nations at war. If they saw, as he had seen, thousands of young men going to death, smiling and unafraid, they would understand that personal gain was a very small thing compared with personal sacrifice."[44] The speech in fact supported a contention quite the opposite of what Streicher wanted. But the average German was not likely to chase down a 1917 issue of *The Times,* and Streicher's argument, creating images of wealthy Jews in distant lands, was persuasive.

As the war neared its end and Germany's position became increasingly worse, the *Stürmer's* tone grew shriller. The semicomical Fips Jew of earlier years was replaced by a deadlier and more sinister caricature. In 1943 Fips drew a Jew's tongue being ripped out. The next issue had Franklin Roosevelt shattering his teeth on a swastika.[45] And all the while, as we shall see in Chapter VII, more and more frequently articles called for the physical annihilation of the Jews.

The *Stürmer* was a far duller newspaper in the 1940s than it had been during its prime. Formerly it had been packed with every manner of lively scandal, sex, bribery, corruption, and dirty dealings, all of which seemed likely to befall any German who failed to keep assiduous watch on every Jew he encountered. But during the war Allied bombs were a more immediate threat than the high prices or decayed meat of the long-departed Jewish shopkeeper. The conspiracy was no longer visible; no longer could a reader act. The *Stürmer* had become a journal of international affairs. In becoming such, it lost its distinctiveness, for the entire German press too denounced Jews around the world. Streicher lost more than half the *Stürmer's* readership during the war, a decline due in part to wartime paper shortages, which by 1944 had reduced it to four pages, down from the sixteen or more of the late 1930s. But at least as importantly, the paper had lost its immediacy. The vivid crudity that was Streicher's hallmark vanished with the Jews who went to Auschwitz.

VII

The Worst Crime: Racial Defilement

Streicher's fascination with sex was notorious. We have already seen that his own conduct did not meet the highest standards, but it was his concentration on the sexual in the pages of the *Stürmer* and in his public speeches that led his fellow citizens to award him the mocking title National Pornographer, and that even today leads writers to call him "a sadistic, pornographic beast." Although past anti-Semites had made sexual charges, and although many Nazis, among them Hitler, had as well, no one before (or since) had focused so large a part of his efforts on accusing Jews of sex crimes. Leon Poliakov, a leading historian of anti-Semitism, considers the emphasis on sex to be the major Nazi addition to the arsenal of anti-Semitism, and he uses Streicher's *Stürmer* as evidence.[1]

Before looking at Streicher's material, one has to understand his bizarre racial theories. There were, he thought, two primary reasons why Jews were interested in German women, aside, of course, from the customary motivation of lust. First, he thought Jews considered the defilement of Gentile women to be a holy act. In 1927 he made the surprising claim that a Jewish woman was pleased to find her husband having sexual relations with German women, since his unfaithfulness was "a deed pleasing to God, not adultery."[2] She reportedly was equally delighted to find her son seducing the German serving girls.

143

To support the argument he relied on a variety of dubious passages from the Talmud. Anything done to a Gentile woman was allegedly pleasing to God, for example. Another passage established that Gentile girls over three years of age could be used sexually, certainly a dreadful-sounding claim. As usual, however, the Talmud passage cited was taken woefully out of context. The full passage concerns whether or not sexual relations with a child cause defilement:

> For R. Zera said: I experienced great trouble with R. Assi, and R. Assi with R. Johanan, and R. Johanan with R. Jannai, and R. Jannai with R. Nathan b. Amram, and R. Nathan b. Amram with Rabbi over this question: From what age does a heathen child cause defilement by sexual emission?—He replied to me: From a day old; but when I came to R. Hiyya, he told me: From the age of nine years and one day. When I then came and discussed the matter with Rabbi, he said to me: Abandon my reply and adopt that of R. Hiyya, who declared: From what age does a heathen child cause defilement by seminal emission? From the age of nine years and one day, for inasmuch as he is then capable of the sexual act he likewise defiles by emission. Rabina then said: It is therefore to be concluded that a heathen girl [communicates defilement] from the age of three years and one day, for inasmuch as she is then capable of the sexual act she likewise defiles by a flux.[3]

The whole discussion sounds strange to the modern ear—but the passage clearly does not contain an injunction to seduce young Gentile girls. Indeed, only shortly before in the discussion the comment is made: "But [the prohibition against] an Israelite having intercourse with a heathen woman is a law of Moses from Sinai, for a Master has said: "If an Israelite has intercourse with a heathen women, zealots may attack him!" Streicher's evidence, as was so often the case, simply did not support his argument, yet he cited the above passage repeatedly as evidence of Jewish depravity.

The second primary reason for Jewish interest in Gentile women rested on Streicher's conviction that they were out to destroy Germany by ruining the purity of the Aryan race. According to Streicher: "Sexual intercourse between a Jew and a German woman is enough to destroy forever the girl's racial purity. Every German girl who even once gives herself to a Jew is lost forever to the German people." In his short-lived anti-Semitic medical journal, Streicher expanded on the argument:

> "Alien albumin" is the semen of a man of another race. As a result of intercourse, the male semen is partially or totally absorbed by the female body. A single incident of intercourse is sufficient to poison her blood forever. She has taken in the alien soul along with the "alien albumin." Even if she marries an Aryan man, she can no longer bear pure Aryan children, but only bastards, in whose breasts dwell two souls, and who physically look like members of a mixed race. . . .
>
> Now we know why the Jew uses every method of seduction he knows to shame German girls as early as possible, why the Jewish doctor rapes his female patients while they are drugged, and why Jewish wives permit their husbands to have intercourse with Gentile women. The German girl, the German woman, who absorbs the alien semen of a Jew can never again bear healthy German children.[4]

Other articles suggested that racial defilement altered not only a woman's children, but also the woman herself, somehow transforming her into a Jewess. In a curious article on a 1938 sex-crimes trial, the *Stürmer* argued: "Racial defilement cannot be washed off like dirt from the hands. No! Racial defilement forces itself into the body, forces itself into the soul, of the Gentile woman. Racial defilement, if repeated again and again, leads to a spiritual as well as a physical transformation. Particularly as the body ages, it gradually loses its own characteristics; the alien spirit takes possession of the Gentile woman." The article supported that incredible claim by examining the Gentile wife of a Jewish sex criminal. "Through years of sexual relations with the Jew, Maria M. lost the last vestiges of German character. She herself gradually became a Jewess."[5]

Stories of German women ruined by Jews filled the *Stürmer*. In 1925 Streicher told of a Jew who raped a fourteen-year-old employee who subsequently became ill: "The doctor says that her blood is poisoned." A 1935 special edition devoted to a racial-defilement trial described the victims of the Jew Hirschland: "One could see the ravages racial defilement had worked on them. The light in their eyes was gone. Gone too was that indescribable glow of sweetness that every German girl has. . . . They looked dead and empty. Their behavior and bearing were dull and indifferent. Their speech was monotonous. . . . Their souls had become Jewish."[6]

The point of the campaign of sexual mayhem was to pollute German blood, to destroy German children, to make Jewesses of once-German women, to eliminate the power of the Aryan race to resist. A 1935 account of a Jewish doctor who allegedly had raped a female patient, for example, concluded: "His goal was attained. He had destroyed a racially valuable woman, forever poisoning her with his Jewish blood" (see figure 21). A children's book described how, at her mother's orders, a girl visited a Jewish doctor, only narrowly avoiding rape and defilement (see figure 22 and Appendix II). When enough women had been ruined, "a racially unified people with its own culture" would no longer exist. The Jews, having bastardized the German race, would be able to take control without open battle.[7]

Why were Jews able to seduce so successfully? Streicher had several answers to what must have been an awkward question for some of the readers. First, he maintained that there was a demonic or supernatural element. Jews could hypnotize women, overcoming them by a mysterious devilish power. Otto Mayer, a favorite target during the Weimar era, relied on "the hypnotic power of the Jew" to work his will on innocent women. A Fips cartoon titled "Under Foreign Control" had a Jew hypnotizing a defenseless girl. When hypnosis failed, Mayer resorted to drugged coffee and 160-proof schnapps. The notorious Hirschland used particularly subtle methods. "To excite his victims he gave them pastries and strong coffee. Thus the Jew excited the Gentile women until they lost their self-control. They looked at his pictures and read his books. It was as if they were hypnotized. A strange and unknown world opened before them, and they tumbled helplessly into it."[8]

Money was naturally a standby. Having robbed Germans of their wealth, Jews used it to destroy German womanhood. A 1930 Fips cartoon had two panels. The first, "Before," showed a well-dressed woman entering a Jew's car. The second, "The End," had the same woman, now poorly dressed and in despair, standing on a street corner with a leering Jew in the background.[9] Dozens of other stories suggested that women succumbed to Jews from the lure of wealth rather than physical charm. The argument combined appeals to envy and sexual pride, a most potent combination—and the German who looked around could find those who would support Streicher's contention. No less than the British ambassador to Germany had this to say in 1933: "Accompanied by his Christian lady friend, the prosperous Hebrew was to be seen at all the expensive seaside resorts, watering places, theaters, restaurants, cabarets and the like."[10] His observation certainly does not suggest that German women were being ruined everywhere, but it does indicate that many felt they saw enough evidence to make Streicher's allegations plausible. We have already noted the persuasive power of an example—the suspicious German who saw Jewish men and Gentile women together could easily grant the rest of Streicher's argument.

If hypnotism, drugs, alcohol, and money were insufficient, Streicher asserted that Jews used force. Ninety-five percent of the German girls in foreign brothels had been taken there forcibly by Jews, he said. Jewish employers allegedly threatened to fire their female employees who reported cases of rape, while German servant girls were regularly raped by their Jewish masters. The reason German women succumbed, then, was never honorable. The unsuccessful German male could assure himself that he could not find a good woman because of Jewish criminality, not his own failings, a more satisfying explanation.

The individual cases Streicher provided were used to support the contention that the same thing was occurring on a vast scale. In 1932 a *Stürmer* writer maintained that hundreds of thousands of German women and girls had been ruined by Jews. Not long after, another writer said that tens of thousands had been ruined in Düsseldorf alone.[11] Individual Jews allegedly seduced large numbers of women. Hirschland and Voss, the subjects of a special edition, reportedly seduced two hundred women over a fifteen-year span. One Obermayer, a homosexual, was accused of eight hundred known cases of sexual offenses against young men—but that was not enough. A *Stürmer* writer asked rhetorically: "How many thousands and thousands of healthy young boys and young men have been destroyed by this Jew?"[12] The 1938 special edition on racial defilement provided the names of 358 persons accused of the crime, along with a full page of photographs titled "Racial Defilers Look at You."

Again, the *Stürmer's* argument was unanswerable, assuming one accepted the premise that Jews were in fact suspect. The many cases the *Stürmer* reported were after all only those that had come to light. Since sexual relations were generally covert, it seemed reasonable for the reader to jump from the hundreds of cases Streicher reported to hundreds of thousands of cases yet concealed, and that is precisely what Streicher urged readers to do. Most major stories claimed that the case under consideration was representative of what was happening everywhere. One *Stürmer* account concluded: "It is the same in Berlin or Hamburg, in Munich or Leipzig, in large cities or small, in market towns, villages and hamlets. The Jew is at work, destroying and ruining German girls, German women and German families."[13] As with charges of ritual murder, lack of evidence became evidence of the power of the "Jewish conspiracy."

As for the victims, they were almost helpless, trapped by sinister methods of seduction. Of one victim in 1930, the *Stürmer* claimed: "No one has the right to throw the first stone at her, for her soul is crushed. Each German has the fundamental obligation to beat his own breast and say to himself that it was his own impiety that abandoned German girls to Jewish scoundrels and rapists."[14] The very innocence of the women made the crime much worse, for it meant that any German woman or girl was in constant danger. The most upright woman might fall afoul of a Jewish rapist. Such an argument has ever been able to rouse men to anger. In the United States the best way to start a lynch mob, for many years, was to accuse a black of having raped a white woman, of which occurrences by the way Streicher took pleased note. A 1935 issue carried a picture of a black hanging from a tree, captioned "People's Justice in the United States."

Over the years the manner in which Streicher used the argument changed. It in fact took him some time to realize its value. Early *Stürmer* issues made occasional reference to sex crimes, but by 1925 they had become a major theme. Streicher discovered that sex sold newspapers, an enlightening if not original insight. His first major account was the Louis Schloss affair, which broke in December 1925. Schloss had had sexual relations with many women and often used whips and lashes on his victims. The attention Streicher gave the affair indicated the direction he took thereafter. The first *Stürmer* report was headlined:

TERRIBLE CRIMES
Discovered in the Torture Chamber on the Bauerngasse
German Girls and Women Whipped and Defiled
The Jew Schloss Arrested

The issue began with a discussion of the Talmud, quoting some of the dubious charges we have already considered. "He who wants to see the Talmud in action need only look into the private chambers and secret rooms of many Jews," the article went on. "There one can clearly and sufficiently see the Talmud in practice, a sight that would make the hair of an honorable citizen stand on end." The fact that Schloss had remained undiscovered for so long was evidence for the Jewish conspiracy, the *Stürmer* thought. The apartments above and below Schloss's were occupied by Jews who must have heard the screams of his victims but had held silence.

Next, one of Schloss's crimes was described in detail and is worth looking at as an example of Streicher's style:

> Schloss's apartment was cared for by a certain Luise H., a small slender girl, scarcely more than a child.
> She invited her girl friend,
> *a 16-year-old girl, pretty as a picture,*
> to visit her at the Jew Schloss's dwelling.
> The girl comes from a respectable family. She is the daughter of upright parents and was raised well. Her eyes displayed her innocence and childlike nature.
> She unsuspectingly accepted the invitation, knowing that the dwelling's owner was not present. Luise H. began cleaning the apartment.
> After a while
> *the Jew Schloss*
> arrived.
> He seemed very friendly, and greeted the girlfriend. He invited both to have a glass of wine. The unsuspecting child lacked the courage to decline. The Jew became more and more friendly and affectionate. He demanded that they drink more and more. One glass became many until the girls scarcely were conscious. Then the Jew ordered Luise H.
> *to take her clothes off.*

This she did with astonishing self-awareness.

With fluttering eyes and animal lust on his face, the Jew now demanded that the other girl do the same. She was so drunk that she scarcely knew what was happening. When she understood what was wanted of her, she turned red with shame. She resisted, defending herself as well as she could, but to no avail.

The Jew and his lackey ripped the clothes from her body.

Then something peculiar happened.

The table in the room had a top which could be turned over. The Jew did that, then forced his sobbing victim to it and, with the help of Luise H., bound her tightly to it. Then he went to a cabinet and selected from among an arsenal of whips and lashes

a dog whip.

The girl begged for mercy with heart-rending cries. The Jew *observed* his victim with a sadistic lust. Then he whipped the *blossoming white body of the girl. She cried and screamed.*

She begged her nearby friend to help her. The friend finally succumbed to pity and begged the Jewish beast to stop. But the Jew only turned on her and whipped her until she was silent.

Again the whip blows fell on the body of the captive, half *senseless girl.*

THEN HE RELEASED THE GIRL, WHO WAS COVERED WITH A THOUSAND STREAMS OF BLOOD, AND CARRIED HIS VICTIM TO THE BED WHERE HE RAPED HER LIKE AN ANIMAL.

As the girl left the dwelling of the Jew Schloss that evening, he knew he could add another to his list of victims. He knew that the girl was now under his devilish power, and was lost eternally to the German race.

This the *Stürmer* claimed was only one of many cases. "The Jew Louis Schloss succeeded in getting one German-blooded girl after another into his secret house. He whipped the bodies of German women and girls, and dirtied their souls with the filth of his perverse swinishness." To make plain who those victims were, the story continued: "The wives of German men are bound and gagged. . . . The daughters of German mothers are delivered to this human swine." The citizens of Nuremberg were warned that their wives and daughters were the kinds of victims Jews chose.

Naturally Schloss was not alone. The story suggested: "These accidentally discovered crimes prove clearly what a terrible danger Jewry is to us. This is, we maintain, no exceptional case. The conditions in Soviet Russia prove that Jewry favors perversity and sadism." Schloss now was part of the international plot. The issue closed with an appeal: "We know that many who read this will shake their heads in disbelief. We know also, however, that there are many who have not until now understood our struggle. We hope this uncovered crime will open the eyes even of the stupidest German."[15]

The next issue reemphasized the points. A Fips cartoon showed a devilish-looking Schloss about his cruel work. An interior article attributed Schloss's success to his "devilish power," which put his victims "under a spell that forced them to return again and again . . . although their consciences urged them to stay away." Already the Jewish conspiracy was at work trying to hide the crimes, claiming, for example, that Schloss was mentally ill, in hopes of securing a lighter sentence. The devastating effects of racial defilement were reviewed. "The girls defiled by Louis Schloss are ruined not only in love, but also in their souls. They are lost not only to their shocked German families, but also are lost forever to the German people." In the past, the story claimed, men like Schloss were hanged.[16]

Schloss's trial began in April 1926. Supposedly great anxiety had been caused in the Jewish community by his arrest, and all possible steps had been taken to free him. His attorneys were, of course, Jewish, and in them the *Stürmer* saw typical Jewish characteristics. After maintaining that racial scientists had proven conclusively that Jews were descended from Mongols, Negroes, and apes, the paper concluded that Schloss displayed more of the ape, while his attorneys were predominately Mongoloid and Negroid, respectively. Schloss's view of German women was indicated by the fact that he branded his victims, just as cattle were branded in the Americas, clear proof that the Talmud's claim that Gentiles were animals remained in force.

Schloss's victims took the stand. One testified that she had been "entirely defenseless because of the suggestive power of the Jew." Others were seduced by candy or alcohol. But each case was a tragedy. The Jewish response was entirely unfeeling. One of Schloss's attorneys attributed his client's misbehavior to the first world war and stated that "all the bodies of the women taken together are worth less

than the body of this sick man." That was only to be expected, the
Stürmer thought, for did not the Jews believe that "a single Jewish
soul is worth more in the eyes of God than the souls of an entire
nation?" When Schloss himself took the stand, he treated the whole
matter lightly. "He was astonished, he said, that people found it so
terrible, for until now he had thought it [sadism] was the general
custom (!!)." His relations with his wife, on the other hand, were
entirely normal, and he refused to practice his perversions on Jewish
women. When his sisters, also in on the plot, though apparently
ignorant of the Talmud, brought Jewish girls to him, he always
refused to seduce them. Meanwhile, the judge said that Schloss's
collection of pornography was the worst he had seen in his professional career.[17]

That was not the end of the matter. For years after, Schloss was a
regular target of the *Stürmer*'s ire. A month after the trial, an article
reported the sad stories of more victims. One was "still alive, but
inwardly she has long been dead.... Her body bears the Jew's brand,
and her dim eyes speak of a murdered soul. She answers the questions
of the judge in a toneless voice. Then she returns mechanically to the
witness area. She gives the impression of being unspeakably tired."[18]
The next issue asserted that the Schloss case and others like it proved
that Jews were about a systematic campaign to destroy German
womanhood. Two months later a Fips cartoon showed a chained,
naked woman with Schloss's brand. Schloss's appeal got considerable
coverage.

In following years, Streicher repeated details of the Schloss affair
whenever a new scandal broke (or when news was thin). In 1929 the
Schloss case served to introduce five more recent cases of Jewish rape,
the claim being that the road to final Jewish victory was not over the
battlefield but "over the bodies of ruined women and girls, and over
their destroyed souls." Schloss's release after his prison term was
reported that same year, and later the *Stürmer* accused him of returning to his old habits. A reader in 1932 reported that Schloss's appearance at a resort in southern Bavaria had aroused great excitement, he
being recognized because people remembered Fips's caricatures. A
1933 Vienna sex-crimes story was prefaced by a discussion of
Schloss's misdeeds, which took most of the front page.[19] Schloss
meanwhile was arrested shortly after Hitler took power and report-

edly "committed suicide" in Dachau. But his death did not end his value. He was mentioned again in 1937, and even at the Nuremberg trials Streicher used Schloss to justify his anti-Semitic career.

The Schloss case was not particularly unusual. It did receive more than the usual publicity, but numerous other cases received attention almost as intense. The frequency with which Streicher returned to the theme could easily suggest to readers that rape was transpiring on a quite remarkable scale. And in each case, the story became more than the evil doings of an individual Jew, but evidence of a huge plot to ruin German womanhood and destroy the German race, part in turn of the larger plot to rule the world. Streicher's entire anti-Semitic argument could be reconstructed from articles on sex criminals. Indeed, only a few issues of the *Stürmer* were necessary before the reader knew the whole of Streicher's argument. The coherence of the system increased its appeal. Everything was connected to everything else. And since convictions often resulted in the cases Streicher considered, particularly after 1933, it became easier for readers to follow the logic to its end.

The Schloss case was a little more explicit than usual. Often Streicher relied more on imagination than on description. A 1924 account, for example, gave a first-person account of a Jew's victim: "One day he forced me into a room behind the office and forced me to a couch. He held both of my hands with one of his and with the other he firmly grasped my breasts . . ." The ellipses are the *Stürmer*'s. The reader filled in his own ending, unlikely to be charitable to the Jew. A later story of a woman summoned to a Jew's private office noted: "From there there was no possibility of escape . . ."[20] Other articles suggested that Jewish deeds were too revolting to be described. Readers were told, for example, that a Jew behaved "in a way that cannot be clothed with words." But deeds that cannot be described can be imagined—and that is what Streicher depended on his readers to do. The process of visualization was aided by Fips's graphic cartoons, often depicting Jews about to rape or seduce (see figure 23).

Hitler's takeover led to a marked increase in Streicher's attention to sex. Many previous arguments were no longer as potent—but sex was a covert activity, just the kind of thing Jews would turn to in difficult times. And now there was hope for firm action. Shortly after Hitler became chancellor the *Stürmer* observed: "Another day has dawned.

The dominance of the Jews is coming to an end, and German law again begins to take command. German law must soon take up racial defilement, the most dangerous and damnable of all crimes. It must ensure that members of foreign races who defile and destroy our women are hanged."[21]

The call for the death penalty was not new. In 1924 Streicher told a public meeting that Jews having sexual relations with Gentiles should be executed. German girls involved should have their hair cut off, and German men ignorant enough to chase Jewish women should be castrated. In 1932 he wrote: "Racial defilers will continue their work until the German people rise up and put a brutal end to the disgrace.... If Adolf Hitler were at the helm, every Jewish racial defiler would be hanged."[22] Now the old call had sudden plausibility.

By 1935, racial defilement was the single most prominent theme Streicher had. This was so, he claimed, because Jews had turned to it as the best way of destroying Nazi Germany. Four of the first eight issues of 1935 demanded the death penalty for racial defilement in lead articles. Approximately half of the issues between January and June had it as their lead theme, and dozens of interior articles spoke about it as well. A long series of cases of Jewish rapists, seducers, and child molesters titillated the German public.

A typical 1935 story told of a Jew who visited a small town where he found a group of young girls keeping watch on their younger brothers and sisters. Under the pretext of getting directions to a neighboring town, he began a conversation that soon turned to other matters. "He succeeded in winning over a nine-year-old girl. She would show him the way. He promised the child a reward for her help. The unsuspecting child went with him quite a ways." Soon the Jew claimed he was tired, and sat down beside the road, persuading his companion to join him. "He told her of his extensive travels and of all sorts of things. He moved closer to the child. His hands made all sorts of immoral moves. Her honor wounded, the girl bit his finger. But the Jew Strauss was not discouraged. He persistently repeated his attacks. He was nearing his aim—only the innate instincts of a pure girl are to be thanked that racial defilement was prevented." At the last moment the girl jumped up, ran home, and told her parents. Upon being arrested, the Jew denied everything.[23] That the story was rather thin bothered Streicher not at all. It made lively reading and gave the reader plenty of opportunity to imagine the dreadful things that might have befallen the innocent young girl.

At the September 1935 Nuremberg party rally, Adolf Hitler announced the Nuremberg Laws, which prohibited sexual relations between Jews and Gentiles and forbade Jewish families from hiring non-Jewish servant girls under the age of forty-five. As we have seen, Streicher was rather offended that the hurriedly drafted laws had been written without his assistance. No one, after all, had been more vocal than he in calling for them. But to the world at large, Hitler's action seemed a personal victory for Streicher. As he left the hall, the crowd joined in chanting "Heil Streicher!" Shortly after, *The New York Times* reporter saw Streicher, "who on his countenance registered his victory." Several days later, the same paper observed: "In view of Mr. Streicher's recent triumph in Nuremberg, his words now must be taken seriously."[24]

Responding to victory can be difficult. Streicher's unexpected triumph left him nonplussed. What was he to say now? Hitler had not ordained the death penalty, it was true, but the principle that sexual relations between Jews and Gentiles were reprehensible was now law. An abrupt falloff in racial defilement stories was evident after the rally while Streicher plotted his strategy. He did print the laws on the front page in place of the Fips cartoon, calling them "an act of significance in world history." And the *Stürmer* soon observed that it would be necessary to continue to speak often about racial defilement, since many Germans did not understand the fundamental significance of the new laws.

Soon articles by Ernst Hiemer made the *Stürmer*'s position even clearer. A month after the rally, he wrote that many in 1933 had thought the *Stürmer*'s role to be over, while those familiar with the Jewish question had known that Jewish criminality would continue. Now some optimists thought the racial laws would end Jewish sex crimes. Instead, Hiemer argued:

> We must now present the Jewish question to the people. The broad masses of the people must be shown the significance of the Law for the Protection of Blood and Race. They must be shown that the Führer had to go this way. We must explain it again and again! We must make the people alert. We must warn them of the dark men who want to misuse

these laws. We must warn everyone who wants to become lazy and inactive. We must constantly tell the people that the new laws do not solve the Jewish question.[25]

A week later Streicher wrote:

National Socialism has won many victories. One of the greatest, and one that will be most valuable in the future, was the Nuremberg Laws. Many feel now that we can return the weapons and flags that won the battles to the arsenals and storehouses. Those who were, and perhaps still are, of that opinion are only soldiers who followed their leaders without knowing the ultimate goals of a wide-ranging plan of war.[26]

Both men argued that Germany could not relax. The racial laws, unprecedented as they were, were only a first step toward a final solution of the Jewish question.

Streicher now set about arguing that Jews were ignoring the Nuremberg Laws. A column titled "Racial Defilement Without End" ran in nearly every issue. A typical 1936 example gave eleven short accounts of the crime from around Germany. Calls for the death sentences had been dropped, but lengthy prison sentences were encouraged. Of a case that resulted in acquittal, a *Stürmer* writer commented: "People of sound human understanding simply cannot understand the acquittal. . . . It is typical proof that in the Third Reich judges need not be the slaves of a legal paragraph when reaching a decision." The defendant, in short, had been innocent under the law, but Streicher thought he ought to have been convicted anyway. A later article asserted that "the people will not be able to understand how the Jew Wolf . . . received only four months" for racial defilement. When the *Stürmer* found unequal sentences were being given, two years in one city and seven weeks in another, it urged that lengthy sentences be the rule. When a Jew was sentenced to one and a half years in prison because his crime had begun prior to the Nuremberg Laws, the *Stürmer* complained that, at the least, he should have gotten penal servitude in place of mere imprisonment.[27] As Streicher put it a year after the laws were introduced: "When National Socialism took control of Germany in 1933, many wanted to say that the work of the *Stürmer* was over. The subsequent years made it clear to those know-it-alls that they had chattered nonsense. . . . With the proclamation of the Nuremberg Laws there were again people who believed that the Jewish question was solved. The events of the past year have proven that those who thought and spoke like that were speaking nonsense."28

It was particularly important, Streicher thought, to warn the young against the Jews. He made sure that German children heard that Jews were to be avoided. His *Stürmer* publishing house printed two illustrated children's books, both of which included stories on the danger of Jewish sexual defilement. In one a repellent Jew accompanies a German girl down the street while several concerned German children watch. In the background is a smirking Jewish boy, himself not old enough to seduce German women but aware of what is going on (see figure 24). The accompanying text has the father's advice to his wayward daughter:

> The father says to his daughter dear:
> "You cause me great distress, I fear!
> The blood of all of us is pure,
> But for the sake of selfish gain,
> For fine dresses and money, too,
> You're always with Sol Rosenfeld, the Jew,
> Thinking maybe to become his wife!
> This means no good. I won't have it, d'ye hear?
> A dachshund is never put between the shafts
> Of a wagon where a cow belongs!
> That's just impossible, I say.
> So mark my words for once and all:
> 'Don't trust a fox on the heath
> And never a Jew on his plighted word.'"29

Another story, the text of which is in Appendix II, told of the almost disastrous visit of a German girl to a Jewish doctor.

Streicher also published a pamphlet on anti-Semitic teaching in the schools, written by his collaborator, Fritz Fink. It maintained: "We all, both parents and teachers, are guilty because of the countless numbers of our women and girls who have been ruined by the Jews." It was the obligation of teachers to be sure their students understood the mysteries of blood and race. "No German teacher today can ignore the problem of 'the Jew and the German girl.' The theme is not a delicate one, as some hypocrites suggest. Why should we, from sinful stupid shame, conceal from our maturing girls in the schools that which five minutes later in the streets, in shops or in the office they may encounter in all its brutality, or what perhaps that same evening may be revealed to them in horrible ways by a criminal Jew?"

The new task of instruction was to prepare German girls for motherhood. Girls needed to understand the significance of racial purity, they had to be aware of the Nuremberg Laws. Biology lessons needed to explain why children of mixed race were inferior. Children should learn that racial defilement "means racial death. Racial defilement is bloodless murder. A woman defiled by a Jew can never rid herself of the transfused poison of foreign blood. She is lost to her people." Fink referred to Talmud passages that, he said, documented the Jewish plot to ruin German womanhood, and concluded with the observation that well-taught German women would, when they had children, pass the message on. "Thus the blessings of our work will benefit future generations."[30]

By the end of the 1930s racial defilement stories were less common. After all, fewer and fewer Jews remained to be accused. With fewer cases to read about, Germans naturally thought less about the matter, a development that greatly worried the *Stürmer* staff. Editor Ernst Hiemer was alarmed to discover at a 1939 racial defilement trial that few female witnesses knew anything at all about the Nuremberg Laws. "Their answers were a catastrophe. Many knew almost nothing. The others had only the barest notion of the fundamental significance of the racial laws."[31]

By 1940 the *Stürmer* had other matters to worry about, fortunately for it, since hardly any new cases of racial defilement were to be found. In the fall of 1940, Streicher ran a lengthy account of a case in Hamburg that proved, he said, "how necessary it is to keep the closest watch on those Jews still living in Germany."[32] The last major trial covered was in the spring of 1942. Ernst Hiemer, obviously relishing a return to what had been so frequent a theme in former years, wrote a long article. Many photographs were carried. The headline was "Death to the Race Defilers," an old theme to which the paper now returned. Though few details of prurient interest were provided, the

Jew's conduct during the trial was given in detail. And the sentence he received was death. The *Stürmer* was delighted: "The physical annihilation of the perpetrator was the only possible atonement." To those who wondered why the *Stürmer* would give over its cover story to the theme in the midst of the war, there was an answer: "When today a Jewish racial defiler is sentenced to death, it proves that years ago the *Stürmer* was a good prophet."[33]

The Hamburg account was the last cover story on racial defilement. Several 1943 issues praised the Nuremberg Laws for having maintained the purity of German blood, but there were to be no further vivid cover stories of rape and defilement. There were few Jews left in Germany, and German womanhood was now "safe." But the *Stürmer* was duller.

VIII

Solutions: Final and Otherwise

In 1921 Streicher wrote: "If we solve the Jewish question soon and thoroughly, then our rise and the happy future of our children is secured."[1] If the Jews were Germany's misfortune, an inferior race, inherently criminal, inclined to every manner of vice, then it was not sufficient to denounce them; something more had to be done. Over the course of his career Streicher needed several ways of dealing with the Jews. To keep his readers at the proper level of fervor, he needed things his readers could do to contribute to solving the problem, but he also needed broader, total solutions to deal with Jewry once and for all.

Hitler made the distinction between the members and the supporters of a political movement. A political party could never have too many supporters, the people who voted for its candidates, but it could easily have too many members, those actively involved in its activity. To allow those without total dedication to join a party only weakened the organization, for lackadaisical members cannot be depended upon in hard times. Streicher made much the same distinction with regard to anti-Semitism. He wanted a core group of men and women who would fight Jews with fervor and enthusiasm, and a much larger group of Germans who simply did not like Jews. Each group had to be supplied with ways of "solving" the Jewish question. Dedicated anti-Semites were fanatics willing to make sacrifices, but most Germans were less eager. Since anti-Semitism to them was not a central attitude, demanding of them actions requiring great commitment could produce a "boomerang effect," provoking less rather than more anti-Semitism. We may have a favorite toothpaste, but would likely switch brands if its price tripled. Similarly, a German not too concerned about the Jews might turn against Nazism if asked to do too much.

On the most basic level, Streicher simply told readers to avoid Jews. The *Stürmer* always carried large-print slogans on the bottoms of its pages such as "Avoid Jewish Doctors and Lawyers" or "German Women and Girls: The Jews Are Your Destruction." During the Weimar era each Christmas brought an appeal not to buy from the "Christ-killers." To assist readers in avoiding Jews, Streicher provided lists of Jewish professionals and shopkeepers. A typical 1935 issue listed Jewish dentists (and Gentile dentists with Jewish wives) practicing in Nuremberg. In providing this sort of information, Streicher was assisted by the whole force of the Nazi state, which through legal methods and propaganda was also persuading people to avoid the Jews. Streicher's task became easier as increasingly Jews were forced to identify themselves as Jews. And as we shall see in the next chapter, Streicher often used intimidation to keep wavering Germans from their Jewish fellow citizens. The nominal anti-Semite, then, could avoid Jews without particular difficulty and feel that he was doing his part in the national effort.

For eager readers Streicher had more demanding activities. A 1936 notice informed readers that they had to do more than simply read the *Stürmer*. "Pass on your *Stürmer* to your neighbor, for only when you can say 'I have helped to spread the knowledge of the Jewish question to the people' will you have done your duty." In 1944 readers were told: "It is the duty of we, the knowing, to spread our knowledge."[2] The loyal reader was an evangelist.

One way to spread the message was to increase the *Stürmer*'s circulation. Early issues carried forms for getting copies to nonreaders, and in 1929 readers were asked to help out in a circulation drive. Thousands of readers erected and maintained the *Stürmer* display cases that made the paper so much a part of everyday life in the Third

Reich (see figure 5). In 1936 an unemployed reader described how he had raised enough money to pay for a showcase's materials, then found people willing to donate the labor to build it. Readers in the Hartberg district of Austria erected fifty showcases within a few weeks of the 1938 *Anschluss*. The dedication of a new case was often made into a considerable affair, particularly in smaller towns. In 1940 the paper appealed to readers for help in maintaining cases that were neglected because their guardian had gone to war.

The showcases really served a double function. They greatly increased readership, but they also strengthened the commitment of those who built and maintained them. They had to persuade themselves each week anew that the *Stürmer* was worth the trouble—and self-persuasion is the strongest persuasion of all.

Stürmer readers also provided large amounts of material. Major articles often were based on material supplied by readers, and Streicher established a column for short items supplied by readers, variously titled "Letterbox" or "News in Brief," which became popular, often including as many as fifty items. In 1933 the *Stürmer* began its infamous pillory column, a list of Jewish men and Gentile women who saw each other socially. Readers were asked to send in the names of such people whom they knew. In 1937 the paper began a campaign against Jewish shopkeepers. One reader helped out by listing thirty-nine people who shopped at a Jewish store in his town, claiming that the Jew "would long since have been bankrupt were there not so many spineless German men and women who give their money to the Jews." Another reported not only the names of his townsmen, but also the amounts they spent. Such reports must have required assiduous watch and surely gained the hostility of the neighbors. Sometimes lists of this type were not sent in to the *Stürmer* but were posted in the local *Stürmer* display case, where the impact was much the same. In 1935 readers were asked to "search the dusty shelves and study the records of past times. They are rich sources for the educational work of the *Stürmer*." At least one reader responded and found records of an 1829 case in which a Jew had been convicted of selling bad meat.[3]

In 1935 an attorney wrote to the *Stürmer* about a racial-defilement case in Berlin in which he was involved. Rather nervously, he observed that he would be violating professional ethics by providing the *Stürmer* information. The *Stürmer* assured him his role would be kept secret, so he provided the information, which led to an article.[4] *Stürmer* informants throughout Germany provided information of a similar confidential nature.

The *Stürmer* archive was another method of reader involvement. Regularly readers were asked to send in materials on the Jews. Thousands of photographs readers sent in survived the war and are now part of the collection of the Nuremberg City Archive. Some were taken from Jewish homes after the owners left or were driven out. Other readers compiled careful photographic essays, denouncing Jews and the friends of Jews in their town. In 1941 readers were told the paper was collecting anti-Semitic proverbs, a book of which later was published. Soldiers in Poland were asked to gather Jewish books and relics from the areas they conquered. As late as January 1945 readers still were being asked to send in material. Once again the *Stürmer* archive served a double function: Aside from its value as a ready source of material, it gave readers the opportunity to express their attitudes in action.

The total amount of material Streicher received from his audience was substantial. In 1934 the *Stürmer* noted that much material recently had been received that could not be acknowledged, as the staff was too small to handle the mail. With the rapid rise in circulation, the staff also increased. In 1935 the *Stürmer* claimed to receive seven hundred letters a day, and two weeks later, eleven thousand a week.[5] Either figure suggests a most active readership. And it was a readership that wanted action. The "Letterbox" sometimes responded to complaints by readers that their attacks on neighbors had not been printed by observing that not all letters could be printed, and that furthermore the paper required "the attestation of a party office that the details given to us conform entirely to the truth."[6] In 1937 readers were told that the mail was so heavy that those who wanted a reply should enclose return postage. Soldiers in 1940 were informed that not all their letters could be printed but that they would at least find their way into the archive. By then the staff had increased to over three hundred, many of whom must have responded to reader mail.[7]

There were other things a faithful reader could do. *Stürmer* advertisers, of whom there were many in the 1930s, needed to be patronized, since they supposedly suffered the wrath of Jews and their friends. Readers could refuse to hire Jews or avoid working for them.

They could keep their children away from Jewish children. In whatever they did, Streicher assured them that they were part of a high crusade. A 1932 Fips cartoon depicted truth, personified as a naked woman riding a horse named the *Stürmer*, leaping across the barrier of confiscation. A Jew hiding behind the barrier exclaims: "The *Stürmer* overcomes every obstacle. It thinks only of its goal." Later, in a New Year message, the paper asserted: "The *Stürmer* will go its way in the new year—straight and true."[8] The reader, whatever he did, participated in that campaign.

Many of Streicher's loyal readers, whom he called the *Stürmer* Guards, were informal volunteers who maintained display cases or informed on their neighbors. But Streicher worked to establish an organized network of representatives around Germany. In 1938, for example, in what must have been part of a general appeal, the *Stürmer* wrote to the mayor of the town of Fellbach: "We want to be sure that the Jewish question reaches every last citizen in your community. To that end we must have a completely reliable party member or citizen who will carry out the educational struggle with particular fervor. . . . Therefore we ask . . . that you provide the name of a local *Stürmer* agent (*Vertrauensmann*)." The mayor complied.[9] In 1939 another loyal reader asked the paper to provide some kind of visible credential that he was the *Stürmer* agent for the area, as that would make his work easier. That same agent, responding to a *Stürmer* inquiry, confirmed that an elderly woman who had been denounced in a letter to the *Stürmer* did indeed buy from Jews, but he urged that there be no story. The woman was old and unaware of the significance of the Jewish question, and besides she had two exemplary Nazi children who would be embarrassed by the publicity.[10] There apparently were many such agents around Germany, who obviously were of great value to a newspaper intent on attacking Jews everywhere in the land.

The gradual disappearance of Jews within Germany not only altered the content of Streicher's rhetoric, it also affected the kinds of solutions he could propose. By 1940 there really was not much his readers could do to solve the mythical Jewish problem, since Jews were no longer to be found in most of the country. Readers could, it is true, continue to spread the message, but that message was of less interest to nonfanatics once Jews could no longer be presented as an immediate threat. The degree of participation fanatic anti-Semites could maintain decreased, certainly part of the reason for the *Stürmer's* loss of circulation after the war began.

The individual actions Streicher's readers could take were not sufficient in themselves to solve the Jewish question. Both national and international solutions also needed to be found. Streicher's leadership of the April 1, 1933 boycott made him a central figure in the campaign to drive Jews out of Germany, a position he attempted to maintain through the *Stürmer*. The paper regularly called for new laws and regulations to restrict the Jews. At various times, for example, it called for a ban on government contracts with Jewish firms, penalties for hotel owners who rented rooms to mixed couples, the exclusion of Jews from the wine trade, and so on. These suggestions became particularly common after 1933, when Hitler's government began implementing a steadily increasing series of anti-Jewish measures. Although Streicher put considerable effort into these kinds of suggestions, he could not really be satisfied with them. As Karl Schleunes observes in *The Twisted Road to Auschwitz*: "Laws, even of the Nazi variety, never quite fit the Nazi style, or for that matter their purposes. Had they restricted themselves to the enforcement of their anti-Jewish laws the continued existence of a separate if second-class Jewish community would have been assured."[11]

National solutions were only half measures—and the *Stürmer* prided itself on its devotion to total solutions. Sometimes the nature of such a total solution was said to be educational. In 1936, for example, a *Stürmer* writer asserted: "The Jewish question can be solved only by constant education for all Gentile peoples. The entire world must know the innate baseness and depravity of the Jews. This would in large part solve the Jewish question."[12] That was a painless solution, but it was also too vague. What would happen to the Jews once the whole world was educated? To that the *Stürmer* alternated between two answers: deportation and annihilation.

At the Nuremberg trials Streicher asserted that he had always wanted a Jewish homeland, that he was at one with the Zionists in that regard. For good reasons the court did not believe him. Still there were times during Streicher's career when deportation was his primary suggestion. It had indeed been the solution proposed by many German anti-Semites. Theodor Fritsch, the old man of German anti-Semitism, wrote: "We do not want to kill the Jews or do violence to them. Rather, we want to tell them peacefully and confidently, 'You will no longer live among us.'"[13] Fritsch went on to suggest possible Jewish homelands. Streicher's early position seems consistent with Fritsch's. During the Weimar era Streicher's primary interest was in immediate solutions, such as electing Nazis and avoiding Jews. When he proposed total solutions, he generally had in mind deportation. A 1931 issue of the *Stürmer*, for example, urged the deportation of all Jews to Palestine.[14]

With Hitler in power Streicher started to think on a broader scale. In late 1933 he took up the idea of sending all the Jews to Madagascar, a large island off the African coast. This became a regular topic for most of the rest of the decade. But *Stürmer* readers came up with other ideas. One thought that removing Jews to Madagascar or New Guinea would be unfair to the inhabitants of those islands, and suggested instead the Russian island of Novaya Zemlya, north of the Arctic Circle. Hardly anyone lived on that island. Another reader suggested the jungles in the North of Brazil.[15] Islands tended to win the most favor, however, since better watch could be kept on the Jews that way. The *Stürmer* seemed to envision an international naval force that would ensure that Jews stayed put. Readers searched their atlases for large and empty islands, the staff reporting in 1939 that many proposals had been received from readers, demonstrating their interest in solving the problem. Streicher was not alone in proposing these schemes, by the way. Many other Nazis, the SS included, gave serious consideration to moving Jews from Germany to Palestine or Madagascar.

By the end of the 1930s Streicher had lost most of his interest in deportation schemes. A 1938 article observed that France and Poland recently had discussed the Madagascar scheme.[16] Streicher recalled that he long had favored that solution but observed that Germany was well on its way to dealing with the problem without resorting to deportation. In 1946 Streicher testified that no articles on the plan were printed after 1939 because censors had banned articles along those lines.

Yet there was something inconsistent in the *Stürmer*'s generous support for a Jewish homeland. If the Jew is the Devil in human form, to allow him to exist, even if only on a well-guarded island, is to admit the possibility of continued Jewish crimes, to perpetuate Satan's hold on earth. If the Jew were demonic, was not death the only logical answer? As the *Stürmer* put it: "The Jew is neither man nor animal. He is the Devil. He cannot be punished, nor can he be reformed. He can only be rendered harmless."[17] The only sure way to render Jews harmless was to kill them. And the *Stürmer* so often compared Jews to bacteria, insects, and vermin, the kinds of pests one kills without a second thought.

Even in his earliest days Streicher's language had been violent. In 1924 he wrote: "The day will come when the German people will awake. . . . This day will come because it *must* come, for it cannot be the will of God, the will of the Creator, that a people such as the Germans, the most beautiful people under the sun, should be the sacrifice of Satan. And that day will be sealed with blood."[18] When a prominent *Stürmer* target committed suicide in 1931, the paper observed: "We see in the fate of this Jew the fate of the Jewish people. . . . The time is coming when they will fall, and end like Alfred Guckenheimer." The unknown Germans who lynched a Jew were said to have done a praiseworthy act of popular justice.[19] Even before 1933, in short, Streicher's rhetoric could be violent—but then it did not seem likely that much would come of his fulminations.

After 1933 all was different. Suddenly it became possible to envision a final solution. Shortly after the takeover a Fips cartoon showed a powerful Nazi shoving a frightened Jew over a cliff (see figure 27). A lead editorial claimed that before Hitler's takeover Jews had denied legality, freedom, and justice to Germany, the very things they cried out for now that Hitler was chancellor. "Shall the past be forgotten? Shall it remain unavenged? The Jew sowed hatred, he shall reap it in return. A driving commandment of National Socialist *Realpolitik* will be to ensure that Monster Jewry forever will be rendered incapable of sowing new seeds of poison." How could Jews be made forever innocuous if they remained alive? By summer 1933, a *Stürmer* article discussing the *Protocols of the Learned Elders of Zion* claimed that Jews were a people of murderers and criminals. "Therefore the Jewish race must be exterminated (*ausgerottet*) from beneath the sun."[20]

In 1935 Streicher spoke to a closed meeting of the Nazi student organization. He gave his typical anti-Semitic sermon, but in conclusion he was more blunt than usual. "All our struggles are in vain if the battle against the Jews is not fought to the finish. It is not enough to get the Jews out of Germany. No, they must be killed (*totgeschlagen*) in the entire world, so that humanity will be free of them."[21]

By 1939 calls for annihilation had become commonplace in the *Stürmer*. That year Ernst Hiemer wrote: The Jewish question is not yet solved. It will not be solved even when the last Jew has left Germany. It will be solved only when world Jewry is annihilated (*vernichtet*)." The following year Streicher, in a lead editorial, concluded that world peace would come only "when the enemy of peace and freedom is annihilated: the world criminal Pan-Jewry." In 1941 he wrote: "The causes of the world's misfortunes will be forever removed only when Jewry in its entirety is annihilated." In January 1944, with the Holocaust raging, he continued his call for destruction: "The National Socialist revolution in Germany has also led to developments in Europe which it can be expected will make the continent forever free of Jewish rabble-rousers and exploiters. Moreover, the German model will, after the successful end to the world war, lead to the annihilation (*Vernichtung*) of the Jewish world tormentor on the other continents as well." And in February 1945, only just before the end, he wrote: "Whoever does what the Jew does is a scoundrel, a criminal. And he who wishes to imitate him deserves the same fate, annihilation, death."[22] The prosecution at Nuremberg submitted more than fifty clear calls for annihilation from Streicher's work, and their collection was not by any means exhaustive.

If, as the *Stürmer* so often claimed, it spoke the language of the people, a language in which words had but one clear meaning, these calls must be taken literally. But were they so intended? In 1946 Streicher argued: "No letter and no correspondence exists in my files where I said or suggested to anybody that Jews ought to be killed."[23] Ernst Hiemer and Adele Streicher, his second wife, joined in testifying that Streicher had never wanted to kill Jews. His vehement language was only a heated response to similar Jewish statements that suggested that Germany would be destroyed. But his response was faulty, for it ignored the context of the statements that allegedly justified his own. Various Allied citizens had indeed called for the destruction of Germany, but they mostly intended not the death of every German, but the end of the Nazi state. Streicher, on the other hand, for many years had argued with his Nazi brethren that each Jew was evil, that every one was a threat. In that context a threat of annihilation is far more ominous.

Did Streicher really mean that all Jews should be killed? The question is difficult to answer. It is probably true that for most of his career he really did not know what he wanted to do with the Jews. He was not alone in his confusion. As Karl Schleunes observes: "During the early years of the Third Reich no one in the Nazi movement, from the Fuehrer down, had defined what the substance of a solution to the Jewish problem might be."[24] Nazism was not an ideology that developed concrete plans before those plans were needed. As a result, for most of his career, Streicher simply tried to do all he could to drive Jews from Germany, to make their lives miserable. The earliest calls for annihilation were more rhetorical flourish than proposals for mass murder. Streicher was not ready for the Holocaust in 1933, nor were other Nazis. The moral weight of millennia stood against it.

The Nazis needed time to persuade themselves as well as others. Streicher was forced over the years to accept mass murder in part by the rhetorical choices he made. In order to present each Jew as a threat to Germany, he was forced to maintain that there were no decent Jews. And having declared all Jews evil, he was forced to propose drastic solutions, lest he find himself in the curious position of maintaining that Jews were Satan's next of kin, yet that they should be allowed to live with the rest of humanity. To maintain mental balance, Streicher (and other Nazis) were led gradually to accept increasingly harsh ways of dealing with the Jews. Every time Streicher told of Jewish ritual murder or the rape of a child, or described the international Jewish conspiracy, it became harder to grant Jews the right to life. The Holocaust could not have occurred in 1933 for many reasons. Surely one of them was that the anti-Semites themselves were not prepared for it.

At the International Military Tribunal Streicher finally admitted the reality of the Holocaust, but never did he accept moral responsibility. Though he had called for the annihilation of the Jews time after time, he saw no personal guilt. In his moral blindness he failed to see that the Holocaust was but the logical consequence of the message he had preached for twenty-five years and to which he himself had fallen prey. Streicher probably did not know the exact details of the death camps. But he knew they existed. And they did not concern him.

IX

A Poisoned Nation:
The Impact of *Der Stürmer*

For twenty-five years Julius Streicher preached hatred. What came of his work? The question is extraordinarily difficult to answer, since Streicher did not work alone, and since it is impossible to determine the exact influence he had on millions of Germans. In looking at Streicher's impact we shall have to consider the larger picture. Yet Streicher was the worst, the most visible, the most prolific Jew-baiter in the land. No less than Heinrich Himmler wrote: "In times to come when the history of the reawakening of the German people is written, and when the next generation will be unable to understand how the German people could ever have been friendly with the Jews, it will be said that Julius Streicher and his weekly newspaper the *Stürmer* were responsible for a good part of the education about the enemy of mankind."[1]

The most obvious result of Streicher's efforts came in converts, men and women who became persuaded that Jews were evil. In 1936 Streicher asserted that "the fifteen-year work of the *Stürmer* has led to an army of millions of National Socialists who understand the Jewish question."[2] That surely was giving himself more credit than he deserved, but many did hear his message and respond. We have already seen that the *Stürmer* was among the most widely circulated newspapers in Germany. The minister of finance under Hitler, Lutz Graf Schwerin von Krosigk, concluded that Streicher had exerted "an influence on Germany that can only be compared with that of Goebbels's propaganda."[3]

Both Streicher's personal files and the letter columns of the *Stürmer* contain many letters from people who attributed their anti-Semitism to Streicher's efforts. A typical letter from a soldier in 1939 ran: "I have read your paper for many years, and came to understand the Jewish question as a result."[4] Streicher's material was easy to read, vivid, and well illustrated, able to reach a far wider audience than the thick books with small print produced by earlier Jew-baiters.

The appeal of the *Stürmer* even reached beyond Germany. For many abroad, of course, the *Stürmer* symbolized the worst of Hitlerism. New outrages from the *Stürmer* were regularly denounced by the world press during the 1930s. But there were many who looked on Streicher's work more sympathetically. A single issue in 1935 contained replies to readers in Greece, Paraguay, Argentina, Brazil, England, Australia, and the United States. Photographs of foreign readers were printed regularly. In the United States, Nazi organizations mailed copies to those interested. Even those unable to read German could absorb much of Streicher's message by looking at the cartoons and photographs. Branch offices of the *Stürmer* were opened in Vienna, Prague, and Strasbourg once Nazi armies had marched in, and a Danish edition was attempted in 1941.

A particularly reprehensible side of Streicher's work was the attention he gave to children. The lively and vivid material Streicher produced had its attractions, and children are susceptible to the appeals to racial pride and group solidarity in which he specialized. To reach those children, for whom even the *Stürmer*'s style was too advanced, Streicher published the children's books we have referred to in previous chapters. The second such book, *The Poisonous Mushroom,* went through at least four printings totaling forty thousand copies.

These materials were widely used by Jew-baiting teachers in the classroom, and Streicher happily printed many photographs of eager children studying the Jewish question. Letters from ardent teachers and students came in regularly. In 1935, for example, a well-indoctrinated boy wrote:

Dear *Stürmer*:

Although I do not have a regular subscription, I have bought each issue of your paper for a full year from a newsstand. You will not believe how eager I am to see each new issue; a week between issues is too long. Although I am young, with your help as a teacher I have recognized with deep conviction the deadly enemy of national life, world Jewry. There is no one I hate or despise more than this devilish Hebrew trash which has brought so much misfortune to our part of the world.... I will close by saying that the battle the *Stürmer* is fighting is the best of its kind.

World Jewry is the Devil in human form. Rip the mask of falsehood from their ugly faces. Reveal them and their criminal law, the Talmud![5]

These kinds of letters were not rare.

Then there were the teachers, happy to report the fruits of their instruction. One teacher had the following to write about a nine-year-old star pupil:

One day he came to school and said, "Herr teacher, I was out walking with my mother yesterday. As we were passing a [Jewish] store, she suddenly remembered that she needed several spools of thread. I told my mother, "I won't go in, you will have to do it yourself. And if you do go in I'll tell my teacher in the morning, and that may not be so very pleasant for you."[6]

The children's books contained particularly clear admonitions to hate Jews. In perhaps the most vicious, an ugly Jewish schoolmaster guides his equally ugly charges past the German school. While the proud German schoolmaster looks on, his pupils mock and torment the Jewish children, several of whom are in tears (see figure 29). Streicher was out to train the next generation—it was to have no pity for Jews. And the last of the children's books, this one without color illustrations, went farther, comparing Jews to every manner of obnoxious creature.

But children were the coming generation. Streicher primarily had to deal with those who were already adults. His readers wanted action, they wanted things to do to battle the Jews. Even before 1933 they looked to Streicher for help. In 1936 a *Stürmer* staff member recalled the early days when regular office hours were held. "It was a day when the office was open. From far and wide, people came to the *Stürmer* with their troubles and needs. . . . They came by the hundreds from the North and South of Germany."[7] Even though the *Stürmer* was unable to help most of them, the writer claimed that all left with new courage.

After 1933 the *Stürmer* was a force to reckon with. The thousands of letters it received each week contained more than weird solutions to the Jewish question. There was as well every manner of denunciation and fulmination. Streicher set up his paper as a national watchdog, ready to report Jewish misdeeds anywhere they were found. Depending on a large staff and on informants and readers throughout Germany, he attacked thousands of Jews, and even more Germans who were friendly with Jews. The latter group, the *Judenknechte* or Jewish-lackeys, were the cause of his greatest ire. To explain how Germans, the pinnacle of Aryanism, could fall prey to so dreadful a disease required some effort. A 1935 *Stürmer* article explained it was because there was Jewish blood in the family tree, even as much as a hundred years in the past, or because they had had too much contact with Jews.[8]

These despicable Germans showed their love of the Jews by reading foreign newspapers, avoiding the "Heil Hitler" greeting, claiming to know decent Jews, laughing at the Jewish question, shopping at Jewish stores, having Jewish friends, disliking Streicher and his *Stürmer*, and so on. *Stürmer* readers were encouraged to tell such people that they were Jewish-lackeys, and no end of them followed their favorite newspaper's advice. Whether from envy, greed, hatred, or perverted faith in anti-Semitism, thousands attempted to vent their complaints through the *Stürmer*. The paper itself admitted that many complaints were from base motives, claiming to ignore the many anonymous denunciations of business competitors or troublemakers, which were "a horror."[9] But those letters the *Stürmer* took seriously were enough to cause great misery.

As we have seen, in 1933 Streicher began the pillory column, giving the names and addresses of German women purportedly having relations with Jewish men. The first column explained that, if good sense were not enough to keep women from the Jews, perhaps fear of publicity would help. The pillory was speedily adopted by other Nazi papers, with powerful effects on the victims. Shortly after the first listing in the *Stürmer*, for example, a woman came in in tears saying that it was not her fault if a Jew followed her about. The unsympathetic paper replied that if that were the case, all she needed to do was seek the assistance of the nearest Storm Trooper. To guarantee that readers could find "pilloried" women, the paper often ran their pictures and even on occasion address corrections.[10] Soon those who shopped in Jewish stores or otherwise violated Nazi sensibilities found themselves pilloried in like manner.

The very popular brief items section of the paper served similar functions. Perhaps the best way to understand the despicable nature of such material is to summarize the twenty items from a typical 1937 issue:

1. Fifteen Germans in a resort area rent their summer homes to Jews.
2. A retired locomotive engineer tips his hat to one Jewess and shakes hands with another. He is a well-known friend of the Jews.
3. In a village the populace is concerned because a well-known Jew-lover has been given the guardianship of a farm.
4. A butcher takes pleasure driving in a Jew's car.
5. A retired accountant has various business dealings with Jews, refuses to contribute to Nazi causes, avoids the "Heil Hitler" greeting, and makes no secret of his opposition to Nazism.
6. The wife of a judicial official talks openly with a Jewess.
7. A woman supplies scrap to a Jew, and a Jew in the same area has a German attorney.
8. Three Germans buy from the Jews.
9. A German works closely with two Jews in the wine trade, and another German in the area is often visited by a Jewish lawyer.
10. The owner of a women's clothing store has business dealings with Jews and is often visited by them.
11. Five Germans work for a Jewish threshing firm.
12. A town councilman lets his daughter date a Jew.
13. A printer is represented by a Jewish attorney.
14. A blacksmith buys supplies and equipment from a Jewish firm.
15. A farmer has business dealings with a Jewish livestock agent.
16. Many officials and farmers in a district still shop at Jewish stores.
17. A postal employee tips his hat to a Jewess.

18. Three Germans have friendly relations with a Jewish woman.
19. Twenty-three farmers deal with the Jews.
20. A German attorney represents a Jew.[11]

In each case, the names of the accused and their towns or districts are given. Sixty-five specific individuals are denounced for conducting business with Jews or extending to them simple friendship or courtesy. Every issue of the *Stürmer* came to carry such items—often there were fifty or more. And in addition many longer letters were printed, and interior articles were based on material supplied by readers. The average issue of the *Stürmer* denounced more than a hundred named individuals.

The fact that so many Germans were attacked for their "spineless" dealings with the Jews is of course evidence that they had a great deal of spine. That thousands refused to bow to the evil of the day is testimony to high courage, for in many cases, the brave people the *Stürmer* denounced had first been warned to cease associating with Jews. In 1935, for example, a reader reported a German butcher who bought his meat from a Jew. Although the butcher had been warned that he would be reported to the *Stürmer* if he continued, the unintimidated merchant conducted business as before.[12] Many Bavarian farmers proved resistant to appeals to avoid Jewish livestock dealers, since the Jews gave better prices and paid in cash.[13]

Men and women of courage were, as everywhere, the minority in Germany, however; the very threat of public disgrace for dealing with Jews was sufficient to cow many Germans. Walter Berlin, for many years a leader in the Nuremberg Jewish community, wrote that Streicher "dominated all spheres of life" there even before 1933. Berlin was often told: "I would like to do this or that, but then I would appear in the suermer [sic]."[14] After 1933, of course, Streicher's impact was nationwide.

And those who feared appearing in the *Stürmer* had good reason. Even if most were not officially prosecuted, they could lose friends and business. As one woman attacked by the paper put it after the war: "There were many people who behaved as I did, but they had to expect the worst consequences."[15] In 1934 a reader reported that a German married to a Jew had been expelled from an organization after the *Stürmer* publicized the marriage. A reader in 1935 wrote that he had recognized in a *Stürmer* photograph the unidentified woman shown buying from a Jewish store. She was his wife. As he traveled a great deal he was not aware of his wife's shopping habits, but he promised to deal with the matter. Editor Ernst Hiemer wrote: "We often receive letters from *Stürmer* fellow workers in every district that tell us that our publication improved things. . . . A few examples! We printed an item in the spring of 1937 which said that landowner . . . in . . . traded with the Jews. Two weeks later we received news from a party office there that, because of our publication, the landowner entirely broke his relations with the Jews." Hiemer gave two other examples of the *Stürmer*'s success.[16] Sometimes brief notices reported that former Jew-lovers had changed their ways, giving further impetus to sinners to avoid Jews. National infamy could be atoned for by national repentance.

Examples could be multiplied. In a 1937 disciplinary procedure against a mayor, the charges against him were in part supported by a *Stürmer* article that accused him of buying a cow from a Jew.[17] It was not even necessary to print accusations. The *Stürmer*'s staff generally checked out reader material before printing it—and a letter from the paper was often enough to get action. When, for example, a reader complained that Jews were involved in his city's gasworks, the paper inquired if that were true. The town's mayor responded, claiming that as a loyal Nazi he had been forced by higher authorities to permit Jews to be involved. Now, however, he sensed that attitudes, if not official policy, had changed. He was removing the Jews forthwith.[18]

For every brave man or woman who resisted the pressure to hate Jews, there were many more ordinary people, the kind who told Walter Berlin that it was too risky to do what they knew was right. The long-term consequences of such behavior are important. The German who walked past a Jewish shop or ignored a former Jewish friend was not likely to attribute his act to cowardice, an unpleasant admission to make after all. We all put the most flattering explanations on our own behavior, and it was far more comfortable for Germans to conclude: "Well, all that Streicher says isn't true, but maybe I should be safe. With all the things you hear . . ." Having taken the first step in rationalization, the individual had accepted part of Streicher's message. Now the individual was on a slippery slope, and it became increasingly easy to avoid Jews more and more, for the critical point is that Streicher did not have to convince all Germans to hate the Jews; indeed, that was impossible. It was enough to make Germans suspicious, to break the bonds of friendship and courtesy that hold society together, to isolate Jews from their fellow German citizens, to make them irrelevant. The many Germans who rejected Streicher's crude anti-Semitism were not by virtue of that fact friends of the Jews. In rejecting the style they were not necessarily rejecting the content. But in failing to reject the content they were in fact being influenced. It is probably true that most Germans did not think much about the Jews, particularly after 1939. But that in itself was a victory for the Nazi anti-Semites. With no one willing to stand by Jews, it became easy to kill them.

If Streicher's impact on Germans was major, his impact on the Jews was devastating. The Germans Streicher attacked might suffer public disgrace and inconvenience; Jews might go to prison or worse. Walter Berlin summarized the effects he saw Streicher have on his Jewish fellow citizens in Germany:

> From the years 1933 to 1938 I frequently met friends who took an active part in Jewish life in various parts of Germany. We exchanged information and tried to analyze the position; it became more and more clear that in most cases new measures persecuting the Jews and interfering with their civil liberties oroginated [sic] from Nuremberg. Prohibiting Jews to enter public baths or places of entertainment; rendering it impossible for Jewish children to attend schools maintained by the state; preventing Jews from acquiring licenses of various kinds; boycotts of Jewish firms and professional men as well as organized social boycott; dismissal of Jewish employees—whatever it was, it was very often found that it was at Nuremberg that the action had been commenced and that the measures then, by and by, had spread throughout the Reich. The friends I met, and I considered that it was JULIUS STREICHER who had initiated the measures, and in the course of time my friends when informed by me of fresh deteriorations of conditions in Nuremberg would confidential [sic] warn Jews in their areas of what had to be expected there.[19]

Berlin's statement is supported by other sources. We have already noted that the pillory columns of the *Stürmer* were widely imitated. In 1933 the paper printed a picture of a city bath that had banned

Jews; other towns were urged to follow. After Streicher spoke in Magdeburg in 1935, Jews were banned from using that city's public transportation.[20] *The New York Times* attributed large anti-Semitic outbursts in Berlin to Streicher.[21] *The Times* of London thought increasing anti-Semitism in Munich to be the result of a recently established *Stürmer* branch office there, and it is in fact true that *Stürmer* agents in Munich were very busy.[22] Streicher himself and the Nuremberg police independently gathered hundreds of foreign press clippings that testified to Streicher's impact on the growing Jew-baiting.

But all this is general. The individual Jews whom Streicher attacked suffered greatly. The horrors of the concentration camps are well known, but what came before often was little happier. Two examples perhaps illustrate the impact of anti-Jewish propaganda. The *Stürmer* printed a story accusing a Jew of cruelty to a cat. Allegedly he had put it in a sack and dashed it against concrete. Then he jumped on the sack, "dancing a genuine Negro dance" atop the still-living animal. Finally he beat it until it died. This, the article concluded, was typical of what Jews did, and it drew a connection to ritual murder. As usual, the name of the Jew and his hometown were given.

After the war, the accused Jew stated that the cat in question had been a nearly dead alley cat that he had put out of its misery. But after the article appeared he received an outraged letter from a reader:

> Full of horror I read in the *Stürmer* of the unheard of way you killed your cat, which goes against all human feelings. Shame on you, you cold-blooded miserable pig-Jew—there is nothing else to call you—treating a poor defenseless animal in this way. All my colleagues agree that the same should be done to you. You should be stomped and beaten until you croak. That by God is only what a miserable, disgusting, detestable, flat-footed and bent-nosed Jew deserves.
>
> We (my acquaintances and I) will therefore see to it that your unheard of deed is known to the Munich newspapers. Go to Palestine where you belong, and behave here in Germany, where you are after all only a guest, as a guest should. You should croak like a worm. All my colleagues agree with this.[23]

Then there was Victor Klemperer, a Jewish linguist who was walking down a Berlin street during the war, wearing the yellow star then required of all Jews still not incarcerated. A father walking with his young son stopped, pointed at Klemperer, and said: "Look here, Horstl! It's all his fault."[24] To many Germans, the Jew was a convenient scapegoat for every trouble.

And then there were the Jewish shopkeepers and professionals who saw their businesses decline as more and more Gentiles walked past. Whether the former customers did so from conviction or cowardice, the effect was the same. There were Jews who saw friends and acquaintances of many years' standing grow colder. The social amenities, a tipped hat, a handshake, disappeared. Many Jews made things easier by themselves breaking relationships, saving awkwardness all around.

Defending his life in 1946, Streicher claimed that he had not incited persecution of the Jews. "It is my conviction," he stated, "that the contents of *Der Stuermer* as such were not incitation. During the whole 20 years I never wrote in this context, 'Burn Jewish houses down; beat them to death.' Never once did such an incitement appear in *Der Stuermer*."[25] In the strictest sense of his words, Streicher was almost correct. His impact came rather through what the *Stürmer* called "holy hate" (see figure 30). Streicher himself did not kill a single Jew, but the words he spoke and wrote were the foundation of the Holocaust. As Otto Finechel wrote:

> The instinctual structure of the average German in Germany was no different in 1935 from what it was in 1925. The psychological mass basis for anti-Semitism, whatever it may be, existed in 1925 too, but anti-Semitism was not a political force then. . . . The principal thing which changed during those ten years was the amount of anti-Semitic propaganda. The effectiveness of this propaganda was the chief thing which altered the attitude of the masses.[26]

As the single most prominent full-time Nazi Jew-baiter, Julius Streicher contributed to that critical development.

The Holocaust was not inevitable; it was not the logical consequence of the flow of German history. It could have been stopped. When in 1940 Hitler began to kill the mentally ill and terminally sick, word got out. Public uproar forced curtailment of the program, for even a totalitarian nation cannot disregard entirely the will of its citizenry. Germans knew about the Holocaust. Not every one, but enough. Many Germans administered it. Others carried it out, or saw it being carried out. More heard rumors. Walter Laqueur's *The Terrible Secret* proves that news of the Holocaust was available throughout Germany—indeed, throughout most of the world. But people did not see what they did not care to see. As Laqueur puts it: "It is, in fact, quite likely that while many Germans thought the Jews were no longer alive, they did not necessarily believe that they were dead. Such belief, needless to say, is logically inconsistent, but a great many logical inconsistencies are accepted in wartime."[27]

Historian Fritz Stern puts it another way. Germans, he writes, knew enough to know that they did not want to know more—but already that requires enough knowledge to guess the truth.[28] To those who hated Jews, of course, the death camps were only what Jews deserved. To the larger number of Germans who had become indifferent, Jews simply were not worth being concerned about. The obituary columns of a newspaper do not affect us until we chance across a familiar name. But those Germans who had become indifferent found it easy to remain indifferent. There were no Jewish obituaries, no front-page newspaper stories, no executions in the middle of Berlin. It took no conscious decision for most Germans to ignore the disappearance of the Jews and then their annihilation. The crucial decision had been made earlier; it had been made when Jews were first ignored. They were not people after all, only Jews. In a deadly irony, the Nazis used the very means to exterminate many Jews that were used to destroy the vermin to which they had so often been compared—poison gas.

Julius Streicher had his way. Germany after World War II contained virtually no Jews. Public-opinion polls found widespread anti-Semitism. Even today Germany has very few Jews. In 1980 there were less than thirty thousand professing Jews in all West Germany. Fifty-three synagogues stood, many new and imposing edifices built with government assistance, but twelve rabbis served the nation and some of the synagogues stood nearly empty.

X

The Illusion
of Immunity

During World War I a French newspaper announced that German depravity was the result of a defective brain. It seemed that the part governing moral behavior was absent from the German cranium. More sophisticated later arguments attributed the German predilection to barbarism to history, culture, authoritarian tradition, or the like. To explain the Holocaust as the product of a German national character defect would be satisfying. It would also be false. The basic reason why Streicher's propaganda worked are as valid in any developed modern society as they were in Hitler's Germany.

My argument is not that the Holocaust could have occurred in any nation in so short a time, for it remains true that a people's past influences its future. Rather, the reasons why Germans came to hate or ignore Jews are the same reasons that render Americans, Russians, other Europeans, or Chinese susceptible to their own brands of propaganda. I shall be following part of the argument developed by Jacques Ellul, whose excellent and unsettling book *Propaganda: The Formation of Men's Attitudes* deserves greater attention than it has had.[1]

Men and women in modern society live far differently than their ancestors did, and not only in the obvious ways influenced by technology and industrialization. The relationships between or among people for many of us have also been transformed. Five hundred years ago, most lives were nasty, brutish, and short, but they were also simpler. For most people the course of life was determined from birth. A man was born, wed, and buried, perhaps in the same house, probably in the same general neighborhood. He had roots in family, Church, and workplace that were enduring. His circle of acquaintances might not be large, but it was permanent.

The average American moves fourteen times, often for considerable distances. To change jobs regularly is the norm, to work in the same place for fifty years is rare. A consequence is that our human relationships are short-term. When I ask my university students how many of them still have a close friend from their kindergarten days, about a fifth raise their hands. Few have more than one from those days. Regular moves mean many Americans live far from their families, seeing parents or siblings several times annually at best, communication in the interval being maintained by infrequent letters or occasional telephone calls. If family and friends have lost force, so too have the churches. Our ancestors who disagreed with the priest faced the wrath of God and society. Today many Christians ignore Church teachings they find inconvenient; the voice of the Lord is of less weight than that of the evening news.

The point is that attitudes need roots. To believe alone is to believe faintly. Earlier generations found support for their attitudes from many sources. To believe weird things required the rejection of family and friends, of Church and society. Today's attitudes are not rooted as solidly in small groups, rather in the more changeable views of "society." But where does society ground its ideas?

The information available to past generations was limited. It is a cliché to assert that we suffer from an "information explosion," referring not only to advances in science but also to the information readily available to the ordinary citizen. Newspapers, magazines, radio, and television provide an astounding amount of information. A single issue of the *New York Times* contains more information about the world than the medieval person encountered in a lifetime. Through the mass media people see and hear events in every part of the world.

And the world's affairs make a difference to us. A peasant in 1400 rarely heard of the doings of the king or of goings-on in far countries. Distant events were irrelevant—they had no impact on everyday life. What was important were those facts that were directly observable. If no rain fell, a farmer knew what drought meant. A townsman who saw his neighbor die of the plague justifiably feared for his own safety. The important facts had immediate consequences. Our situation is less happy. People we have never met and events far distant may have immediate, perhaps disastrous consequences. A war in the Middle East may mean lines outside a filling station, inflation, economic uncertainty, even world war. We have very practical reasons for wanting to know what the rest of the world is about. As a result, news is important and we consume large amounts of it.

But do we understand the facts we receive? Past generations certainly knew fewer facts than we, but that does not mean we understand more, for facts and wisdom are never identical. The critical difference between us and our ancestors is not that we have more facts, but that we know different kinds of facts, facts we believe not because we have firsthand knowledge but because someone has told us they are so. The old phrase "All I know is what I read in the papers" is embarrassingly true. But to know only that is to depend on others to do our thinking and observing. We are proud to be "well informed," but what that means for most people is to read a newspaper and a newsweekly, to watch the evening news, and perhaps to subscribe to one or two journals of opinion.

Consequently we form opinions quickly and easily. Not to have an opinion on the economy, the President, or international politics is to be disgraced. Since few have firsthand experience with such matters, we rely on others to select information and relay it to us. We become consumers of other people's opinions. Instances are easy to find. One of the clearest came with the 1979 seizure of the American embassy in Iran. Formerly most Americans probably could not have pointed to Iran on a map, yet within twenty-four hours a remarkably firm national consensus formed. The opinion was based not on experience, but on what we were told. Americans almost instantly despised an entire nation. On my own campus, large crowds of Americans gathered around groups of Iranians in the student union. A small incident would have led to violence.

Opinion based on secondhand sources, in short, is easy to manipulate. If I tell a man it is raining outside, he can go to the window to see if I am telling the truth. If I tell him the Soviet Union has invaded Malaysia he is unlikely to fly there to see for himself. It simply is not possible to check out every fact. We have little choice but to accept most of them. We may claim to be critical readers, but it is difficult to be critical when we cannot examine the evidence on which an argument rests.

Moreover, many facts are not necessarily representative facts. A careful selection of information can lead an audience to a quite mistaken conclusion, even though none of the information is false. One can simply omit inconvenient facts, of course, but leaving that aside, it is easy to draw improper conclusions in other ways. For example, people greatly overestimate the incidence of disasters, murders, and diseases like cancer, and underestimate the occurrence of home accidents or diabetes. A plane crash or an earthquake gets front-page coverage and full play on the evening news, and cancer is the great evil of the day. Such vivid happenings are remembered, overshadowing less dramatic facts.

Julius Streicher's ability to provide a profusion of facts suggesting that Jews were committing crimes on a startling scale was well suited for the modern media. His standards of evidence were, as we have seen, unimpressive, but some of what he accused Jews of doing was true. It did not matter to him and his readers that infractions committed by Jews were certainly not more numerous or even proportionally higher than crimes committed by "Aryans." During the Weimar era his targets sometimes were convicted. And after 1933 convictions became almost predictable, for reasons perhaps not entirely evident to the average citizen. His material was not representative, but its vividness was far more persuasive than a mere statistic.

On a lower level, given complete knowledge of the behavior and thoughts of any individual, one could construct a highly unflattering portrait, relying entirely on those facts that suggested the individual's depravity. The ability to select is the ability to persuade. Streicher could present cases of Jewish evil with reasonable assurance that his readers would make the desired inductive leap from the given case to the general. If a large number of Jews seemed to be criminal, then all Jews probably were. Of course, the well-known human tendency to perceive selectively is also at work. One who expects to see Jews about evil deeds will find just that, overlooking consciously or not the more impressive evidence to the contrary. The anti-Semite who, in reading the Talmud, was struck only by the small number of passages he perceived as supporting his prejudices, was only following to a greater degree a mental and emotional process that everyone commonly practices.

A distinctive trait of modern society is the widespread loss of a sense of meaning, in part the consequence of increased education and leisure, in part the result of the breaking up of traditional society. Medieval society was properly called Christendom, for the larger society was rooted in Christian practices and values. With the loss of that consensus, much of the foundation of Western culture also was lost. As Chesterton observed, when men cease to believe in God, they do not believe in nothing, they believe in anything. The record of the twentieth century offers no refutation. Every manner of religion, political and social philosophy, and psychology offers meaning to a befuddled world. The common phrase of the 1960s, "It doesn't matter what you believe as long as you are sincere," speaks to the emptiness caused by the loss of faith, a void that men feel they must fill. With what matters little to them.

Then there are the changes brought on by the Industrial Revolution, which led to enormous advances in productivity and human comfort but also reduced the sense of personal accomplishment on the part of many workers. The shoemaker who makes the whole shoe feels greater pride than the worker who attaches eyelets. Few of us anymore have the sense of accomplishment that comes from doing all of a task, indicated perhaps by the remarkable popularity of crafts and pseudocrafts, which after all provide some outlet for personal creativity. There are exceptions—farming, for example. Although farmers regularly complain about their lot, surprisingly few leave their occupation by choice, and many who would like to enter it are unable to make the necessary investment. A farmer still has total responsibility for his crop, from planting to harvest. He needs to be a jack-of-all-trades, able to care for plants, fix machinery, and handle increasingly complicated finances. In that there is satisfaction.

Our ancestors believed their family, their neighbors, and their clergy. We believe the evening news. We think of past generations as gullible, believing the most outrageous things. But every age is gullible in its own way. The shallowness with which even our most important attitudes are sometimes rooted makes them remarkably easy to sway. In the United States, recent and widespread transformations in the prevailing views of morality indicate weak foundations. Interestingly, those who most protest social change are generally those who are "traditional," who still set more store by family or Church than by the changing currents of the larger society.

It was Hitler's genius to speak to a confused and alienated nation in ways that restored lost community, that put a confusion of facts into a coherent framework, that gave meaning and purpose. With different content, his techniques are with us today. *Mein Kampf* is difficult reading at best, repetitious, wandering, absurd—except for the sections on propaganda. The masses, Hitler wrote, are simple. They do not like confusion, they want clarity, black and white, yes and no. Propaganda has to be straightforward, it must say only a few things, but they must be repeated over and over again until the message has been pounded into the masses. It must appeal to the emotions, and it must show the world as a meaningful whole. Hitler specifically rejected the idea that merely anything could be done with propaganda. Even a great movement, he thought, had to watch anxiously lest it lose contact with the broad masses. To mock French soldiers during World War I, for example, had been a mistake, for the propaganda succeeded in convincing some German soldiers, who were rudely surprised to find that the French soldier in the trenches was a dangerous and determined foe. Finally, propaganda had to be total; it could not tolerate naysayers.

To render their propaganda effective, the Nazis needed to remove the foundations of non-Nazi attitudes. William Sheridan Allen's illuminating book *The Nazi Seizure of Power: The Experience of a Single German Town* describes the "atomization of society," Nazism's campaign to destroy small groups, clubs, and family ties that could sanction anti-Nazi attitudes. These ancient and intimate groups were replaced by a nationwide pseudocommunity of like-feeling, like-thinking men and women. The hundreds of thousands who annually gathered in Nuremberg for the party rally were told they were part of a mystical national community of blood and race, but that community was not one to support much individual differentiation.

We should not conclude that, in practice, Western democracies are necessarily better at solving the problem of the individual in mass society. We have already noted societal changes. People come to identify with "everyone else," a vague entity at best. David Riesman's evocative phrase, now thirty years old—"the lonely crowd"—describes the emptiness many feel. It is interesting that even on university campuses, where students are surrounded by thousands, even tens of thousands of people of like age and interests, loneliness and a sense of isolation are among the more frequent problems counseling centers encounter.

Julius Streicher's anti-Semitic crusade provided one way of overcoming the sense of isolation. The dedicated followers who were his *Stürmer* Guards had a sense of participating in a struggle of immense importance. The feelings engendered by such cooperative endeavor, however misguided, remain powerful. They are the kinds of feeling that make men look back on wartime military service with pride—a sense of having been a small yet significant part of an important enterprise, a transcendent fellowship of the trenches. Both Hitler and Streicher looked back with satisfaction on those deadly days. The devoted *Stürmer* reader had a purpose in life, something of greater import than his factory or office job, an ultimate meaning to an otherwise hollow life.

Most *Stürmer* readers were less rabid, finding other ways to deal with modern society. Yet many of them also accepted and acted on what Streicher urged. It must be remembered that the anti-Semitic propaganda they received was *total*. So far we have looked only at Julius Streicher's work, but there was an enormous amount of anti-Semitic propaganda coming from other sources. The earliest Nazi documents speak of a hatred of the Jews. The "Twenty-five Points" of the 1920 party platform already state that only those of German blood are to be citizens and that Jews are to be excluded from public office and the mass media. Nazi propaganda before 1933 constantly accused Jews of responsibility for Germany's ills. A standard speech titled "Lenin or Hitler," which Goebbels regularly gave in the late 1920s, contains over thirty specific uses of the term "Jew," the thesis of the speech being that Jews were Germany's central problem.

With Hitler as chancellor, the whole force of party and state turned to Jew-baiting. Anti-Jewish legislation developed steadily, both because Hitler understood that immediate drastic measures would lead to popular hostility and because the Nazis themselves were not sure what to do with the Jews. But the forces of propaganda heated up immediately. The *Stürmer* was only the most notorious. There was the *Schwarze Korps,* the SS weekly, almost as crude as the *Stürmer* but not devoted with such single-mindedness to assailing Jews. The many local and national Nazi newspapers and magazines joined in, and so with time did the entire German press.

We have already seen that Streicher's materials were used in the schools, but even in those areas where his material was thought unsuitable for children, less blunt ways of presenting anti-Semitism were available. Nazi racial theory became a standard part of the biology curriculum, and history found in anti-Semitism an explanation for much of the past. Bernhard Rust, the Nazi minister of education, directed teachers in 1935 to instruct students in "the nature, causes, and effects of all racial and hereditary problems." Teachers were to see to it "that no boy or girl should leave school without complete knowledge of the necessity and meaning of blood purity."[2]

Culture was transformed. During the Weimar era many leaders in the arts were Jewish. Nazism resolved that difficulty by establishing a Reich Chamber of Culture, with subsections for the various arts and media. To be employed in any aspect of culture required membership in the relevant subsection, for which membership Jews were ineligible. Nazism speedily produced novels, films, and plays in which Jews went about dastardly deeds. Art that was the work of Jews was proscribed. Many thousands of paintings were burned along with books, and music by Jewish composers was no longer played.

Leading officials of party and state (whose roles often overlapped) attacked the Jews. Hitler, Goebbels, and Streicher, the big three Jew-baiters, were joined in their calumnies by men like labor leader Robert Ley, Alfred Rosenberg, Heinrich Himmler, and hosts of lesser party functionaries. We have already noted the anti-Semitic legislation that restricted Jewish civil liberties in many ways, which legislation continued even into the war. In 1939, for example, Hitler ordered all Jewish males to adopt Israel as their middle name, and all Jewish women Sarah. Later those Jews still in Germany had to wear a yellow star.

The churches lamentably contributed to the general campaign. A third of German Protestantism joined to form the German Christian movement, dedicated to the challenging task of reconciling the teachings of Christ with those of the Führer. The German Christians, of course, refused membership to Jews. Even those Catholics and Protestants who saw the contradiction between their faith and Hitler generally lacked the will, the interest, or the courage to proclaim their opposition publicly and forcefully, though there were some shining exceptions among them.

As a consequence Germans encountered anti-Semitism almost everywhere, in schools and churches, newspapers and magazines, films and literature. Streicher was distinctive not in the message he preached, but in the vehemence and energy with which he spread it. Few were the naysayers. The occasional jurist or cleric, or the tens of thousands of courageous Germans who refused to bow to the spirit of the day did not outbalance the far greater weight of anti-Semitic propaganda coming from every channel of influence. The early years, 1933–35, were milder in tone and the effects of anti-Semitism less evident, but by the time the war was on most of the nation had come to accept enough of the propaganda to render it indifferent to the fate of the Jews.

It is not surprising that so many Germans came to accept at least part of the Nazi gospel. The torrent of facts was most impressive. A person did not have to believe all or even most of it to become uninterested in the fate of the Jews. "Where there's smoke there's fire," the saying goes—and it was difficult to believe that the entire public-opinion apparatus was lying about the Jews, particularly given the distressing but undeniable popularity Hitler enjoyed. To remain resistant to Hitler's propaganda required rejecting the full force of the mass media. Even those who are suspicious of what they read rarely go that far. There simply was no easy way to corroborate non-Nazi views.

Before concluding that the citizens of a democracy are better prepared to resist the propaganda that reaches them, consider several things. In recent American history there have been many cases in which public opinion shifted almost instantly. Besides the Iranian situation, consider the Gulf of Tonkin incident, the *Mayaguez* incident, or the Cuban missile crisis. What is important is not so much the rightness or wrongness of the attitude as the speed with which it was reached. More than that, Americans face a centralized mass media that differs in its effective power surprisingly little from that of Hitler's Germany. Two major wire services and three major networks along with several newspapers and magazines with their own staffs of foreign correspondents determine most of the domestic and foreign news Americans receive. These sources have a common bond to the status quo. Of course, they differ on specific policies, but in every case they are controlled by people with understandable interests in the existing system. The *Washington Post* is unlikely to urge that the Constitution be replaced with a Marxist dictatorship of the proletariat, and were it to do so its circulation would drop markedly. Of course, there are many less powerful sources of opinion in the United States, with every shade of politics, but their circulation and influence are limited.

This is not to disparage the virtues of an open society or to suggest that it makes no difference whether one lives in Chicago or Moscow. A person who stood up in Red Square to advocate the overthrow of the Soviet state would receive immediate and drastic punishment. A Communist in the United States may proclaim his message with limited fear of legal harassment. But in either case the message reaches few people. It goes against the prevailing propaganda, and it fails even to affect most of those who chance upon it.

A remarkably comprehensive set of forces joins to produce loyal American citizens, without the central planning characteristic of totalitarian states, but effective nonetheless. From the "Pledge of Allegiance" in the schools to the placement of a Christian flag next to the national flag in the churches, from evening television to the Bicentennial, Americans hear of their country's greatness. The Boy Scouts and the Girl Scouts foster patriotism. Advertising, whatever the product, is also a brief for the system that made such plenty possible. Frances FitzGerald's work on American history textbooks has demonstrated how they are rewritten each generation, in a real sense changing history, to meet the demands of a new day.

The barrage of facts Americans receive testifying to the greatness of their society is enormous, but it is surprising how many are uncertain of the principles upon which their society rests. In some of my university classes I take on the role of a visiting citizen of the Soviet Union who, in typical Soviet fashion, denounces capitalism and the United States. Remarkably few of my students can respond with a cogent defense. They *know* their nation is superior, they have been told so all their lives, but when the few arguments they have are dealt with they are suddenly confused and alarmed. They have many facts but few arguments.

Julius Streicher too depended not on careful argument, but on a barrage of facts consistent with the larger currents of the nation. Even those who did not accept his entire argument remained influenced. To assume that we in the same situation would remain immune is pleasant but dangerously false. Anti-Semitism surely would have greater difficulty succeeding on a mass scale in the United States, but the reason is not our lesser susceptibility to propaganda. Rather there are differences in our society that would make it harder, but not impossible, to get anti-Semitism across. Antiblack rhetoric has always been more popular in the United States than Jew-baiting, but there is an indigenous American anti-Semitic tradition that remains to this day. Organizations like the Ku Klux Klan spread anti-Semitic material as noxious as any Streicher put out and seem to be gaining adherents today. And the Middle East situation has produced serious advances in the appeal of anti-Semitism.

As Ellul observes, propaganda formerly was thought to modify attitudes, but today its primary interest is in behavior. Often attitudes are constructed to explain, after the fact, why we did something. The man who cheats on his income-tax return the first time may feel guilty about his dishonesty, but by the next time he will have modified his attitudes in such a way that he believes cheating the government is no longer dishonest. When we stand to sing the National Anthem, when we vote, when we pay our taxes, we are performing actions that in turn strengthen our attitudes.

The German situation was much the same. Germans needed ways in which they could express their union with Hitler's national community. We have seen that Streicher's most dedicated followers, by actively attacking the Jews, could find purpose to life. Yet the far greater number who responded more with indifference than with outright hatred were also persuaded by their own actions. The German who walked past a Jewish shop, the woman who ignored a Jewish neighbor, the child who mocked a Jewish child, these and a multitude of everyday actions were critically significant. Whatever their cause, the person had behaved in anti-Jewish ways, and this behavior would influence his later actions, inevitably making the next step easier.

Interestingly, the greatest opposition Nazism encountered in its Jew-baiting policies came when sudden steps were taken. The April 1933 boycott, for example, offended many Germans. In 1938, after five years of crude anti-Semitic propaganda, large numbers of Germans were still disgusted by the violence of Crystal Night. Even during the war there was difficulty. When, for example, Berlin authorities attempted to close down a retirement home for elderly Jews, a large crowd gathered to protest the operation, much to Goebbels' horror. These kinds of actions required a greater commitment to anti-Semitism than many Germans had. But those same Germans accepted gradually increasing sanctions against the Jews. Slow growth gave time for inconspicuous shifts in attitude.

Anti-Semitism also provided meaning, even faith. For rabid anti-Semites it was a world view by itself, but even nominal anti-Semites could explain goings-on in much of the world by partially accepting the Nazi dogma of Jewish conspiracy. The flood of particular bits of information we receive needs general explanations, or else the universe is simply a chaotic and random collection of unrelated facts. Regrettably, many things are not easily explained. Economists have difficulty explaining to a confused public how a national economy works. To understand the Soviet Union or Islam is the work of a lifetime. Religion provides exactly the kind of overarching explanation that makes the significance of particulars clear, demonstrated by the continuing appeal of traditional religions as well as the rise of forces like the cults.

For those who cannot accept traditional answers, or for those to whom they are of insufficient power, a second source of transcendent truth can be a political movement. Hitler specifically maintained that religion and politics were close kin, filling many of the same needs. The party, the state, or the revolution can give sanction to the individual life. Conspiracy theories equally provide a simple framework that explains much. Conspiracies do of course exist, but the enthusiasm with which even improbable ones are accepted suggests the satisfactions they provide. The popularity of conspiratorial explanations for John F. Kennedy's assassination is intriguing. To assume a popular President could be killed by a lone crank suggests that the world is a cold, uncaring place where chance rules more than virtue, an uncomfortable theory. To believe instead that Kennedy was killed by an organized conspiracy of great power is more satisfying—at least the magnitude of the cause is now commensurate with that of the effect. A conspiracy makes "sense" of otherwise inexplicable happenings. At various times in American history large numbers of people believed in conspiracies of Masons, Catholics, water fluoridators, Communists, anarchists, socialists, new and old rights and lefts; the list could go on.

Streicher's anti-Semitism drew on each of the strains we have discussed. It appealed to the religious legacy that had long derogated Jews, incorporating into it the political faith of National Socialism. To that was added the modern "scientific" anti-Semitism and the notion of a powerful worldwide conspiracy of evil Jews. Once one accepted the premise that Jews were suspect, the whole structure had remarkable power. World wars, economic crises, governmental corruption, and crime had a common cause. Such a conclusion greatly simplifies a person's world view. Each problem would be blamed on the Jews, and to solve the Jewish question would be to solve a host of others.

Finally there is the matter of emotional appeal. Propaganda, though superficially it may be based on facts and reason, best speaks to the emotions, and the easiest emotions to reach are pride, envy, and anger, three of the medieval canon of cardinal sins. For propaganda cannot take time to reason logically; that is a commitment to dialogue, to reaching individuals one by one, a slow and uncertain process. It is more effective to reach people in masses, and that takes emotional appeal. Getting people to hate, or at least dislike, their neighbor has never been difficult. We need not look as far as Germany for examples, as the American record is not innocent of harsh prejudice. The matter of antiblack prejudice is familiar, but the Irish, the Italians, the Jews, the Chinese and Japanese, all these and more have suffered.

The case of the Japanese is particularly instructive, for while Germans were incarcerating Jews because they were Jews, Americans were imprisoning Japanese because they were Japanese, even though many were U.S. citizens. That the United States did not resort to mass murder is of course critical, but the affair remains unsettling. Talking with a woman whose father had administered such a camp in California during World War II, I asked her about the justice of the policy. When she supported it I asked why we had not done the same to Americans of German descent. Though she was unwilling to make the argument plainly, it was clear that her reason was that Japanese looked different. Germans looked like most other Americans. Before too readily assuming that the Holocaust represents a peculiar German depravity, one should consider the rest of history. There has never been a time in human history, certainly not today, when it has not been possible to get one group of humanity so aroused against another that death was the result.

The point is not that emotional appeals are bad. They are not necessarily bad. Nor is it true that people can be convinced of any and all absurdities by using propaganda. Of course not. There are presuppositions of every age to which propaganda must attend. Ellul rightly observes that most modern people believe that man is naturally good, that his chief goal is happiness, that history progresses, and that all is material. Each culture in addition has its own traditions and convictions that propaganda will not prudently ignore. A nation committed to democracy will demand at least a democratic veneer.

But the principles that Streicher, and Nazism as a whole, used to wage war against the Jews are the same principles that, in different causes, are used in Western democracies or in China. The content differs, in very significant ways. Yet McLuhan's catchphrase "the medium is the message" is in important ways true. Regardless of the content, modern propaganda does things to people that in the long run are unfortunate. To be committed to democracy without knowing why is to be, as Ellul puts it, "a totalitarian man with democratic convictions."

The lesson to be learned from Julius Streicher's propaganda, and from the horrendous effects his work and that of others like him had, is not that people believe nonsense. That has been evident for millennia. It is instead that we are no more immune to the forces of propaganda than were the citizens of Hitler's Germany. The Holocaust was inevitable only in retrospect. Future disasters of perhaps equal magnitude may even now be forming. To assume that we are critical and rational human beings, making decisions on the evidence before us, is comfortable. It is also the conviction many readers of the *Stürmer* held.

Afterword to the Cooper Square Press Edition

Since I wrote this book nearly twenty years ago, two developments need amplification, one briefly, the other in more detail.

The first is the Internet as a medium for promoting racism. While American racists have always reprinted some of Streicher's material, bigots now have a less expensive way to reach a wider audience. Some sites have revived Streicher's brand of anti-Semitism in particular. One person even plagiarized sections of the first edition of this book. He chose material he could twist to present Julius Streicher in a favorable light.

Fortunately, the Internet also makes it possible to provide a virtual appendix to this book. In 1996 I established the German Propaganda Archive (www.calvin.edu/academic/cas/gpa/) a large collection of translations of Nazi and East German propaganda. My goal is to make available, in English, the original materials of the two German dictatorships of the twentieth century. The site includes translations from the *Stürmer* and other products of Streicher's publishing house.

The longer matter concerns the controversy occasioned by Daniel Jonah Goldhagen's 1996 book *Hitler's Willing Executioners: Ordi-*

nary Germans and the Holocaust. His thesis is that the great majority of ordinary Germans were characterized by an "eliminationist anti-Semitism" that would have led them to kill Jews had they had the opportunity. He states his case directly:

> Germans' anti-Semitic beliefs about Jews were the central causal agent of the Holocaust. They were the central causal agent not only of Hitler's decision to annihilate European Jews (which is accepted by many) but also of the perpetrators' willingness to kill and to brutalize Jews. The conclusion of this book is that anti-Semitism moved many thousands of "ordinary" Germans—and would have moved millions more, had they been appropriately positioned—to slaughter Jews. Not economic hardship, not the coercive means of a totalitarian state, not social psychological pressure, not invariable psychological propensities, but ideas about Jews that were pervasive in Germany, and had been for decades, induced ordinary Germans to kill unarmed, defenseless Jewish men, women, and children by the thousands, systematically and without pity.[1]

Most scholars of the Holocaust criticize Goldhagen's book. None of them deny that large numbers of Germans held to varying degrees of anti-Semitism, but they doubt that most Germans were anti-Semitic with the intensity necessary for Goldhagen's case to stand. The eminent historian Saul Friedländer, for example, wrote in 1997: "It seems, however, that the majority of Germans, although undoubtedly influenced by various forms of traditional anti-Semitism and easily accepting the segregation of the Jews, shied away from widespread violence against them, urging neither their expulsion from the Reich nor their physical annihilation."[2]

As I followed the controversy, it astonished me that the *Stürmer* came down on Friedländer's side. This book centers on the anti-Semitic side of Streicher's activity, but the *Stürmer* also provides ample evidence that many Germans were not, by any reasonable definition, "eliminationist anti-Semites." The major part of the *Stürmer*'s activities were directed against Jews, but as this book notes (174–178), a smaller part targeted Germans who were not sufficiently hostile to Jews. I gave that aspect relatively little attention in writing *Julius*

Streicher, but have since revisited the *Stürmer* to look for evidence of opposition to Nazi anti-Semitic views. There is a great deal of it.

Stürmer readers denounced their fellow citizens with considerable energy for having relations with Jews. In this activity they were not alone. A variety of recent works have looked at denunciations in the Third Reich, generally based on Gestapo or court records. Robert Gellately, after surveying Gestapo files for the Würzburg area, concludes:

> The enforcement of Nazi anti-Semitic policies required—once the regime set the tone of official "line" on the "Jewish Question" and could count on enough zealous officials in place to press anti-Semitism home—that a sufficient number of people come forward, for whatever reason, to offer information when they witnessed non-compliant acts of any kind. Nazi anti-Semitism would in all likelihood have remained impossible to enforce if this requirement had not been met.[3]

The Gestapo, however, was only part of the process that enforced Nazi anti-Semitic policy. At least as important were the acts of people who did not go so far as to involve the Gestapo, but rather made it clear to fellow citizens that they were being watched. The *Stürmer* was a major outlet for such denunciations.

Some wrote from private motives. As noted earlier, the *Stürmer* received many anonymous letters, which supposedly were immediately thrown away. Only letters that were signed and contained evidence (e.g., the names of witnesses or the testimony of local Nazi Party officials) were considered for publication.[4] But enough met the *Stürmer*'s guidelines to fill about 10 percent of its editorial content with denunciations not of Jews, but of Germans.

Between January 1935 and September 1939, Germans denounced 6,586 of their fellow citizens by name in the *Stürmer* for being insufficiently hostile to Jews. Those denounced were ordinary people. Some knew the risk they were taking and were not deterred; others changed their ways after facing public opprobrium. The number of denunciations increased markedly each year until 1939, at which point most Jews had emigrated or had been concentrated in larger cities; those remaining in Germany had been driven out of almost every area of public life. The following chart shows the growth in denunciations:

Year	Number of Germans Denounced in the *Stürmer*
1935	367
1936	417
1937	2,309
1938	3,029
1939	464

The increase in 1937 was largely the result of a column of brief items supplied by readers, a typical example of which is on pages 175–176. The first such column appeared in December 1936, the last in August 1939. The columns provided the names and addresses, if necessary, of citizens and companies who had dealings with Jews.

There were also hundreds of reader reports, often only slightly longer than the brief items, but sometimes running several paragraphs. The subjects of these reports were the same as the brief items, but more detail was provided. A group of readers in Silesia made regular reports in 1937 and 1938, often attacking Jews in the area, but also giving considerable attention to those having dealings with Jews. The *Stürmer* office in Berlin made biweekly reports focusing on Jews, but also listed Germans who dealt with them. Readers in other areas reported at occasional intervals.

With the exceptions of regular reports from a few large cities (e.g., Berlin, Cologne, Hamburg), the majority of these reports came from smaller towns and villages, places where everyone knew everyone else. When reports did arrive from large cities, sometimes they were lengthy. A March 1938 report listed 204 Germans who patronized Jewish shops in Berlin; four months later, a report from Münster named German patients of Jewish doctors.[5] But these were unusual. The overwhelming majority of reports gave a small number of names. The 1,122 brief items for 1938 identified a total of 1,700 people, their names always highlighted in bold type.

Many of these reports are clearly the work of "true believers," dedicated anti-Semites not seeking personal gain (though some certainly were out to settle scores or to advance their own interests), but rather in "educating" their fellow citizens. Often, the anti-Semites began along the lines of this 1937 report from Dresden: "We have warned the public often enough and asked them to buy only from German merchants. Since our warnings and requests have not been followed, we have no choice but to publish the names of those Jew-lovers who shop at the Jewish firm Salm-Spiegel."[6] These letter writers suggest that only after their long-suffering efforts at persuasion failed did they turn to naming names.

These denunciations suggest fairly widespread indifference—and sometimes hostility—toward Nazi anti-Semitic policies. The thousands of citizens named are only a fraction of those whom readers could have named. Repeatedly, articles note that a list is partial; the writers hope that the yet-unnamed citizens will draw the proper conclusion from the publication of the names of others.

What were the offenses that moved readers to report their neighbors to the *Stürmer*? Unlike the remainder of the paper's content, which included some quite implausible material, the denounced offenses were always believable. *Stürmer* readers were not interested in allegations of ritual murder or vast international conspiracies, but in day-to-day human social interaction.

Of those named, 68 percent were accused of business dealings with Jews. Nine percent had visited a Jewish professional; 5 percent were German professionals who accepted Jewish clients. Eighteen percent had friendly relations with Jews or extended simple courtesies. Two hundred twenty-four priests, pastors, or other religious citizens were accused of offenses ranging from baptizing Jews to protecting their belongings during the pogrom of November 9, 1938, to denouncing anti-Semitism or the *Stürmer* from the pulpit. Some citizens had their marriages to Jews pilloried in print.

Two-thirds of the complaints about business dealings included every aspect of commerce. *Stürmer* readers were often from rural areas; many accused farmers of selling or buying livestock from Jews. In towns and cities readers collected lists of customers of Jewish shops. Hotel owners who accepted Jewish guests or merchants who bought from Jewish wholesalers were other common offenders. Surprisingly, the *Stürmer* sometimes carried the responses of such people. Some of the accused claimed that Jews provided better quality at lower prices. A farmer who took Jewish children for a cart ride asserted, "The government does not ask me where the money came from when I pay my taxes."[7] To *Stürmer* readers, such comments emphasized stubborn refusal to relinquish contact with Jews. The criticized behavior sometimes displayed clear opposition to Nazi anti-Semitic policies, at other times only the person's economic self-interest. Those denounced in the *Stürmer* might still have harbored anti-Semitic attitudes.

Still, the behavior is clearly not what one would expect of those holding eliminationist anti-Semitic views. This was particularly true by 1937, when Hitler had been in power for more than four years. Those who had thought that the Nazis were anti-Semites of the traditional variety had had sufficient time to learn otherwise. To shop at a Jewish store or to trade with a Jewish livestock dealer by 1937 took a conscious decision to ignore the considerable pressures of the state and society.

Fellow citizens who attempted to conceal their Jewish business dealings particularly aggravated *Stürmer* readers. A report from Silesia, for example, complained that many citizens ordered goods from Jewish shops by telephone and had their purchases delivered in plain wrappers.[8] Regularly, readers encountered the excuse that the buyer had not known the shop in question was Jewish. A variety of articles warned citizens that, in the future, such excuses would no longer prevent public exposure. Concealing the transaction indicated an awareness that not only was the exchange risky, but also that the buyer was disregarding the Nazi argument that buying from Jews was treasonous.

Those accused of social relations with Jews were of even greater alarm to loyal readers. Any form of social contact was objectionable. Readers supplied lists of neighbors who attended Jewish funerals and frequently noted that the attendees were grief-stricken. One woman, for example, was so moved by the loss of her friend that "tears ran down to her neck."[9] From the informant's point of view, this was evidence of particular depravity. There were regular reports of people who walked or played cards with Jews or received them as guests. The percentage of such denunciations increased in 1939 as Nazi pressure made it impossible for Jews to own shops or to practice their professions. Germans might no longer have economic relations with Jews, but to the *Stürmer*'s distress some held to friendship and common decency.

Another sign of public opposition to official, Nazi-generated anti-

Semitism came in the often-expressed sense loyal readers had that they were fighting a hard fight against a recalcitrant audience. Long after 1933, the newspaper's loyal readers, the *"Stürmer* Guards," portrayed themselves as lonely battlers for the "truth." In the summer of 1936, three years into the Third Reich, a *Stürmer* informant wrote:

> The village of Bundorf in Franconia belongs to those areas in which National Socialist thinking as yet has little footing. Those of foreign race are still welcome guests here. Many Bundorf farmers do business almost exclusively with the Jews. Even party members and members of the women's organization have friendly relations with the descendants of the Christ-killers. . . . The few upright German citizens who live in Bundorf are ashamed to have to live with people who betray the New Germany every day.[10]

Even into 1939, letters noted that a great deal of educational work remained to be done before every last "decent German" had joined the anti-Semitic cause. Those who dealt with Jews were called cowards—a peculiar accusation given the overwhelming pressure the Third Reich exerted to separate Germans and Jews in every sphere of life.

Some correspondents reported being insulted when they attempted to encourage people to avoid Jews. A 1938 letter gave the response of a woman in Silesia who, when reproached for buying in a Jewish shop, replied, "You're drunk, aren't you?"[11] A farmer criticized in 1939 for dealing with Jews responded bluntly, "Hang me from the church steeple if you want, but I'm not going to stop dealing with the Jews."[12] Many letters noted that well-meaning attempts to dissuade citizens from dealing with Jews were simply ignored. Often they wrote, in apparent astonishment, that someone had conversed with a Jew "in broad daylight" or "in the fifth year of National Socialism" or visited a Jewish shop "on November 10, [1938]!"

Readers often complained about their social betters and took particular pleasure in reporting the names of the upper class who had relations with Jews. A vivid example appeared in 1938:

> The *Stürmer* is warning these "ladies" today. If the warning bears no fruit, the *Stürmer* will have to secure the customer list of the Jewish

dressmaking shop Aronheim. It will have to make public the names of all of these "ladies." And to avoid confusion, it will have to give the addresses where these "ladies" live. It will have to provide the names and occupations of their dear husbands.[13]

There were many similar comments. The upper classes were those with the most to lose by flouting the prevailing anti-Semitism, yet many seem to have avoided becoming eliminationist anti-Semites.

It is also interesting that the number of denunciations increased with time. Before 1933, and in the early years of the Third Reich, those who dealt with Jews were often presented as ignorant. Dennis Showalter's excellent book on the *Stürmer* in the years before Hitler's takeover in 1933 demonstrates that most letters from readers denounced Jews, not Germans.[14] There were exceptions, but before Hitler's takeover the *Stürmer* was far more interested in attacking Jews than Germans.

After 1933 anti-Semitism became the nation's established policy. The *Stürmer* was no longer a voice in the wilderness, but rather a newspaper with mass circulation and the outward support, at least, of the leading figures of party and state. Perhaps Streicher expected that, if given only a little encouragement, the mass of Germans would join his loyal readers in hating Jews. In the first several years of the Third Reich, the *Stürmer* was relatively cautious in attacking Germans. When accusations were made, reports often gave only the initials of those involved. Even in 1935 comparatively few names of Germans were provided.

It became clear, however, that a significant percentage of the population was not prepared to hate Jews. Yet as the number of Jews in Germany decreased and as they were driven from public life, the number of denunciations also grew, driven by the sheer momentum of anti-Semitic sentiment that refused to recognize the ever-diminishing pool of victims. The calendar year 1938 had the most denunciations, perhaps reflecting prewar anxiety toward a country's outsiders. It marked the culmination of prewar, Nazi anti-Semitic policy. It was the year Jews were finally prohibited from most professions and driven from businesses. It was also the year of the "spontaneous" *Kristallnacht*, or "Night of Broken Glass," the Nazi-organized pogrom that resulted in the arrests, incarcerations, and murder of Jews and in the destruction of synagogues and Jewish-owned businesses across Germany and the recently annexed Austria. The single three-month period with the greatest number of names—over 1,300—was January through March 1938. That five years into the Third Reich there were still so many denunciations is evidence that many Germans refused to view Jews in the way that the Nazis wanted.

The *Stürmer* was not alone in denouncing Germans for dealing with Jews. Other Nazi newspapers and party offices excoriated those who associated with Jews. Studies of Gestapo denunciations and of anti-Nazi resistance by ordinary Germans provide further evidence. The Catholic and Protestant churches did too little, but still some clergy and believers—fueled by the moral imperatives of their own individual consciences—resisted Nazi anti-Semitism. All this in no way denies that the considerable majority of the German population held to varying levels of anti-Semitism. It does show, however, that there was no widespread public sentiment in favor of killing Jews.

When Goldhagen argues that most Germans were eliminationist anti-Semites, he overstates the case. Some *Stürmer* readers met his definition, but even most of them disliked Jews without giving evidence of wanting to kill them. Increasing numbers of villages announced themselves "free of Jews," but readers who reported that fact did not seem concerned that their former Jewish neighbors, though relocated, were still alive. Those very readers provided evidence in their letters that they were not typical of the German population as a whole. In denouncing their decent and compassionate fellow citizens, they felt themselves members of a crusade that lacked universal support and predicted it would take a long time before they could win the struggle to remake all Germans to their anti-Semitic image. Hitler found his willing executioners—a number ample enough to slaughter millions—but he did not have the whole citizenry of Germany from which to choose.

RANDALL L. BYTWERK
Grand Rapids, Michigan
January 2001

Appendix I

Three *Stürmer* Articles

The first article comes from special edition No. 4 of 1936, devoted to Alfred Fabian, accused of numerous crimes. It is titled "The Jewish Race."

Alfred Fabian does not belong to the German people. German blood does not flow in his veins. He is a Jew. He is a member of the Jewish race. Of all the races on earth, the Jewish race stands in greatest contrast to the German race. The German works and creates in an honorable way; the Jew is the great enemy of productive work. The German tills the soil, builds houses, establishes industries; the Jew practices low trades, speculation, usury, and exploitation. This he has done since the beginning. He has to, for he can do nothing else. His blood carries not honor, uprightness, and honesty, rather criminality, fraud, hypocrisy, lies, the lust for defilement, and the lust for murder. From the beginning the Jew has committed crime after crime. He ruined the Egyptians and killed their firstborn. He destroyed Canaan and made the land subject to him. He ruined Babylon and Persia. He incited the terrible and murderous revolutions against Rome. He lived in all nations during the Middle Ages, his criminality leading to repeated barbaric punishments and persecutions. He does the same today, for he has inherited the blood of his forefathers, and with their blood, their criminality. The Jew Fabian is a worthy son of his fathers. He is a splendid example of his race. He has in his blood the characteristics of his forefathers, the characteristics of the Jewish race, and is therefore a great criminal. He is a great criminal because he is a Jew.

But it is not only the inherited Jewish characteristics that drove Fabian to criminality. He who wants to understand the Jewish question and to understand entirely the Jew Fabian's drives must uncover a second secret. It is the secret of the Jewish law book, the Talmud. The Jewish people do not live in their own state, but among other nations. These nations have their own laws. The Jews obey these laws outwardly. In their own minds, however, they reject these laws. The Jew's blood, characteristics, and race rebel against them. A race that has drives toward the unnatural and toward criminality cannot recognize natural moral laws. Therefore the Jew created his own laws. Corresponding to the Jewish blood and character, these laws permit any crime against Gentiles. These laws are fifteen hundred years old. For fifteen hundred years the Jews have been taught and raised according to these laws. They are as holy and valid to them today as they were fifteen hundred years ago. In the Talmud it is written: "The Laws of the Talmud have precedence over all other laws. They are more important than the laws of Moses." (Rabbi Ishmael and Rabbi Chan bar ada, and others). In another place it says: "Anyone who acts contrary to the Talmud deserves death." (Erobin F. 21b Sanhedrin 46.) Thus he who wants to understand the Jewish question must know the Jewish race and the Jewish law book. As the Jewish question is the key to world history, the Talmud is the key to understanding the Jewish question.

If the *Stürmer* is to present the following story of Fabian in the proper way, it must refer constantly to the Talmud. The Talmud will reveal all the hidden relations that until now have been unseen by those who only superficially understand the Jewish question.

The next article is from the notorious 1934 ritual murder special edition of the *Stürmer*. The translation is from the 1976 "Julius Streicher Memorial Edition" of the *Christian Vanguard* and is reprinted with its permission. I have not corrected the numerous errors. (See figure 16 for the cover.)

Jewish Murder Plan
Against Gentile Humanity Exposed

The Murderous People

The Jews are under a terrible suspicion the world over. Who does not know this, does not understand the Jewish problem. Anyone who merely sees the Jews, as Heinrich Heine (Chaim Bueckburg) described them, "a tribe which secures its existence with exchange and old trousers, and whose uniforms are the long noses", is being misled. But anyone who knows the monstrous accusation which has been raised against the Jews since the beginning of time, will view these people in a different light. He will begin to see not only a peculiar, strangely fascinating nation; but criminals, murderers, and devils in human form. He will be filled with holy anger and hatred against these people.

The suspicion under which the Jews are held is murder. They are charged with enticing Gentile children and Gentile adults, butchering them and draining their blood. They are charged with mixing this blood into their masses [sic] (unleaven [sic] bread) and using it to practice superstitious magic. They are charged with torturing their victims, especially the children; and during this torture they shout threats, curses, and cast spells against the Gentiles. This systematic murder has a special name. It is called

Ritual Murder

The knowledge of Jewish ritual murder is thousands of years old. It is as old as the Jews themselves. The Gentiles have passed the knowledge of it from generation to generation, and it has been passed down to us through writings. It is known of throughout the nation. Knowledge of ritual murder can be found even in the most secluded rural villages. The grandfather told his grandchildren, who passed in on to his children, and his children's children, until we have inherited the knowledge today.

It is also befalling other nations. The accusation is loudly raised immediately, anywhere in the world, where a body is found which bears the marks of ritual murder. This accusation is raised only against the Jews. Hundreds and hundreds of nations, tribes, and races live on this earth, but no one ever thought to accuse them of the planned murdering of children or to call them murderers. All nations have hurled this accusation only against the Jews. And many great men have raised such an accusation. Dr. Martin Luther writes in his book "Of the Jews and Their Lies": "They stabbed and pierced the body of the young boy Simon of Trent. They have also murdered other children ... The sun never did shine on a more bloodthirsty and revengeful people as they, who imagine to be the people of God, and who desire to and think they must murder and crush the heathen. Jesus Christ, the Almighty Preacher from Nazareth, spoke to the Jews: 'Ye are of your father the devil, and the lusts of your father ye will do. He was a murderer from the beginning.'"

The Struggle of Der Stürmer

The only newspaper in Germany, yes, in the whole world, which often screams the accusation of ritual murder into the Jewish face is *Der Stürmer*. For more than ten years *Der Stürmer* has led a gigantic battle against Judaism. This has caused *Der Stürmer* to be under constant attack by the Jews. Dozens of times it has been confiscated and prohibited. Its workers, most of all its editor Julius Streicher, have been dragged to court hundreds of times. They were convicted, punished, and locked into prisons. *Der Stürmer* has come to know the Jew from the confession which Dr. Conrad Alberti-Sittenfeld, a Jew, wrote in 1899 in No. 12 of the magazine *Gesellschaft*:

> "One of the most dangerous Jewish qualities is the brutal, direct barbaric intolerance. A worse tyranny cannot be practiced than that which the Jewish clique practices. If you try to move against this Jewish clique, they will, without hesitating, use brutal methods to overcome you. Mainly the Jew tries to destroy his enemy in the mental area, by which he takes his material gain away, and undermines his civil existence. The vilest of all forms of retaliation, the boycott, is characteristically Jewish."

Der Stürmer has never been stopped. Just in Nuremberg alone there have been fought dozens of Talmudic and ritual murder cases in the courts. Because of the Jewish protests the attention of the whole world was focused on these cases. Thereafter heavy convictions followed. At first no judge had the guts to expose the Jewish problem. Finally in 1931 (court case lasting from Oct. 30th to No. 4th) *Der Stürmer* won its first victory. The jury found the following:

1. Der Stürmer is not fighting against the Jewish religion, but against the Jewish race.
2. The Talmud and Schulchan aruch are not religious books. They have no right to be protected under the religious paragraphs.
3. The laws of the Talmud which are quoted and published in Der Stürmer are exact quotations from the Talmud.
4. The laws of the Talmud are in harsh contradiction to German morals.
5. The Jews of today are being taught from the Talmud.

With this verdict *Der Stürmer* brought about the first big breach in the Jewish-Roman Administration of Justice, which was given the job before the National Socialist revolution to protect Judaism and its government. The Jews, of course, became greatly agitated about it all. But for *Der Stürmer* this success was an omen of the victory yet to come. Of course, *Der Stürmer* does not stop half way. It knows what must be done. It is our duty! to frustrate the gigantic murder plot of Judaism against humanity. It is our duty! to brand this nation before the whole world, to uncover its crimes and to render it harmless. It is our duty! to free the world from this national pest and parasitic race. *Der Stürmer* will fulfill its mission. It will light up the darkness with the truth which shall rule the world. And it will always direct itself according to the following proverb: "He who knows the truth and does not speak it truly is a miserable creature."

The third article is the lead article titled "Against the Death Blow," from the *Stürmer*, No. 12 (1943), signed by Julius Streicher.

He who lives the life of a criminal is always careful not to appear that way. His dark handiwork forces him to put on the mask of the honest man, the mask of the harmless.

The Jews live the lives of criminals. They have been told by their desert god El-Schaddei-Jahwe that it is their destiny to take to themselves the wealth produced by the work of the nations, to make themselves masters. At the moment the Jews began to enslave the peoples, and therefore to commit a crime against the world, they realized that they were in great danger. They were in danger of being annihilated if a threatened humanity became aware of their criminal deeds. It became necessary for the Jews to conceal their campaign for world domination so that the Gentiles would not be aware of the abyss before which they stood.

The course of world history is clear proof that the Jews actually succeeded in deceiving Gentile humanity about the worldwide danger of world Jewry. The Jews were masters at always understanding how to escape the danger they deserved. Indeed, they even succeeded in getting the Gentile peoples to believe that Jewry had through divine providence received a message for the salvation of humanity. The Jews have this spiritual conquest of the Aryan people who converted to Christianity to thank for the toleration that enabled them bit by bit to carry out their plan to enslave the world. The Christian command to love thy neighbor, which even demanded of its adherents that they include their enemy as an object of Christian love, made the rising hate against the Jews lose itself repeatedly in suicidal toleration.

Even so, world history proves that the voice of the blood could break down the barriers holding back racial and national self-consciousness. For thousands of years, in every century, popular uprisings have tried to remove the foreign-raced tormentors. But the popular uprisings lacked unified leadership. And so in the end the Jew could ever rest triumphant.

It was reserved for the twentieth century to defend the European peoples at the very brink of the abyss. Under the leadership of a German people awakened by National Socialism, Europe has undertaken total war. A total war that will give the death blow to the world-tormentor, Pan-Jewry.

Appendix II

Two Children's Stories from *The Poisonous Mushroom*

The first story is titled "What is the Talmud?" It accompanies figure 10.

Solly is thirteen years old. He is the son of the livestock-Jew Blumenstock from Langenbach. There is no Jewish school there. Solly therefore has to go to the German school. His schoolmates don't like him. Solly is fresh and insolent. There are always fights. And Solly is always responsible for them.

Today Solly doesn't have to go to school. He has to visit a rabbi in the city. A rabbi is a Jewish preacher. And this Jewish preacher wants to see if Solly has diligently studied the teachings of the Jewish religion. Solly has gone to the synagogue. A synagogue is the church of the Jews. The rabbi is waiting for him. He is an old Jew with a long beard and a genuine devil's face. Solly bows. The rabbi leads him to a reading table where there is a large, thick book. It is the Talmud. The Talmud is the secret law book of the Jews.

The rabbi begins the examination.

"Solly, you have a non-Jewish teacher in school. And every day you hear what the Gentiles say, what they believe, and the laws by which they live . . ."

Solly interrupts the rabbi.

213

"Yes, rabbi, I hear that every day. But that doesn't concern me. I am a Jew. I have laws to follow that are entirely different from those of the Gentiles. Our laws are written down in the Talmud."

The rabbi nods.

"Right! And now I want to hear what you know about them. Give me a few sayings or proverbs that you have heard in the Gentile school!"

Solly thinks. Then he says:

"A proverb of the Gentiles is: 'Work is no disgrace.'"

"What do the Gentiles mean by that?"

"They mean to say that it is no disgrace when one has to work."

"Do we Jews believe that?"

"No, we don't believe that! In our law book the Talmud it is written:

Work is noxious and not to be borne.

"Therefore we Jews don't work, but mostly engage in commerce. Gentiles are created to work. In the Talmud it also says:

The rabbi teaches: There is no lower occupation than farming. A Jew should neither plow the field nor plant grain. Commerce is far more bearable than tilling the soil."

The rabbi laughs.

"You've learned very well. But I know another Talmud passage that you must learn."

He opens the Talmud. Solly must read:

The Gentiles are created to serve the Jews. They must plow, sow, weed, dig, reap, bundle, sift, and grind. The Jews are created to find everything ready.

The rabbi continues his examination.

"Tell me several more principles or proverbs of the Gentiles!"

Solly answers:

"The Gentiles say: 'Be ever loyal and upright. Honor is the surest defense.'"

"What do the Gentiles mean by that?"

"They mean that one should always be honest in life. One should not lie and cheat. That's what the Gentiles say."

"And what do we Jews do?"

"We may lie and cheat Gentiles. In the Talmud it says:

It is permitted for Jews to cheat Gentiles. All lies are good.

"And furthermore it is written:

It is forbidden for a Jew to cheat his brother. To cheat a Gentile is permitted.

"When we loan the Gentiles money, we must demand usurious interest. For in the Talmud it is written:

Concerning robbery it is taught: Gentiles may not rob each other. The Gentile may not rob the Jews. But the Jews may at any time rob the Gentiles.

"It further says:

If a Jew has stolen something from a Gentile and the Gentile discovers it and demands it back, the Jew should simply deny it all. The Jewish court will stand by the Jew.

"It is also permitted for us Jews to buy stolen goods from a thief, when they come from Gentiles. We Jews may also be fences without sinning before our God. Smuggling and tax evasion are also permitted for us Jews. In the Talmud it is written that we may cheat Gentile authorities of customs and taxes. It says:

Smuggling is permitted, for it is written: You need not pay what you owe.

"Also thievery is permitted for Jews. But we may steal only from the Gentiles. The Talmud says:

The words "Thou Salt Not Steal" in the text refer only to thievery from Jews. Stealing from Gentiles is not meant.

"What does that mean?" the rabbi asked.

"That means that we cannot steal from or cheat Jews. But we can cheat Gentiles at any time. That is permitted for us."

The rabbi is satisfied.

"Excellent! In conclusion, give me several more laws from the Talmud."

Solly is delighted with the rabbi's praise. Solly says: "In the Talmud it is written:

Only the Jew is human. The Gentile peoples are not called people, rather they are named animals.

"And because we see Gentiles as animals, we call them *goy*. It is also permitted for us at any time to perjure ourselves before a Gentile court. In the Talmud it is written:

The Jew is permitted to swear falsely before a Gentile court. Such an oath is always to be seen as compelled. Even when a Jew swears by the name of God, he is allowed to tell a lie, and in his heart to reject the oath he has made.

"Furthermore, in the Book of Sirach it says:

Terrify all the nations, O Judah! Lift up your hands against the Gentiles! Incite the wrath of the Gentiles against each other and pour out anger! Shatter the princes who are enemies to the Jews.

"Enough!" interrupts the rabbi. He comes up to Solly and shakes his hand. Then he says:

"You are a fine Talmud student. You will become a real Jew. Always think about what the Talmud demands of you. The teachings and laws of the Talmud are more important and more to be obeyed than the laws of the Old Testament. The teachings of the Talmud are the words of the living Jewish god. He who breaks the laws of the Talmud deserves death. You should think about that throughout your whole life. If you always follow the Talmud laws diligently, you will join our biblical fathers in the Jewish heaven. Amen!"

> Murder, thievery, and lies
> Robbery, perjury, and cheating
> These are all permitted for the Jews,
> As every Jewish child knows.
>
> In the Talmud it is written,
> What Jews hate and what they love,
> What Jews think and how they live,
> All is ordained by the Talmud.

The second story is titled "Inge's Visit to a Jewish Doctor" and is accompanied by figure 22.

Inge is sick. For several days she has had a light fever and a headache. But Inge did not want to go to the doctor.

"Why go to the doctor for such a trifle?" she said again and again when her mother suggested it. Finally her mother insisted.

"March! Go to Dr. Bernstein and let him examine you!" her mother ordered.

"Why Dr. Bernstein? He is a Jew! And no real German girl goes to a Jew," Inge replied.

Her mother laughed.

"Don't talk nonsense! Jewish doctors are all right. They are always chattering nonsense about it at your BDM [League of German Girls] meetings. What do those girls know about it?"

Inge protested.

"Mother, you can say what you want, but you can't slander the BDM. You should know that we BDM girls understand the Jewish question better than many of our parents. Our leader gives a short talk about the Jews nearly every week. Just recently she said: 'A German may not go to a Jewish doctor! Particularly not a German girl! Because the Jews want to destroy the German people. Many girls who went to a Jewish doctor for healing found instead sickness and shame!' That's what our leader said, Mother. And she's right!"

Her mother grew impatient.

"You always think you know more than the grown-ups. What you said just isn't true. Look, Inge. I know Dr. Bernstein well. He is a fine doctor."

"But he is a Jew! And the Jews are our deadly enemies," Inge replied.

Now her mother became really angry.

"That's enough, you naughty child! Go to Dr. Bernstein right now! If you don't, I'll teach you how to obey me!"

Her mother screamed and raised her hand.

Inge did not want to be disobedient, so she went. Went to the Jewish doctor Bernstein!

Inge sits in the waiting room of the Jewish doctor. She had to wait a long time. She leafs through the magazines that are on the table. But she is much too nervous to be able to read more than a few sentences. Again and again she thinks back on the conversation with her mother. And again and again she recalls the warning of her BDM leader: "A German may not go to a Jewish doctor! Particularly a German girl! Many girls who went to a Jewish doctor for healing found instead sickness and shame!"

As Inge entered the waiting room, she had had a strange experience. From the examination room of the doctor came crying. She heard the voice of a girl:

"Doctor! Doctor! Leave me alone!"

Then she heard the scornful laugh of a man. Then all was suddenly silent. Breathlessly Inge had listened.

"What does all that mean?" she asked herself, and her heart beat faster. Once again she thought of the warnings of her BDM leader.

Inge has been waiting for an hour. Again she picks up the magazines and tries to read. Then the door opens. Inge looks up. The Jew appears. A cry comes from Inge's mouth. In terror she lets the newspaper drop. Terrified, she jumps up. Her eyes stare in the face of the Jewish doctor. And this face is the face of the Devil. In the middle of this devilish face sits an enormous crooked nose. Behind the glasses glare two criminal eyes. And a grin runs across the protruding lips. A grin that wants to say: "Now I have you at last, little German girl!"

The Jew comes toward her. His fat fingers grasp for her. But now Inge has recovered. Before the Jew can grab her she hits the fat face of the Jew-doctor. Then a leap to the door. Breathlessly Inge runs down the steps. Breathlessly she dashes out of the Jew-house.

In tears she returns home. Her mother is shocked to see her child.

"For God's sake, Inge! What happened?"

It is a long time before the child can say anything. Finally Inge tells about her experience with the Jew-doctor. Her mother listens in horror. And when Inge finishes her story, her mother lowers her head in shame.

"Inge, I shouldn't have sent you to a Jewish doctor. When you left I regretted it. I couldn't relax. I wanted to call you back. I suspected suddenly that you were right. I suspected that something would happen to you. But everything came out all right, thank God!"

Her mother moans, and tries to conceal her tears.

Gradually Inge calms down. She laughs again. "Mother, you've done a lot for me. Thank you. But you have to promise me something: about the BDM . . ."

Her mother doesn't let her finish.

"I know what you want to say, Inge. I promise. I'm finding that one can learn even from you children."

Inge nods.

"You're right, Mother. We BDM girls, we know what we want, even if we are not always understood. Mother, you taught me many sayings. Today I want to give you one to learn." And slowly and significantly Inge says:

> The Devil, it was he
> Who sent the Jew-doctor to Germany.
> Like a devil he defiles
> The German woman, Germany's honor.
>
> The German people, they'll not be sound
> Unless very soon the way is found
> To German healing, German ways,
> To German doctors in future days.

Notes

I: The Making of an Anti-Semite

1. *Fränkische Tageszeitung,* February 13, 1939. There is surprisingly only one published biography of Streicher, *The Number One Nazi Jew Baiter* by William Varga, though Klaus Kipphan has been working on one in German for some years. A helpful dissertation which has looked at Streicher's career is Carol Jean Ehlers' "Nuremberg, Julius Streicher and the Bourgeois Transition to Nazism, 1918–1924," Colorado, 1975.
2. Julius Streicher, "Das politische Testament Julius Streichers," *Vierteljahrshefte für Zeitgeschichte,* 26 (1978), 670.
3. Streicher, "Das politische Testament," 671.
4. The letter is in Offiziers-Personalakt No. 50.016 für Julius Streicher, Bayerisches Hauptstaatsarchiv, Munich.
5. Two accounts of the year's events, based on conversations with Streicher, are found in Heinz Preiss, *Die Anfänge der völkischen Bewegung in Franken,* diss. Erlangen 1937 (Erlangen: Verlag F. Willmy, 1937), p. 43, and Karl Holz, *Die Freiheitskampf in Franken* (Nuremberg: Stürmerverlag, 1933), pp. 5–6.
6. II National DSP Convention Report, Nachlass Streicher, folder 9, Bundesarchiv Koblenz.*

---

*Future references to Streicher's surviving personal files will take the form NS 9.

7. Julius Streicher, *Ruf zur Tat* (Nuremberg: Stürmerverlag, 1937), pp. 11–13.
8. II DSP Convention Report, NS 9.
9. Anonymous letter to Streicher, May 19, 1921, NS 9.
10. Dickel to Streicher, September 3 and September 5, 1921, NS 13.
11. Nuremberg police report of an April 4, 1922 meeting, Hauptarchiv der NSDAP, Hoover Institution Microfilm Version, reel 84, folder 1730.†
12. Kellerbauer to Streicher, August 27, 1922, NS 13.
13. Böhrer to Hitler, 28 September 1922, NS 52.
14. Streicher, *Ruf zur Tat,* p. 75.
15. Streicher, "Das politische Testament," 682–83.
16. The best account of the unpleasantness is in Robin Lenman, "Julius Streicher and the Origins of the NSDAP in Nuremberg, 1918–1923," in Anthony Nicholls and Erich Mattias, *German Democracy and the Triumph of Hitler* (London: George Allen & Unwin, 1971).
17. The documents are reprinted in Adolf Hitler, *Sämtliche Aufzeichnungen 1905–1924,* ed. Eberhard Jäckel and Axel Kuhn (Stuttgart: Deutsche Verlags-Anstalt, 1980), pp. 1057–58.
18. Julius Streicher, *Kampf dem Weltfeind* (Nuremberg: Stürmerverlag, 1938), pp. 24–25.
19. Kellerbauer made the charge during a July 22, 1924 DAP meeting, on which there is a police report in the HA, 17A/1731.
20. See a Nuremberg police report of an October 31, 1924 GVG meeting in Beckengarten, HA, 17A/1731.
21. Strasser's complaint is found in a Württemberg police report on radical movements, May 7, 1930, HA, 58/1403.
22. The affair is described in Luppe's autobiography in the Nachlass Luppe, Bundesarchiv Koblenz, folder 10, pp. 548–49.
23. Cited in an unpublished manuscript by Heinz Preiss, HA, 25/508.
24. See the Nuremberg police report of an April 16, 1929 Nazi meeting in the HA, 85/1733.

†Future references to the Hauptarchiv documents will take the form HA, 84/1730.

25. Luppe's autobiography, folder 10, p. 536.
26. Nuremberg police report of an April 4, 1922 DW meeting, HA, 84/1730.
27. Statement by Walter Berlin to the International Military Tribunal, December 27, 1945, in the Wiener Library Eyewitness Collection, P. III, f. 6.
28. See Randall L. Bytwerk, "Rhetorical Aspects of the Nazi Meeting: 1926-1933," *Quarterly Journal of Speech,* 61 (1975), 307-18.
29. Cited by Varga.
30. Würzburg police report of an October 15, 1929 Nazi meeting there, HA, 85/1733.
31. *Der Angriff,* August 16, 1935, cited from a typescript copy in NS 3.
32. *The New York Times,* November 10, 1937, p. 24.
33. The statement, by a Principal Grimm, dated December 4, 1924, is in the HA, 97/AL 13.
34. The clipping is in the HA, 85/1732.
35. *Völkischer Beobachter,* October 20, 1930.
36. See the police reports of an April 29, 1922 DW meeting in Bottenheim and an October 13, 1932 meeting in Nuremberg, HA, 84/1730 and 85/1734.
37. *Völkischer Beobachter,* August 23, 1927.
38. Bimonthly report of the Mittelfranken government, HA, 85/1734.
39. Munich police report of a February 19, 1932 Nazi meeting there, HA, 88/1846.
40. Fürth police report of an April 17, 1924 DAP meeting, HA, 17A/1731.
41. See Erwin Hilbig, "Sind Feierstunden notwendig?" *Unser Wille und Weg,* 9 (1939), 164-65.
42. See Koch to Streicher, September 18, 1922, NS 91, and Lacher to Streicher, March 9, 1929, NS 81.
43. Otto Strasser and Michael Stern, *Flight from Terror* (New York: R. M. McBride, 1943), p. 107.
44. Nuremberg police report of a June 16, 1924 GVG meeting in Nuremberg, HA, 17A/1731.
45. Franz Buchner, *Kamerad! Halt aus!* (Munich: F. Eher, 1942), pp. 103-4.

46. Konrad Heiden, *A History of National Socialism* (New York: Alfred A. Knopf, 1935), p. 48.

II: The Bloody Czar of Franconia

1. Edward Peterson, *The Limits of Hitler's Power* (Princeton, N.J.: Princeton University Press, 1969), p. 228. Peterson has a fascinating chapter on Streicher's career during the 1930s.
2. The best account of the affair is Utho Grieser's *Himmlers Mann in Nürnberg: Der Fall Benno Martin* (Nuremberg: Stadtarchiv Nürnberg, 1974), pp. 14–71.
3. Grieser, p. 10.
4. *The Trial of the Major War Criminals before the International Military Tribunal,* Vol. 28 (Nuremberg: U.S. Government Printing Office, 1947–49), p. 149.
5. *The New York Times,* December 23, 1938, p. 12.
6. See David Pryce-Jones, *Unity Mitford* (New York: Dial Press/ James Wade, 1977), pp. 121–36.
7. *Der Stürmer,*‡ No. 7 (1933) and No. 13 (1933).
8. Cited by Peterson, p. 231.
9. *International Military Tribunal,* Vol. 28, pp. 55–234.
10. *Fränkische Tageszeitung,* February 13, 1939.
11. Streicher to Göring, August 2, 1939, NS 127.
12. Streicher to Hess, November 7, 1939, NS 127.
13. The best account of the tribunal is in Grieser, pp. 179–96.
14. Adolf Hitler, *Hitler's Table Talk: 1941–1944,* ed. H. R. Trevor-Roper (London: George Weidenfeld & Nicolson, 1953), pp. 155–56.
15. Joseph Goebbels, *Final Entries 1945,* ed. H. R. Trevor-Roper, trans. Richard Barry (New York: G. P. Putnam's Sons, 1978), p. 227.
16. *Evening Standard,* April 24, 1945. A clipping is in the Wiener Library files.
17. *The New York Times,* May 24, 1945, p. 1.
18. Werner Maser, *Nuremberg: A Nation on Trial,* trans. Richard Barry (New York: Charles Scribner's Sons, 1979), pp. 51–52.

‡Future references to *Der Stürmer* will take the form DS.

19. Julius Streicher, "Das politische Testament," 662.
20. *The New York Times,* July 31, 1945, p. 6.
21. Streicher, "Das politische Testament," 693.
22. *International Military Tribunal,* Vol. 5, p. 118.
23. G. M. Gilbert, *Nuremberg Diary* (New York: Farrar, Straus & Company, 1947), p. 419.
24. *Nazi Conspiracy and Aggression,* Supp. B (Washington, D.C.: U.S. Government Printing Office, 1946–48), p. 460.
25. *C. V. Zeitung,* 7 (November 8, 1929), 600.
26. See, for example, Rainer Hambrecht, *Der Aufstieg der NSDAP in Mittel- und Oberfranken (1925–1933)* (Nuremberg: Stadtarchiv Nürnberg, 1976), p. 430, and Peterson, p. 225.
27. Streicher, *Kampf dem Weltfeind,* p. 118; the hotel story is found in the Wiener Library Eyewitness Accounts Collection, P. II. c., No. 1,176; Gilbert, p. 41; and Burton C. Andrus, *I Was the Nuremberg Jailer* (New York: Coward-McCann, 1969), p. 105.
28. Kelly, p. 143; *Der Nazi-Spiegel,* No. 2 (December 1932), a copy of which is in the HA, 85/1734; and Baldur von Schirach, *Ich Glaubte an Hitler* (Hamburg: Mosaik Verlag, 1967), p. 71.
29. The article is translated into German in the HA, 25/508.

III: *Der Stürmer:* "A Fierce and Filthy Rag"

1. The story is in a manuscript version of Preiss's dissertation in the HA, 98/AL 18. The final version omits the story.
2. Amann to Streicher, August 16, 1923, NS 105.
3. *Nürnberger Zeitung,* November 8, 1925. A clipping is in the HA, 17A/1731.
4. The undated circular is in NS 71.
5. Nuremberg Police to State's Attorney, December 12, 1927, HA, 85/1732.
6. Hitler, *Table Talk,* pp. 31–32.
7. Preiss, p. 79.
8. *DS,* No. 17 (1935).
9. Wolfgang Sauer, ed., *Dokumente über die Verfolgung der jüdischen Bürger in Baden-Württemberg durch das nationalsozialistische Regime 1933–1945,* Vol. 1 (Stuttgart: Verlag W. Kohlhammer, 1966), p. 103.
10. *DS,* No. 5 (1936).

11. Hermann Rauschning, *Hitler Speaks* (London: Thornton Buttersworth, 1939), pp. 233–34.
12. *DS,* No. 11 (1937) and No. 27 (1937).
13. See the September 4, 1937 Gestapo memo in the HA, 91/1891, and *DS* to Düsseldorf Gestapo, September 2, 1940, in the Wiener Library Collection, VB 5, Nazi Anti-Semitic Propaganda at Home.
14. Horowitz to *DS,* February 5, 1939, Stadtarchiv Nürnberg, Stürmerarchiv, folder 1,681.
15. *DS,* No. 41 (1937).
16. *DS,* No. 47 (1935) and No. 5 (1938). Various complaints from doctors are found in the Bundesarchiv, Reichskanzlei file R 43 II. One attacks Streicher for suggesting insulin was part of the Jewish plot.
17. *DS,* No. 3 (1936).
18. See Peterson, p. 230, for a discussion of Lammers's difficulties.
19. Fred Hahn, *Lieber Stürmer! Leserbriefe an das NS-Kampfblatt 1924 bis 1945* (Stuttgart: Seewald Verlag, 1978), p. 105.

IV: The German Anti-Semitic Tradition

1. Friedrich Nietzsche, *Basic Writings of Nietzsche,* ed. and trans. Walter Kaufmann (New York: Modern Library, 1968), p. 377.
2. Heinrich von Treitschke, *Ein Wort über unser Judenthum* (Berlin: G. Reimer, 1880), p. 4.
3. The three best books on the history of German racism, on which I depend heavily in this chapter, are Joshua Trachtenberg, *The Devil and the Jew* (New Haven, Conn.: Yale University Press, 1943); Jacob Katz, *From Prejudice to Destruction: Anti-Semitism, 1700–1933* (Cambridge, Mass.: Harvard University Press, 1980); and George L. Mosse, *Toward the Final Solution* (New York: Howard Fertig, 1978). Mosse's is the most readable.
4. Martin Luther, *Luther's Works,* Vol. 47, ed. Franklin Sherman, trans. Martin H. Bertram (Philadelphia: Fortress Press, 1971), p. 275.
5. Theodor Fritsch, *Handbuch der Judenfrage,* 30th ed. (Leipzig: Hammerverlag, 1931), p. 497.
6. Werner Jochman, "Die Ausbreitung des Antisemitismus," in

Deutsches Judentum in Krieg und Revolution 1916–1923, ed. Werner E. Mosse and Arnold Paucker (Tübingen: J. C. B. Mohr [Paul Siebeck], 1971), p. 494.

V: Children of the Devil: Streicher's Image of the Jew
1. Fritz Fink, *Die Judenfrage im Unterricht* (Nuremberg: Stürmerverlag, 1937), p. 21.
2. *DS,* No. 22 (1934) and No. 34 (1938).
3. The Wiener Library Clipping File has a lengthy newspaper account of the speech.
4. *DS,* No. 27 (1930), No. 23 (1934), and No. 45 (1934).
5. *DS,* No. 22 (1938).
6. *DS,* No. 40 (1939).
7. *DS, Sondernummer* 8 (1938).
8. The document is reprinted in Hahn, p. 152.
9. *DS,* No. 1 (1943) and No. 28 (1937).
10. Ernst Hiemer, *Der Pudelmopsdackelpinschern* (Nuremberg: Stürmerverlag, 1940), p. 61.
11. *DS,* No. 35 (1929) and No. 11 (1941).
12. *DS,* No. 5 (1934).
13. *DS,* No. 10 (1935), No. 27 (1935), No. 23 (1937), and No. 45 (1933).
14. *DS,* No. 13 (1929) and No. 9 (1943).
15. *DS,* No. 5 (1936) and No. 37 (1938).
16. *DS, Sondernummer* 9 (1938) and No. 2 (1940).
17. *DS,* No. 11 (1934).
18. *DS,* No. 26 (1935) and No. 30 (1937).
19. Alexander Guttmann, *Enthüllte Talmudzitate* (Berlin: Philo Verlag, 1930), p. 179.
20. *DS,* No. 43 (1927) and *Sondernummer* 7 (1937).
21. *DS,* No. 6 (1937).
22. *DS,* No. 31 (1935) and No. 33 (1935).
23. *DS,* No. 24 (1939).
24. *DS,* No. 36 (1936).
25. Fink, p. 25.
26. *DS,* No. 44 (1936).
27. *DS,* No. 15 (1938).
28. Gilbert, p. 125.

29. Joseph Wulf, *Presse und Funk im Dritten Reich* (Reinbek: Rowohlt, 1966), p. 103.
30. *DS,* No. 23 (1926) and No. 30 (1926).
31. *DS,* No. 1 (1935).
32. *DS,* No. 14 (1929), No. 8 (1935), No. 7 (1939), and No. 51 (1938).
33. *DS,* No. 17 (1943).
34. Hitler, *Table Talk,* p. 154.

VI: Fraud, Conspiracy, and Murder
1. *DS,* No. 52 (1934) and No. 28 (1938).
2. Richard Hofstadter, *The Paranoid Style in American Politics and Other Essays* (New York: Alfred A. Knopf, 1965), pp. 29–37.
3. *DS,* No. 4 (1929).
4. *DS,* No. 28 (1939).
5. *DS,* No. 11 (1931).
6. The poem is from Elwira Bauer, *Trau keinem Fuchs auf seiner Heid und keinem Jud bei seinem Eid* (Nuremberg: Stürmerverlag, 1936). I am using an anonymous translation in the University of South Florida library. The bad-meat story is from *DS,* No. 7 (1935).
7. *DS,* No. 2 (1929).
8. *DS,* No. 12 (1935).
9. Bauer.
10. *DS,* No. 12 (1935).
11. *DS,* No. 20 (1939) (*Ritualmordnummer*). It was used in other ritual murder issues as well.
12. *DS,* No. 31 (1936).
13. *DS, Sondernummer* 1 (1934). I am using the English translation published in the *Christian Vanguard,* No. 50 (February 1976).
14. *DS,* No. 4 (1935).
15. *DS,* No. 17 (1938) and No. 20 (1939).
16. The best book on the *Protocols* is Norman Cohn, *Warrant for Genocide* (New York: Harper & Row, 1966).
17. Editions of the *Protocols* tend to be rather makeshift. The one I am using, currently available, cites no publisher and no publication date but is sold by a number of right-wing groups. The quotations are from Protocols 1 and 5.
18. Cited by Cohn, pp. 152–53.
19. Cited in the preface to my edition of the *Protocols.*

20. Robert Körber and Theodor Pugel, *Antisemitismus der Welt in Wort und Bild* (Dresden: Verlag M. O. Groh, 1935), p. 316. The book is dedicated to Streicher.
21. Streicher, *Ruf zur Tat,* p. 59.
22. *DS, Sondernummer* 5 (1936).
23. *DS,* No. 8 (1931).
24. Police report of a November 23, 1922 Nazi meeting in Nuremberg, HA, 25/508.
25. *DS,* No. 1 (1929) and No. 6 (1929).
26. *DS,* No. 46 (1934).
27. Karl A. Schleunes, *The Twisted Road to Auschwitz* (Urbana: University of Illinois Press, 1970), pp. 178–79.
28. *DS,* No. 3 (1929) and No. 31 (1940).
29. *DS,* No. 42 (1928) and No. 40 (1934).
30. *DS,* No. 5 (1938) and No. 10 (1940).
31. *DS,* No. 1 (1941).
32. Nuremberg police report of a January 29, 1926 Nazi meeting, HA, 25/508 and *DS,* No. 21 (1929).
33. *DS, Sondernummer* 3 (1935).
34. *DS,* No. 16 (1936).
35. *DS,* No. 3 (1937).
36. *DS,* No. 19 (1939).
37. Wulf, p. 106.
38. *DS,* No. 7 (1940).
39. *DS,* No. 38 (1941).
40. *DS,* No. 5 (1934).
41. *DS,* No. 4 (1939).
42. *DS, Sondernummer* 10 (1938) and No. 37 (1939).
43. *DS,* No. 1 (1942).
44. *DS,* No. 39 (1944). *The Times* article appeared on March 3, 1917.
45. *DS,* No. 11 (1943) and No. 12 (1943).

VII: The Worst Crime: Racial Defilement
1. Leon Poliakov, "The Weapon of Anti-Semitism," in *The Third Reich* (London: George Weidenfeld & Nicolson, 1955), p. 840.
2. Nuremberg police report of a March 4, 1927 Nazi meeting in Nuremberg, HA, 85/1733.
3. *'Abodah Zarah,* trans. A. Mishcon and A. Cohen (London: The Soncino Press, 1935), pp. 178–79.

4. *Deutsche Volksgesundheit aus Blut und Boden,* III (January 1, 1935), 3.
5. *DS,* No. 19 (1938).
6. *DS,* No. 26 (1925) and *Sondernummer* 2 (1935).
7. *DS,* No. 8 (1935).
8. *DS, Sondernummer* 2 (1935).
9. *DS,* No. 30 (1930).
10. Rumbold to Simon, April 13, 1933, in E. L. Woodward and Rohan Butler, eds., *Documents on British Foreign Policy,* Second Series, Vol. 5 (London: Her Majesty's Stationery Office, 1956), p. 41.
11. *DS,* No. 34 (1932) and No. 1 (1933).
12. *DS,* No. 52 (1936).
13. *DS,* No. 48 (1936).
14. *DS,* No. 40 (1930).
15. *DS,* No. 52 (1925).
16. *DS,* No. 53 (1925).
17. *DS,* No. 16 (1926).
18. *DS,* No. 20 (1926).
19. *DS,* No. 8 (1929), No. 49 (1932), and No. 6 (1933).
20. *DS,* No. 25 (1924) and *Sondernummer* 1 (1928).
21. *DS,* No. 16 (1933).
22. *DS,* No. 32 (1932).
23. *DS,* No. 29 (1935).
24. *The New York Times,* September 16, 1935, p. 11, and September 19, 1935, p. 9.
25. *DS,* No. 42 (1935).
26. *DS,* No. 43 (1935).
27. *DS,* No. 9 (1936), No. 11 (1936), and No. 4 (1936).
28. *DS,* No. 39 (1936).
29. Bauer.
30. Fink, pp. 41–46.
31. *DS,* No. 23 (1939).
32. *DS,* No. 33 (1940).
33. *DS,* No. 14 (1942).

VIII: Solutions: Final and Otherwise

1. Streicher, *Ruf zur Tat,* p. 112.

2. *DS,* No. 31 (1936) and No. 39 (1944).
3. *DS,* No. 42 (1935) and No. 48 (1935).
4. The correspondence is in the Stadtarchiv Nürnberg, Stürmerarchiv, folder 1,213.
5. *DS,* No. 31 (1935) and No. 33 (1935).
6. *DS,* No. 45 (1935).
7. Streicher to Goebbels, January 20, 1938, HA, 25/508.
8. *DS,* No. 30 (1932) and No. 1 (1937).
9. Sauer, p. 111.
10. Tausch to *DS,* April 5, 1939, Stadtarchiv Nürnberg, Stürmerarchiv, folder 1,216.
11. Schleunes, p. 131.
12. *DS,* No. 31 (1936).
13. Theodor Fritsch, *Handbuch der Judenfrage,* 29th ed. (Leipzig: Hammerverlag, 1923), p. 484.
14. *DS,* Nos. 17–18 (1931).
15. *DS,* No. 48 (1933), No. 20 (1934), and No. 2 (1939).
16. *DS,* No. 1 (1938).
17. *DS,* No. 9 (1937).
18. *DS,* No. 22 (1924).
19. *DS,* No. 53 (1931) and No. 12 (1933).
20. *DS,* No. 8 (1933) and No. 27 (1933).
21. Streicher's speech on July 23, 1935 is summarized in a report in the National Archives microfilm series of captured German documents, Series T-81, reel 75, frames 86592–99.
22. *DS,* No. 4 (1939), No. 30 (1940), No. 36 (1941), No. 1 (1944), and No. 8 (1945). Other passages calling for annihilation are found in No. 45 (1931), No. 32 (1937), No. 50 (1937), *Sondernummer* 7 (1937), No. 13 (1938), No. 13 (1939), No. 31 (1939), No. 20 (1942), No. 1 (1943), and No. 32 (1944). There are many more.
23. *Nazi Conspiracy and Aggression,* Supp. B, p. 1,429.
24. Schleunes, p. 257.

IX: A Poisoned Nation: The Impact of *Der Stürmer*
1. *DS,* No. 14 (1937).
2. *DS,* No. 39 (1936).
3. Lutz Graf Schwerin von Krosigk, *Es Geschah in Deutschland*

(Tübingen: Rainer Wunderlich Verlag Hermann Leins, 1951), p. 265.

4. *DS*, No. 38 (1939).
5. The letter is reproduced in Hahn, pp. 172–73.
6. *DS*, No. 35 (1935).
7. *DS*, No. 38 (1936).
8. *DS*, No. 14 (1935).
9. *DS*, No. 28 (1935).
10. *DS*, No. 30 (1933), No. 31 (1933), No. 32 (1933), and No. 33 (1933).
11. *DS*, No. 42 (1937).
12. *DS*, No. 12 (1937).
13. Ian Kershaw, "Antisemitismus und Volksmeinung: Reaktion auf die Judenverfolgung," in Martin Broszat et al., *Bayern in der NS-Zeit, II* (Munich: R. Oldenbourg Verlag, 1979), p. 300.
14. Statement by Walter Berlin to the International Military Tribunal, a copy of which is in the Wiener Library Eyewitness Collection, P. III. f. 6.
15. Hahn, p. 231.
16. *DS*, No. 41 (1937).
17. Sauer, p. 152.
18. The letters are in Hanz-Joachim Fliednor, ed., *Die Judenverfolgung in Mannheim 1933–1945* (Stuttgart: Verlag W. Kohlhammer, 1971), Vol. 1, pp. 187–88.
19. Berlin statement to the IMT.
20. *The New York Times,* August 26, 1935, p. 5. According to the article, Streicher was "barnstorming the country."
21. *The New York Times,* June 17, 1935, p. 1.
22. See Kershaw, p. 293.
23. Sauer, p. 63.
24. Viktor Klemperer, *Die unbewältige Sprache* (Darmstadt: Melzer, 1966), p. 310.
25. *International Military Tribunal,* Vol. XII, p. 320.
26. Otto Finechel, "Elements of a Psychoanalytic Theory of Anti-Semitism," in *Anti-Semitism,* ed. Ernst Simmel (New York: International Universities Press, 1946), pp. 11–12.
27. Walter Laqueur, *The Terrible Secret* (London: George Weidenfeld & Nicolson, 1980), p. 201.

28. J. P. Stern, *Hitler: The Führer and the People* (Berkeley: University of California Press, 1975), p. 215.

X: The Illusion of Immunity
1. Jacques Ellul, *Propaganda: The Formation of Men's Attitudes,* trans. Konrad Kellen and Jean Lerner (New York: Alfred A. Knopf, 1971).
2. George L. Mosse, ed., *Nazi Culture* (New York: Grosset & Dunlap, 1966), pp. 283–84.

Afterword to the Cooper Square Press Edition
1. Daniel Jonah Goldhagen, *Hitler's Willing Executioners: Ordinary Germans and the Holocaust* (New York: Alfred A. Knopf, 1996), p. 9.
2. Saul Friedländer, *Nazi Germany and the Jews: The Years of Persecution, 1933–1939* (New York: HarperCollins, 1997), p. 4.
3. Robert Gellately, *The Gestapo and German Society: Enforcing Racial Policy 1933–1945* (Oxford: Oxford University Press, 1990), p. 259.
4. *DS*, No. 28 (1935).
5. *DS*, No. 10 (1938") and No. 28 (1938).
6. *DS*, No. 25 (1937).
7. *DS*, No. 36 (1938).
8. *DS*, No. 19 (1938).
9. *DS*, No. 8 (1937).
10. *DS*, No. 24 (1936).
11. *DS*, No. 39 (1938).
12. *DS*, No. 39 (1939).
13. *DS*, No. 8 (1938).
14. Dennis Showalter, *Little Man, What Now?* Der Stürmer *in the Weimar Republic* (Hamden, Conn.: Archon, 1981).

Bibliography

Archival Sources

Bayerisches Hauptstaatsarchiv, Munich
    Interior Ministry files
    Offiziers-Personalakt No. 50.016 für Julius Streicher
Bundesarchiv Koblenz
    Nachlass Streicher
    Nachlass Luppe
    Reichskanzlei file R 43 II
Hauptarchiv der NSDAP (Hoover Institution Microfilm Edition)
National Archives, Washington, D.C.
    Captured German Documents, Series T-81
    Streicher's Nachlass is also available in Series T-580
Stadtarchiv Nürnberg
    Stürmerarchiv
Wiener Library, London
    Clipping and Document files
    Eyewitness Accounts Collection

Newspapers and Magazines

C. V. Zeitung, 1922–32
Deutsche Volksgesundheit aus Blut und Boden, 1934–35
Fränkische Tageszeitung, 1933–40
Der Stürmer, 1923–45
Völkischer Beobachter, 1927–32

Works by Streicher and His Associates

Bauer, Elwira. *Trau keinem Fuchs auf seiner Heid und keinem Jud bei seinem Eid.* Nuremberg: Stürmerverlag, 1936.

Deeg, Peter. *Hofjuden.* Nuremberg: Stürmerverlag, 1938.

————. *Vor 50 Jahren: Für und wider den Russen-Pakt.* Nuremberg: Stürmerverlag, 1940.

Fink, Fritz. *Die Judenfrage im Unterricht.* Nuremberg: Stürmerverlag, 1937.

"FIPS." *Juden Stellen sich vor.* Nuremberg: Stürmerverlag, 1934.

Hiemer, Ernst. *Der Giftpilz.* Nuremberg: Stürmerverlag, 1938.

————. *Der Pudelmopsdackelpinschern.* Nuremberg: Stürmerverlag, 1940.

————. *Die Juden im Sprichwort der Völker.* Nuremberg: Stürmerverlag, 1942.

Holz, Karl. *Die Freiheitskampf in Franken.* Nuremberg: Stürmerverlag, 1933.

————. *Des Stürmers Kampf.* Nuremberg: Stürmerverlag, 1937.

Streicher, Julius. *Ruf zur Tat*, ed. Heinz Preiss. Nuremberg: Stürmerverlag, 1937.

————. *Kampf dem Weltfeind*, ed. Heinz Preiss. Nuremberg: Stürmerverlag, 1938.

————. "Das politische Testament Julius Streichers," ed. Jay W. Baird. *Vierteljahrshefte für Zeitgeschichte*, 26 (1978), 660–93.

Other Books and Articles

'Abodah Zarah, trans. A. Mishcon and A. Cohen. London: The Soncino Press, 1935.

Allen, William Sheridan. *The Nazi Seizure of Power,* repr. ed. Chicago: Quadrangle Books, 1965.

Ball-Kaduri, Kurt Jacob. *Vor der Katastrophe: Juden in Deutschland 1934–1939.* Tel Aviv: Olameau, 1967.

Bein, Alex. "The Jewish Parasite—Notes on the Semantics of the Jewish Problem with special reference to Germany," *Year Book IX.* Publications of the Leo Baeck Institute. London: East and West Library, 1964.

Bondy, Louis. *Racketeers of Hatred: Julius Streicher and the Jew-Baiters International.* London: Newman Wolsey, 1946.

Broszat, Martin, et al. *Bayern in der NS-Zeit, I.* Munich: R. Oldenbourg Verlag, 1977.

Buchner, Franz. *Kamerad! Halt aus!* Munich: F. Eher, 1942.

Bytwerk, Randall L. "Rhetorical Aspects of the Nazi Meeting: 1926–1933," *Quarterly Journal of Speech,* 61 (1975), 307–18.

———. "Julius Streicher and the Impact of *Der Stürmer*," *Wiener Library Bulletin,* 29 (1976), 41–46.

———. "The Early History of *Der Stürmer,* 1923–1933," *Journalism History,* 5 (1978), 74–79.

Cohn, Norman. *Warrant for Genocide: The Myth of the Jewish World-Conspiracy and the Protocols of the Elders of Zion.* New York: Harper & Row, 1967.

Davidowicz, Lucy. *The War Against the Jews 1933–1945.* New York: Holt, Rinehart & Winston, 1975.

Ehlers, Carol Jean. "Nuremberg, Julius Streicher and the Bourgeois Transition to Nazism, 1918–1924." Diss. Colorado, 1975.

Ellul, Jacques. *Propaganda: The Formation of Men's Attitudes,* trans. Konrad Kellen and Jean Lerner. New York: Alfred A. Knopf, 1971.

Fliednor, Hanz-Joachim, ed. *Die Judenverfolgung in Mannheim 1933–1945,* 2 vols. Veröffentlichungen des Stadtarchivs Mannheim. Stuttgart: Verlag W. Kohlhammer, 1971.

Fritsch, Theodor. *Handbuch der Judenfrage,* 29th ed. Leipzig: Hammerverlag, 1923.

———. *Handbuch der Judenfrage,* 30th ed. Leipzig: Hammerverlag, 1930.

Gilbert, G. M. *Nuremberg Diary.* New York: Farrar, Straus & Company, 1947.

Gliksman, Shlomo. *The Forgeries and Falsifications in the Anti-semitic Literature and My Lawsuit against Julius Streicher & Co.* New York: People's Institute for Dissemination of Biblical and Talmudic Jurisprudence—Jud Judaicum, 1939.

Goebbels, Joseph. *Final Entries 1945,* ed. Hugh Trevor-Roper, trans. Richard Barry. New York: G. P. Putnam's Sons, 1978.

Grieser, Utho. *Himmlers Mann in Nürnberg: Der Fall Benno Martin.* Nürnberger Werkstücke zur Stadt- und Landesgeschichte, Vol. 13. Nuremberg: Stadtarchiv Nürnberg, 1974.

Guttmann, Alexander. *Enthüllte Talmudzitate.* Berlin: Philo Verlag, 1930.

Hahn, Fred. *Lieber Stürmer! Leserbriefe an das NS-Kampfblatt 1924 bis 1945.* Schriftenreihe der Studiengesellschaft für Zeitprobleme, e.V., Vol. 19. Stuttgart: Seewald Verlag, 1978.

Hambrecht, Rainer. *Der Aufstieg der NSDAP in Mittel- und Oberfranken (1925-1933).* Nürnberger Werkstücke für Stadt- und Landesgeschichte, Vol. 17. Nuremberg: Stadtarchiv Nürnberg, 1976.

Hanschel, Hermann. *Oberbürgermeister Hermann Luppe: Nürnberger Kommunalpolitik in der Weimarer Republik.* Nuremberg: Selbstverlag des Vereins für Geschichte der Stadt Nürnberg, 1977.

Heiden, Konrad. *Der Fuehrer.* Boston: Houghton Mifflin, 1944.

Hitler, Adolf. *Mein Kampf.* New York: Reynal & Hitchcock, 1941.

————. *Hitler's Table Talk: 1941-1944,* ed. H. R. Trevor-Roper. London: George Weidenfeld & Nicolson, 1953.

————. *Sämtliche Aufzeichnungen 1905-1924,* ed. Eberhard Jäckel and Axel Kuhn. Quellen und Darstellungen zur Zeitgeschichte, Vol. 21. Stuttgart: Deutsche Verlags-Anstalt, 1980.

Hofstadter, Richard. *The Paranoid Style in American Politics and Other Essays.* New York: Alfred A. Knopf, 1965.

Jochman, Werner. "Die Ausbreitung des Antisemitismus," *Deutsches Judentum in Krieg und Revolution 1916-1923,* ed. Werner E. Mosse and Arnold Paucker. Tübingen: Verlag J. C. B. Mohr (Paul Siebeck), 1971, pp. 409-510.

Katz, Jacob. *From Prejudice to Destruction: Anti-Semitism, 1700-1933.* Cambridge, Mass.: Harvard University Press, 1980.

Kelly, Douglas M. *22 Cells in Nuremberg.* New York: Greenburg, 1947.

Kershaw, Ian. "Antisemitismus und Volksmeinung: Reaktion auf die Judenverfolgung," *Bayern in der NS-Zeit, II,* ed. Martin Broszat et al. Munich: R. Oldenbourg Verlag, 1979, pp. 218–348.

Kipphan, Klaus. "Julius Streicher: Propagandist of the Holocaust," *Juniata Studies: Peace, Justice, and Conflict,* ed. Ralph Church and Klaus Kipphan. Huntingdon, Pa.: Juniata College, 1976.

Klemperer, Viktor. *Die unbewältige Sprache.* Darmstadt: Melzer, 1966.

Kolb, Bernard. "Die Juden in Nürnberg." Nuremberg: Carbon typescript, 1946.

Körber, Robert, and Pugel, Theodor. *Antisemitismus der Welt in Wort und Bild.* Dresden: Verlag M. O. Groh, 1935.

Laqueur, Walter. *The Terrible Secret.* London: George Weidenfeld & Nicolson, 1980.

Lenman, Robin. "Julius Streicher and the Origins of the NSDAP in Nuremberg, 1918–1933," *German Social Democracy and the Triumph of Hitler,* ed. Anthony Nicholls and Erich Mattias. London: George Allen & Unwin, 1971, pp. 129–59.

Luther, Martin. *Luther's Works,* Vol. 47, ed. Franklin Sherman, trans. Martin H. Bertram. Philadelphia: Fortress Press, 1971.

Maser, Werner. *Die Frühgeschichte der NSDAP.* Frankfurt: Athenäum Verlag, 1965.

————. *Nuremberg: A Nation on Trial,* trans. Richard Barry. New York: Charles Scribner's Sons, 1979.

Mosse, George L. *Nazi Culture.* New York: Grosset & Dunlap, 1966.

————. *Germans and Jews.* New York: Howard Fertig, 1970.

————. *Toward the Final Solution.* New York: Howard Fertig, 1978.

Müller, Arnd. *Geschichte der Juden in Nürnberg 1146–1945.* Nuremberg: Selbstverlag der Stadtbibliothek Nürnberg, 1968.

Nadler, Fritz. *Eine Stadt im Schatten Streichers.* Nuremberg: Fränkische Verlagsanstalt und Buchdrückerei, 1969.

Nazi Conspiracy and Aggression, 10 vols. Washington, D.C.: U.S. Government Printing Office, 1946–48.

Nietzsche, Friedrich. *Basic Writings of Nietzsche,* ed. and trans. Walter Kaufmann. New York: Modern Library, 1968.

Orlow, Dietrich. *The History of the Nazi Party 1919-1933.* Pittsburgh: University of Pittsburgh Press, 1969.

Peterson, Edward N. *The Limits of Hitler's Power.* Princeton, N.J.: Princeton University Press, 1969.

Podro, Joshua. *Nuremberg: The Unholy City.* London: Anscombe, 1937.

Poliakov, Leon. "The Weapon of Anti-Semitism," *The Third Reich.* London: George Weidenfeld & Nicolson, 1955.

Preiss, Heinz. *Die Anfänge der völkischen Bewegung in Franken.* Diss. Erlangen 1937. Erlangen: F. Willmy, 1937.

Pridham, Geoffrey. *Hitler's Rise to Power: The Nazi Movement in Bavaria, 1923-1933.* London: Hart-Davis, MacGibbon, 1973.

Protocols of the Learned Elders of Zion, trans. Victor E. Marsden. N.p., n.d.

Pryce-Jones, David. *Unity Mitford: An Enquiry into Her Life and the Frivolity of Evil.* New York: The Dial Press/James Wade, 1977.

Rauschning, Hermann. *Hitler Speaks.* London: Thornton Buttersworth, 1939.

Rühl, Mannfred. "Der Stürner und sein Herausgeber." Diplomarbeit Erlangen-Nürnberg, 1960.

Sauer, Wolfgang, ed. *Dokumente über die Verfolgung der jüdischen Bürger in Baden-Württemberg durch das nationalsozialistische Regime 1933-1945,* 2 vols. Veröffentlichung der Staatlichen Archivverwaltung Baden-Württemberg, Vol. 16. Stuttgart: Verlag W. Kohlhammer, 1966.

Schleunes, Karl A. *The Twisted Road to Auschwitz: Nazi Policy Toward German Jews, 1933-1939.* Urbana: University of Illinois Press, 1970.

Schwerin von Krosigk, Lutz Graf. *Es Geschah in Deutschland.* Tübingen: Rainer Wunderlich Verlag Hermann Lein⸴, 1951.

Smith, Bradley F. *Reaching Judgment at Nuremberg.* New York: Basic Books, 1977.

Stern, J. P. *Hitler: The Führer and the People.* Berkeley: University of California Press, 1975.

Trachtenberg, Joshua. *The Devil and the Jew.* New Haven, Conn.: Yale University Press, 1943.

The Trial of the Major War Criminals Before the International

Military Tribunal, 42 vols. Nuremberg: U.S. Government Printing Office, 1947–49.

Varga, William. *The Number One Nazi Jew Baiter.* New York: Carlton, 1981.

von Schirach, Baldur. *Ich Glaubte an Hitler.* Hamburg: Mosaik Verlag, 1967.

von Treitschke, Heinrich. *Ein Wort über unser Judenthum.* Berlin: G. Reimer, 1880.

Warburg, G. *Six Years of Hitler.* London: George Allen & Unwin, 1939.

Woodward, E. L., and Butler, Rohan. *Documents on British Foreign Policy 1919–1939,* Second Series, Vol. 5. London: Her Majesty's Stationery Office, 1956.

Wulf, Joseph. *Presse und Funk im Dritten Reich.* Reinbek: Rowohlt, 1966.

The Yellow Spot. London: Victor Gollancz, 1936.

Index

THE JEHOVAH'S WITNESSES
AND THE NAZIS
Persecution, Deportation, and Murder,
1933–1945
Michel Reynaud and Sylvie Graffard
Introduction by Michael Berenbaum
304 pages, 40 b/w photos
0-8154-1076-X
$27.95 cloth

THE MEDICAL CASEBOOK OF ADOLF HITLER
His Illnesses, Doctors, and Drugs
Leonard L. Heston, M. D. and
Renata Heston, R. N.
Introduction by Albert Speer
192 pages, 3 b/w photos, 4 graphs
0-8154-1066-2
$17.95

HITLER
The Survival Myth
Updated Edition
Donald M. McKale
296 pages, 12 b/w photos
0-8154-1128-6
$17.95

THE HITLER YOUTH
Origins and Development, 1922–1945
H. W. Koch
382 pages, 40 b/w photos
0-8154-1084-0
$18.95

HITLER'S WAR
Edwin P. Hoyt
with a new preface
440 pages, 60 b/w photos, 4 maps
0-8154-1117-0
$18.95

MENGELE
The Complete Story
Gerald L. Posner and John Ware
New introduction by
Michael Berenbaum
400 pages, 41 b/w photos
0-8154-1006-9
$18.95

THE MEMOIRS OF FIELD-MARSHAL
WILHELM KEITEL
Chief of the German High Command,
1938–1945
Edited by Walter Gorlitz
New introduction by Earl Ziemke
296 pages, 4 b/w maps
0-8154-1072-7
$18.95

THE WEEK FRANCE FELL
June 10–June 16, 1940
Noel Barber
336 pages, 18 b/w photos
0-8154-1091-3
$18.95

CORREGIDOR
The American Alamo of World War II
Eric Morris
560 pages, 23 b/w photos
0-8154-1085-9
$18.95

CANARIS
Hitler's Master Spy
Heinz Höhne
736 pages, 21 b/w photos, 1 map,
2 diagrams
0-8154-1007-7
$19.95

HITLER'S COMMANDERS
Officers of the *Wehrmacht*, the *Luftwaffe*, the
Kriegsmarine*, and the *Waffen–SS
Samuel W. Mitcham Jr. and
Gene Mueller
384 pages, 52 b/w photos, 8 maps
0-8154-1131-6
$18.95

HITLER'S FIELD MARSHALS
and Their Battles
Samuel W. Mitcham Jr.
456 pages, 26 b/w photos, 22 maps
0-8154-1130-8
$18.95